Peace in Sri Lanka:
Obstacles and Opportunities

World Alliance for Peace in Sri Lanka (WAPS)
P.O. Box 4066, Mulgrave, Victoria VIC 3170, Australia

Sansadaya (The Forum)
16/10A, Pagoda Road, Nugegoda, Sri Lanka

Online web orders:
www.vijithayapa.com
vybooks@sri.lanka.net

ISBN 955-1165-00-4

First Edition January 2005

Printed by Piyasiri Printing Systems, Nugegoda

Peace in Sri Lanka:
Obstacles and Opportunities

WAPS

World Alliance for Peace
in Sri Lanka (WAPS)
London, New York, Oslo, Melbourne, Tokyo, Toronto

This book is dedicated
to all Sri Lankans who have sacrificed their lives
for the sovereignty of the country

PREFACE

The World Alliance for Peace in Sri Lanka (WAPS) is a forum for all Sri Lankans, mainly living overseas, who are determined to counter the false and organized pro-separatist, pro-terrorist and anti-Sri Lanka propaganda disseminated internationally. The member organizations of WAPS include:

Society for Peace, Unity and Human Rights for Sri Lanka (SPUR), Australia, Sri Lanka United National Association of Canada (SLUNA), Japan-Sri Lanka Association for Peace in Sri Lanka, Sri Lankans Against Terrorism, Australia, Veera Parakramabahu Foundation, Australia, International Campaign for the Liberation of the Nation, United Kingdom, New York Society of United Sri Lanka, USA, United Sinhalese Association in Italy, Ape Shakthi Sanvidanaya, New Zealand and several other organizations in the Middle East, Europe, the Americas, Australasia and Asia.

One of the most important steps among many others taken by WAPS was to hold the OSLO Conference on "Road Map to Peace in Sri Lanka" on 20th August 2004. WAPS, with the ready assistance of R-Sentor, a Norwegian human rights organization held the conference on the very soil of Norway, recognized as a safe haven for terrorist organizations, especially the LTTE.

Norway is the leader among some other members of the 'international community' who after overtly and covertly providing succor to the separatist terrorist movement is now actively trying to usher a particular brand of "peace" in Sri Lanka. WAPS considers, given Norway's past history, that it is the duty of all who desire genuine peace in Sri Lanka to be aware of the dangers in any Norway-led prescription. Given the facts that we document in this book, very possibly some of the attacks on Sri Lanka would have been planned within Norway and would have been probably financed by Norwegian money. Norwegian remedies point to being more lethal than their diagnosed disease.

At the conference, papers were presented by Mr. F. Rovik, Mr H.L.D.Mahindapala, Prof. Shantha Hennayake, Prof Asoka Bandarge, Dr Susantha Goonatilake, Mr. Paul Harris, Dr. Peter Chalk and Mr. Stewart Bell. Apart from the formal papers, there were presentations by representatives of the democratic Tamil parties, EPDP and PLOTE on the state of democracy in the North and East of Sri Lanka. Although Mr. Eric Solheim, the self designated "special Norwegian peace envoy" was invited, he did not attend. The Norwegian foreign ministry however sent their Ms. Liza Golden to give the perspective of the Norwegian Government on its role.

All the formal papers are reproduced here except those of Dr. Peter Chalk (of Rand Corp, USA) "LTTE's use and institutionalization of suicide terrorism" and of Mr. Stewart Bell (of the National Post news paper, Canada) "The Snow Tigers: The Canadian Tamil Tiger network and how it supports violence in Sri Lanka". These two authors are publishing their papers elsewhere and for copyright reasons, they are not carried here. (However, a summary of their speeches and those of Golden together with members of Tamil democratic parties are included).

The different speakers spelt out the threats posed by the LTTE to democracy and the stability of the region and the world. Material presented at the conference showed the LTTE, molly coddled by Norway and some other members of the 'International Community', to be gathering attack capabilities and serving as a critical benchmark for other terrorist organizations.

Falk Rovik, an Amnesty International activist in his speech covered many details on the complicity of the Norwegian

Government in supporting terrorism against Sri Lanka. These facts proved beyond reasonable doubt that Norway is not a neutral party in Sri Lanka and had brazenly violated basic diplomatic norms, human rights regulations and Security Council resolutions on terrorism. In fact, Norway was found in effect to be an LTTE activist trying to score its own goal against Sri Lanka while leading its "Peace Team".

While Mahindapala, Bandarage and Hennayake, in their presentations discussed various facets of the conflict such as the history of the separatist movement, erroneous facts and concepts, issues of democracy and pluralism, Susantha Goonatilake traced the role of Norway as it evolved as an actor in the re-colonization of Sri Lanka. Paul Harris, expelled from Sri Lanka for his forthright views on the LTTE, described how Sri Lanka's sovereignty has been ransomed by an imprudent set of friends and foes. The representatives of PLOTE, EPDP and EPRLF participating in the discussion stressed the importance of having space for non-LTTE forces among the Tamil population and explained in detail how Norwegian authorities are helping the LTTE to spread hate against them in Norway. Some democratic Tamil speakers stated that Norway should grant refugee status to their members threatened by the LTTE.

Since the Oslo Conference, WAPS has taken a number of key steps. These include reporting Norway to the Anti-Terrorism Commission in the UN and preparing documents to take a class action suit against Norway and criminal action against the LTTE for their activities in sponsoring and/or carrying out terrorist acts. In the Colombo Conference in December 2004, WAPS has forged links with Sanasadaya, a group of professional Sri Lankan men and women fighting the injustices perpetrated on Mother Lanka. We also intend taking our message to the broad masses of Sri Lanka who are being short changed by their political leaders as they appease terrorists. We at WAPS believe that all Sri Lankans must resolve to liberate themselves from terror and institute full democracy.

We take this opportunity to give our special thanks to *Sanasadaya*, to our well wishers and colleagues in Sri Lanka and overseas and to numerous others who made this publication a reality within a period of two months.

Ranjith Soysa
Co-ordinator, WAPS
Melbourne, Australia

Contents

PART I

PART II

PART III

Contributors

F. Rovik of the R-Senter is a lawyer and has served in the council of Amnesty International Oslo. He has been in the forefront in exposing official Norway's supporting role for the LTTE in the military, training and political spheres.

Dr. Susantha Goonatilake's academic work has been primarily on knowledge systems. He has authored 14 books, published internationally in this area. His writings have been translated to Arabic, French, German and Japanese. He has taught or researched in a number of universities in Asia, Europe and the US. He has worked at the UN and has also been a senior consultant to all the UN organs dealing with knowledge, science and technology issues. He is a former General President of the Sri Lanka Association for the Advancement of Science.

H. L. D. Mahindapala is a former Editor of the daily Observer and the Sunday Observer, a past President of the Sri Lanka Working Journalists' Association and a past Secretary-General of South Asia Media Association. His political analyses and commentaries have been published in academic and other outlets. He has participated in the UN and other international forums, presenting critical perspectives on the on-going North-South conflict in Sri Lanka.

Professor Shantha K. Hennayake is at the Department of Geography at the University of Peradeinya. In 1993, he was a Visiting Senior Scholar at University of California, Los Angeles researching on the "Federal Experience and Ethno-nationalist Conflicts". In 1994, he was awarded a Visiting Professorship by the Asia Center and Geography Department at University of

Kentucky, Lexington USA. He has been an active researcher in the field of ethno-nationalist theory and politics in Sri Lanka. He has published in a number of local and international journals and has published books on the subject in Sinhala.

Paul Harris works internationally as a writer and conflict analyst, presently based in Shanghai, China. As specialist contributor on global insurgency & terrorism for Jane's Intelligence Review, he has written on Sri Lanka, Bosnia, Kosovo, Aceh, East Timor, Nepal, NE India, Nagorno Karabakh, the Sahara, Uganda and Algeria. He has authored over thirty books including *Fractured Paradise: Images of Sri Lanka.*

Dr. Asoka Bandarage is a professor of Asian Studies at Mount Holyoke College and Visiting Scholar at the Elliott School for International Affairs at George Washington University. She is the author of *Colonialism in Sri Lanka* and many other publications on Sri Lanka, global peace and development. She is currently writing a book on the conflict and the peace process in Sri Lanka.

Lisa Golden is an Advisor in the Norwegian Ministry of Foreign Affairs and has been working in the Norwegian peace Broker delegation since it started. She has an in-depth knowledge of the conflict, ceasefire agreement and the Peace negotiations in Sri Lanka.

Stewart Bell is Chief Reporter of Canada's National Post newspaper, where he covers the national security beat. An award-winning investigative reporter and foreign correspondent, he has travelled on assignment to more than two dozen countries. His bestselling book, Cold Terror, reveals how terrorist groups, from the Tamil Tigers of Sri Lanka to Al Qaeda, have used Canada as a base for exporting violence around the world.

Dr. Peter Chalk is a policy analyst working in the Project Air Force and National Security divisions of the RAND Corporation,

Washington DC. During the past year, he has worked on projects examining unconventional security threats in South East Asia, new strategic challenges for the US Air Force (USAF) in Latin America and evolving trends in national and international terrorism.

Rohan Gunaratna is one of the leading global experts on international terrorism. His books have covered both the activities of the LTTE and Al Qaeda. He is the author among others of *Inside Al Qaeda: Network of Terror; War and Peace in Sri Lanka: With a Post-Accord Report from Jaffna; Global Terror: Unearthing the Support Networks That Allow Terrorism to Survive and Succeed and of Combating Terrorism.* He is currently an Associate Professor, Institute of Defense and Strategic Studies, Singapore.

Mahinda Weerasinghe, a Norwegian-Sri Lankan, was a pioneer among overseas Sri Lankan activists who in the wake of corrosive and false Tamil Tiger propaganda in Europe decided to organize themselves. He wrote articles, met political leaders and staged demonstrations. With the support of other Lankans he was able to form a strong Sri Lanka organization to show that the balkanization of Lanka was not the solution to LTTE terrorism.

Professor D.G. Harendra de Silva is the Professor of Pediatrics at the University of Kelaniya. He is a leading activist against violations of human rights of children in Sri Lanka and the region. He has authored and co-authored several books on child health and child abuse. Prof Harendra de Silva is the author of the book Power Games in War & Peace.

Neville S. Ladduwahetty, a political analyst is an engineer by profession, and has held high posts in engineering and planning in Sri Lanka. Later he was a consultant in the US. He authored the book *Sri Lankan Issues* and has published nearly 60 articles in the press on Sri Lanka's national question.

Photo credit – Paul Harris – Bombing of the Central Bank

PART I

CONFERENCE PAPERS

Norway: A Terrorist Safe Haven?

F. Rovik

The liberal Norwegian asylum policies combined with a police force that has lost track of thousands of illegal immigrants have created a major headache for those who fight terrorism. Terrorist leaders live freely in Norway today with the consent and approval of the Norwegian Government. The US and other countries have asked for extradition of terrorists, but to no avail. Norway has thus become a terrorist safe haven where terrorists can plan and finance terror[1].

Al-Qaeda, Ansar al-Islam, Al-Aqsa, Hamas, PKK (Kurdistan Worker's Party), UCK (Kosovo Liberation Army), LTTE and several other terrorist groups are found to be active in Norway. Some operate openly, some engage in criminal activities, and some act as sleeping terrorist cells. Al-Aqsa and Hamas have raised funds several times in Norway for suicide missions in Israel[2]. Both Israel and the US have complained but little, if anything, has been done to stop this activity.

The former leader and founder of Ansar al-Islam, Mullah Krekar, lives and works in Norway. He has openly admitted meeting and having contacts with Osama Bin Laden. The numerous terror attacks and atrocities done by the Ansar al-Islam are well documented. There are links to Mullah Krekar and Norway, both in the Madrid terror bombings and the 9/11 attacks on New York[3]. The US is upset that Norway has allowed Krekar to work freely, promoting Jihad through the Internet and through his network of sympathizers[4] .

PKK and UCK have been present in Norway for a considerable period of time and are heavily involved in the sale and smuggling of narcotics. Even though the PKK is on the US terrorist organisations list, Norway has allowed it to broadcast from the Norwegian Kvitsøy radio station[5]. A well known Chechen terrorist from the Barajeev guerrilla movement is currently seeking asylum in Norway. The asylum seeker is wanted by the Russian Intelligence services, FSB. The Barajeev have been involved in 170 murders, kidnappings and terror acts.

Norway has also become a home for several hijackers and war criminals. Several Iranian and Palestinian hijackers have been granted asylum in Norway. War criminals from former Yugoslavia[6], Lebanon and Rwanda also have found a safe haven in Norway. The Norwegian Government attorney Arne Willy Dahl estimates that there are more than 100 war criminals living in Norway; at least 10 more arrive every year[7].

According to a Norwegian police report, the police suspect twenty-five individuals to be involved in funding of terrorism[8]. They are working in six different networks. Funding of terrorism is mostly done through criminal activities, extortion of legitimate business, fraud, smuggling, trafficking and prostitution. We have also seen funds being raised in religious congregations and cultural organisations.

Norway a terror target

Most terrorism experts believe the risk for a terror attack in Norway is low. But Brynjar Lia at the Norwegian Defence Institute thinks that Al-Qaeda will attack Norway within 10-15 years and that suicide attacks are likely[9].

Norway has had several terror threats:

- On 21 May 2003, Ayman al-Zawahri, the number two, next to Osama Bin Laden, threatened Norway and Norwegian interests abroad
- On 4 June 2003, detailed terrorist plans to attack and bomb the Norwegian embassy in Addis Ababa were revealed
- On 24 May 2003, NTB (Norway's primary wire service) reported that sources in the Norwegian Police told NTB, that organized crime groups in Norway are suspected to have terror support functions

Norway is already a victim due to the financing of terrorism. Norway has 15,000 drug addicts injecting narcotics. Several hundred Norwegian youths die every year due to drug abuse. The exploding number of drug addicts has become very visible in Oslo[10]. The drugs are bought from terrorist cells that use Norway to raise funds for more war and terror. It is a paradox that Norway cannot afford to take care of drug addicts, but can afford to support foreign dictators and terrorist groups with billions of dollars.

Norwegian support to LTTE

There are many instances of direct and indirect Norwegian support for the LTTE:

1. Direct financial support

Through NORAD the Norwegian Government has given millions directly to the LTTE. Norway has also paid for LTTE propaganda trips to Europe. There are also numerous rumours about funds channelled from secret Norwegian funds to the LTTE. Colonel Karuna Amman told the *Asian Tribune* that Norway and Denmark was essential in the LTTE funding of terrorism in Sri Lanka[11].

2. Equipment

A total of six tons of electronic equipment was delivered to the LTTE in 2002, allegedly including V-Sat equipment used in satellite communications. The circumstances related to the import of the electronic equipment were highly dubious. The Norwegian embassy in Colombo imported the equipment through diplomatic channels, allegedly because the LTTE did not want to pay import taxes to the Sri Lankan government! Ambassador Jon Westborg made a deal with then Sri Lankan government functionary Bradman Weerakoon and the equipment was given to the LTTE. Bradman Weerakoon was sold a story that the electronic equipment was important for the peace process and he seems to have been unaware of the military use of the Norwegian gift.

The conversation between Ambassador Jon Westborg and the LTTE had been tapped and is available on the Internet[12]. The conversation also revolves around a document that has been signed by Tamil Chelvam and another is requested to be mailed to the ambassador's residence and not to the Norwegian Embassy! Unprecedented and strange "diplomatic" procedures are revealed.

The equipment received from Norway is according to Indian intelligence sources, contacted by the Asian Tribune, used actively in the murders of the Tamil political opposition. India has warned Sri Lanka of the facilities LTTE possess to track down telephone conversations and locations, even telephone conversations by officials in the Presidential Secretariat of Sri Lanka through the remote sensing radio transmitting device provided by Norway in 2002. India has also pointed out that the LTTE was able to locate telephone conversations between Satchi Master and the Thamil Broadcasting Corporation through their remote sensing device and subsequently managed to slay him inside the Batticaloa prison through one of their inmates – a fellow prisoner." [13]

3. Financial support to LTTE front organisations in Norway

The LTTE front organisations in Norway annually receive Government and Municipality Funds. Since 2000, organisations sympathetic to the LTTE in Oslo have received 1.7 million Norwegian kroner in support from the Oslo Municipality[14]. These funds are used for their rent, for computers and to provide "bread and circus" for the LTTE propaganda and fund-raising events.

4. Military training and intelligence information

General Trygve Tellefsen leaked information about the Navy's pursuit of a LTTE arms smuggling ship to the Tamil rebel group allowing them to escape. After the incident, President Chandrika Kumaratunga wrote to the Norwegian Prime Minister, Kjell Magne Bondevik to remove the Head of the Sri Lanka Monitoring Mission, Retired Major General Trygve Tellefsen[15]. The Norwegian generals Trygve Tellefsen and Trond Furuhovde have been involved in the conflict in Sri Lanka and have regularly favoured the LTTE. How biased the Norwegian generals have been is revealed in the so called "Colombo voice documents". In the phone call between General Furohovde and the LTTE, it is obvious that the general is ordering the LTTE to withdraw their forces and then blame the terror incident on a fictitious "third party" with stolen uniforms[16].

Norway invited on April 1st 2003 the Tamil Tigers to the Rena Military camp to observe the Norwegian military demonstrate their skills and equipment. The LTTE was allowed to film all of the demonstrations[17]. The Norwegian ex-Special Forces have also been used to instruct Sea Tigers in underwater demolition. The IPS news service said the LTTE is known to have used Thailand's Andaman coast "to strengthen its capability to attack Sri Lanka's Navy. That included the training members of its sea Tiger Wing allegedly received from Norwegian ex-special forces to launch underwater demolition strikes."[18]

The Norwegian Tamil, Christy Reginold Lawrence was arrested in Thailand on 9th April 2000 by the Phuket Marine Police. He was driving his 17 meter long speedboat loaded with food and petrol heading for international waters. When the police accompanied him to his shipyard, Seacraft Co. Ltd, they found a half-built mini submarine. The hull was 3.6 meters and the tail, which has a rudder and designed to hold a propeller, was 1.6 meter long. Its total length of 5.2 meters was capable of accommodating 2-3 persons. The Thai police also discovered sophisticated sonar and GPS systems, satellite phones, combat training videos in Tamil, LTTE calendars and uniforms. Sri Lanka's ambassador to Thailand Karunatilaka Amunagama said the submarine was similar to one seized by the Sri Lankan Government Forces from the LTTE in Jaffna in the early 1990's. Lawrence was released on bail put up by the Norwegian Government[19].

5. Providing a safe haven for LTTE operatives and sympathisers

The liberal Norwegian asylum policies combined with corrupt Norwegian bureaucrats have converted Norway to a safe haven. With their political and bureaucratic contacts, the LTTE have created obstacles for anti LTTE Tamil refugees. It is a well known fact that a bureaucrat in the Norwegian Foreign Ministry and Justice department has sold visas and travel documents to the LTTE and criminal organisations[20]. Interpol and Sri Lankan Intelligence have contacted the Norwegian police related to this scandal and three Norwegian police officers participated in a meeting in Colombo where this matter was discussed.

6. Giving LTTE credibility and being a door-opener internationally for the LTTE

Maybe the most important support Norway has given to the LTTE is in its role of an international door opener. Norway has used substantial resources to give the LTTE credibility. While the LTTE assassinates the Tamil political opposition in Sri Lanka, the LTTE political leaders travel around Europe, with Norwegian Diplomats as door openers, explaining to the European leaders how great the LTTE's democratic ideas are.

The LTTE in Norway

The LTTE has been active in Norway for the last two decades through several front organisations and companies. They have skilfully lobbied Norwegian politicians and organisations. Their work has been successful and they have been able to get support from several political parties. They invite politicians and organisations to their cultural organisations which are used for promotional activities.

The LTTE in Norway has collected substantial amounts from the Tamil Diaspora to fund their activities in Sri Lanka. Officially, the funds collected in Norway are used to build hospitals and help war invalids. Unofficially, we know that at least part of the collection go to fund the LTTE war and terror. Some Tamils voluntarily give funds to the LTTE, others reluctantly because they are afraid of the LTTE. The funds collected from the Tamil Diaspora can legally be transferred to the LTTE in Sri Lanka. There are **no** restrictions on transfers from Norway to Sri Lanka[21].

The LTTE often uses threats and intimidation to those who refuse to contribute funds to the LTTE or do not support them. They have also attacked anti-LTTE political meetings and beaten up the participants. A total of 50 LTTE sympathisers were involved in the attack. Even though they admitted to the crime, they were not punished by the police.

The Norwegian police have done very little, if anything, to stop LTTE threats and extortion of the Tamil Diaspora in Norway. Some of the threats are even radio broadcasted and fatwas are issued against Tamils that do not support the LTTE. Anti-LTTE Tamils have complained several times about the intimidation and threats from the LTTE in Norway to both the police and to the Foreign

Ministry. Erik Solheim, for example, has ignored these complaints and refused to answer their numerous phone calls and messages.

After the Norwegian police raided the LTTE Norwegian head office in the area Toyengata 35 in February 1992, the police officers and their families received several death treats. A police officer involved in the raid was also stalked by LTTE operatives for a period of time. In the police report one also even reads how the LTTE intended to use their contacts in the Foreign Ministry to remove the police officers involved in the raid of the LTTE Norwegian head office[22]!

Amnesty International Norway is one of the few organisations that have dared to confront the LTTE in Norway. They have had several mail campaigns against the LTTE front organisations in Norway and Anton Balasingham in order to stop the LTTE use of Child soldiers[23]. Yet, we know that the LTTE has ignored the Amnesty International, HRW and UNESCO demands, and still continue to kidnap and abuse children.

Conclusion: Lawsuit against Norway?

Norway has provided a safe haven for the LTTE. In Norway, the LTTE has skilfully lobbied politicians and organisation with great success. In Norway, the LTTE can collect and legally transfer funds to the LTTE in Sri Lanka. The complaints filed by anti-LTTE Tamils about the LTTE threats seem to have been ignored both by the Foreign Ministry and the Police.

Norway has openly supported the LTTE morally, financially and with equipment enabling the LTTE to trace and kill their opponents. Norway has been, and is, the LTTE's most important door opener. Norway has used its foreign aid funds to lubricate journalists, organisations and individuals in Sri Lanka in order to help the LTTE to create their own State.

Norway has continued to support the LTTE despite the thousands of Cease Fire Agreement violations, ethnic cleansing in

LTTE controlled areas, genocide against the Tamil opposition and numerous human rights violations. Norway has several times used financial pressure on Sri Lanka and also lobbied internationally to get other countries to use financial pressure against Sri Lanka to accommodate the LTTE. Norway must immediately disclose all its secret files (and there are many such files) and information about their funding, gifts and services provided to the LTTE. It should be in Norway's interest to get all the facts revealed.

A lawsuit has been successfully filed against Libya for their support of terrorism. Libya has made a settlement with their victims, awarding them billions of US dollars. There is overwhelming evidence that many of the atrocities done by the LTTE are acts of terror. There is also overwhelming evidence that the LTTE has raised funds for more than two decades in Norway. There is also evidence from Norwegian intelligence reports that Norwegian authorities were aware of LTTE fundraising and did nothing to stop it[24]. There is also evidence that the Norwegian gift of electronic equipment had a dual purpose, at least one LTTE murder can be traced directly to the use of this equipment. There **are sufficient grounds** to have a lawsuit against Norway for their support of LTTE terrorism.

Victims of terrorism must seek compensation from countries supporting and/or funding terrorism.

End notes

1. Norway's terrorist haven by Michael Ragu, FrontPage magazine www.frontpagemag.com/Articles/ReadArticle.asp?ID=9910

2. The US Treasury May 29 2003 , www.ustreas.gov/press/releases/js439.htm

3. Source: Aftenposten 15 March 2004 http://www.aftenposten.no/english/local/article753543.ece

4. Source: Newsweek 7th January 2004, http://msnbc.msn.com/Default.aspx?id=3899582&p1=0

5. Source: VG 5th June 2003, (In Norwegian) www.vg.no/pub/vgart.hbs?artid=62430

6. Source: Aftenposten; Croatia is asking to have a Yugoslav war criminal extradited www.aftenposten.no/english/local/article671611.ece

7. P4 radio interview with Government attorney Arne Willy Dahl : http://www.p4.no/txo/104182.asp

8. Source: Aftenposten 28 January 2004. www.aftenposten.no/english/local/article718795.ece

9. Source: Norwegian Broadcasting http://presse.nrk.no/nyheter/innenriks/2887755.html (In Norwegian)

10. Norway's Heroin Lows By Jeffrey Fleishman, Los Angeles Times Staff Writer http://www.latimes.com/news/nationworld/world/la-fg-heroin29nov29,0,2616070.story?coll=la-home-world

11. Source: Asian Tribune 14th July 2004 Colonel Karuna interview www.asiantribune.com/show_article.php?id=1602

12. Phone conversation between LTTE and Ambassador Jon Westborg www.svik.org/Videos/ambatamil.mp3

13. Source Asian Tribune 22 July 2004: India refused to arrange direct talks with the LTTE www.asiantribune.com/show_news.php?id=10493

14. Source: Oslo Municipality, Flyktningeetaten

15. Source: The Hindu 30 October 2003 www.hindu.com/2003/10/30/stories/2003103004181200.htm

16. The sound file of the telephone conversation between the LTTE and General Furuhovde is available on the Internet. www.svik.org/Videos/GENTAMIL.mp3

17. Source: The Norwegian Military, www.mil.no/languages/english/start/article.jhtml?articleID=43041

18. Source: Lankaweb 12 November 2003 by Walter Jayawardhana www.lankaweb.com/news/items03/121103-5.html and Canadian Security Intelligence www.csis-scrs.gc.ca/eng/comment/com77_e.html

19. Source: Police Captain Pailin Jamjamrat of Phuket Town Police Station (Nation June 7, 2000)

20. Source: Several Norwegian police reports described the

illegal activities of this individual and his travels to Jaffna Police report dated 18 December 1992, Narcotics department.

21. Source: Bank of Norway, Letter to the WAPS conference dated 2 August 2004

22. Source: The Norwegian police, report dated 25 November 1992

23. Source: Amnesty International Norway, www.amnesty.no/web.nsf/pages/4DBBFE6D73BCB9DCC1256B61004298B2

24. Norwegian intelligence report dated 22 March 1993 describing in detail the LTTE front organisations in Norway, the LTTE criminal activities in Norway and terror in Sri Lanka.

Norway, a 25 Year Odyssey: From Sympathizer to Colonial Intruder

Susantha Goonatilake

My presentation poses the question up-front: Is there a role for Norway in building a secure, democratic, multi-ethnic and multi-cultural Sri Lankan society?

Let me begin the search on a detour with Norway. Norway's history compared to the around 2,500 year history of Sri Lanka is very short. Its early antecedents were the Vikings - popularized in Western literature as barbarous hordes fond of raping women they captured on their raids. The Norwegians' toast "skoll" which is widely believed to come from their drinking out of the skulls of their captives (possibly after a cannibalistic feast) also arrives from this past.

Yet, today Norwegians are rightly proud of their only recent history and celebrate with much pageantry 17th May, the Norwegian National Day. Twenty years ago I myself participated in these celebrations and observed the sheer pride of Norwegian natives. Sometimes they have even gone to extra extents in their patriotism. For example they banned the film "What's New, Pussycat" in Norway in 1965 because of a scene where Peter Sellers tries to commit suicide by burning himself wrapped in a Norwegian flag. Some sophisticates might consider this a silly action. But Norwegians wear their patriotism very transparently.

Yet ...

Norwegians are directly and indirectly seen in many quarters as burning Sri Lanka and subverting Sri Lankan integrity. They are also some of the major source of funds to organizations that have questioned Sri Lankan sovereignty and have attempted to subvert it and weaken patriotism.

President Chandrika Kumaratunga has talked about "these busy-body, salmon-eating Norwegians". And Sri Lankans have organized hugely against Norwegian interference. The first major demonstration against Norway was held by the then main opposition party in April 2002[1]. Ethnic Tamils have protested with hundreds carrying bodies of those slain by LTTE to the Colombo Norwegian Embassy to protest Norway's pro LTTE partiality.

A series of massive demonstrations – people power – against Norwegian intervention in Sri Lanka have thus occurred. These are possibly the largest ever demonstrations against Norway in Norway's history. As for Sri Lanka, they come close to the large numbers that demonstrated against the Indian incursion into Sri Lanka, titled the Indian Peace Accord. Next to that, the anti-Norway protests were the largest ever demonstrations against a foreign power in Sri Lanka's 2,500 year history. In one, 50,000 marched to the Norwegian Embassy in Colombo carrying black flags while police guarded the Norwegian embassy. As posters in the demonstrations loudly proclaimed, Norway had become the new "Ugly American". Norway's image in Sri Lanka, except for those elements controlled by Norwegian money in the form of NGOs funded by it, had declined to an unprecedented level. It is worse than the image India had after its brief incursion into the country in the late 1980s.

But ...

Norway's self image is that of a sensitive nation, sympathetic to developing countries devoting over 1% of its oil generated GNP to aid. (Well actually not quite, it has declined from this once high figure). The present paper traces this shift of Norway to colonial intruder, partly through an exercise in participant observation. In the late 1970s and early 1980s, the author interacted closely with Norwegian academics to attempt equal academic partnerships not only with Sri Lanka, but also with the rest of the Third World.

I attempted to build a non-colonial academic situation in Sri Lanka.

By the late 1970s, the global critique of academic colonialism, of which I was a pioneer, was being heard in mainland Europe. Soon, I found European collaborators willing to work under our guidance. One offer was from within the University of Trondheim, Norway. During that interaction, which I found to be between equals, I discussed with Norwegian authorities how to build up correct collaborative relationships. I suggested to then sympathetic Norwegians how to attempt real academic equality. And I helped establish collaborative research between Norway and Sri Lankan universities on a fully equal, transparent basis.

But, as we have seen, Norway is today perceived to have drastically changed its relations. There are reasons for this perception. Norway has indeed become a "subverter", in two ways. This has occurred directly through attempted control of Lankan Government structures. Norwegian subversion has also occurred through unrepresentative NGOs that Norway funds and sponsors and who have been against Sri Lanka sovereignty.

Let me recall a few examples of direct interference.

The Norwegian Deputy Prime Minister Vidar Helgesen suspended the Sri Lanka "peace drive" claiming the then Prime Minister and the President were at logger heads (Friday, 14-Nov-2003). But this was hardly news. The Sri Lankan President, the executive head of the country had already accused the Prime Minster of violating the Constitution by showing her the Norwegian brokered truce only after the Tamil rebels' leader had signed it[2]. And the Norwegian Foreign Ministry had been directly involved in this. Eric Solheim, a self appointed adventurer on Sri Lankan soil (for his personal background see my article in this volume), had announced publicly in Norwegian media in June 2000 that he had "produced a proposal of peace and is ready to present it to the Tamil Tigers".[3] Solheim together with the Norwegian Foreign Ministry had drafted and crafted the final Ceasefire Agreement along with the LTTE's Balasingham. They had then got it signed by Prabhakaran without the concurrence of the Executive Head of State[4]. And Kumaratunga complained, "The powers and functions which by this agreement are vested in the Norwegian Government travel far beyond the role of facilitator."[5]

Helgesen in a published interview had also placed himself on record above the Sri Lanka President. Thus in a reporter's question to Helgesen: "The President [Head of State] has said that she was not shown the Memorandum of Understanding [between the LTTE and the Prime Minister] until the last minute. Is not the responsibility of the Norwegian Government to inform both the President and the Prime Minister at the same time?" He had imperiously replied "When the Prime Minister asks Norway to inform the President we will do that."[6]

The *Economist*, published from a country which had been used to a colonial empire labeled Norwegian interference simply as "Viking rule". It revealed that "but nor, curiously, was [Prime Minister] Mr. Wickremesinghe consulted about the wording of the memorandum [with the LTTE]. It appears to have been composed by the Norwegian Foreign Ministry after discussions with the Tigers. The Tigers' leader, Prabhakaran … [first] signed the memorandum ... It was then brought to Colombo for Mr. Wickremesinghe's signature."[7] And Kumaratunga summarized "The nature of the Norwegian Government's status has changed to such an extent as to make it incompatible with the sovereign status of Sri Lanka."[8]

The Norwegians' pro-LTTE stance was clearly shown in the wording of the memorandum. The LTTE was allowed to have no-go areas whereas the 'cleared areas' under Government control were opened to LTTE operatives to indulge, not really in political work but in all manner of direct subversive activity. They were in fact thus allowed to violate the Ceasefire Agreement with impunity. To make this possible, the pro-LTTE Norwegians brought in Ceasefire monitors from Nordic countries. They have been totally partial towards the LTTE[9].

The impunity with which the LTTE was allowed to go around the country freely contrasted itself with the then UNF Government leader literally swearing in public just before the Parliamentary General Election in 2001 that the ban on the LTTE would not be lifted. But the Norwegians had other plans, as the following question and answer between Helgesen and a reporter revealed.

Q [to Helgesen]: Is there a condition that the ban on the LTTE should be lifted if they were to attend the talks?

A: It is important that when you bring parties to the negotiating table, they have the feeling of being treated equally.[10]

Soon thereafter the LTTE ban was lifted.

Norwegians exposed themselves also clearly as torch bearers for the LTTE in Europe and in Geneva at the Human Rights Commission. Their facilitation of the peace process "was without precedent. They would never have taken the liberties they took with Sri Lanka with any other country."[11]

Norwegians had for several years supported the LTTE designs on the country through its NORAD and Red Barna (Norwegian "Save the Children") activities. Norwegians had a UNDP Resident Representative in the mid 1990s who was a former Red Barna man who was very supportive of the LTTE[12]. Aggression on Sri Lanka's territorial integrity had occurred earlier through the later-to-be Ambassador Jon Westborg. As head of Redd Barna, Westborg transported thousands of estate (Indian origin) Tamils to the jungles of the Vanni to illegally change the country's ethnic geographical distribution. Those transported later became soldiers of the last stronghold of Prabhakaran.

Norwegians had let the LTTE establish their international communication headquarters in Oslo. After the ceasefire the Norwegian embassy soon secretly smuggled in very sophisticated radio equipment for their LTTE protégés. This was done under diplomatic privilege violating any accepted behavior under the Vienna Convention. This electronic equipment had the highest possible degree of security from interception by the security forces. In contrast, the Sri Lankan Government's radio equipment was far less sophisticated. This new equipment from the Norwegian embassy would allow future attacks to be better coordinated and to be more effective. Westborg who had done much to undermine Sri Lanka was now, personally involved in the import of radio equipment to Prabhakaran. Further, under the conditions of the Norwegian ceasefire, the LTTE had installed a radar system and a satellite telephone centre in the sea coast.[13]

Norway had, as shown by videos in this conference, also taken the LTTE delegates to its infamous Oslo meeting to Norwegian army camps for briefing on weapons. The IPS News Service reported that Norway had trained Sea Tigers in the seas of Thailand to attack the Sri Lanka Navy[14]. Previously in 1993, 1994 and 1995 they had provided training to the LTTE in a distant Malaysian island[15]. Norwegian colleagues critical of the Norway-LTTE connection have unearthed some strange facts. The LTTE has begun having the same weapons as the Norwegian Special Forces! LTTE cadres have been arrested by Thai authorities with one of the favorite weapons of the Norwegian Special Forces ("Marine jegerne") namely the HK MK23 pistol. They have been also arrested LTTE cadres with a Swedish rocket launcher, the Carl Gustav 84mm rocket launcher that is the standard launcher used by the Norwegian military. These are weapons normally used by NATO Special Forces and SWAT teams combating terrorists. Thai police have wondered how these got into LTTE hands.[16] The answer appears very obvious. The Norwegian Government gave it.

The Norway Foreign Minister Petersen warned the Sri Lankan President according to the English language Norway Post on "her continuous interference in the peace process."

When Helgesen was confronted about reports of the LTTE bringing arms including long range missiles and was asked whether he had talked to the LTTE about it, he replied simply "No"[17]. When asked about the continuous breaking of the cease-fire by the LTTE Helgesen replied that he cannot give a guarantee that they would not do that[18]. When Helgesen was asked about reports from Amnesty International that the LTTE are recruiting child soldiers, his reply was that the LTTE "are telling us that it is not true."[19]

While the Norwegians, by deed and propaganda, had surreptitiously worked hard for a separate Tamil State they became disingenuous when asked about LTTE's true intentions. Thus when Helgesen was asked whether the LTTE had changed its minds from its stated objectives of settling only a separate State, he replied "you have to ask that from them."[20]

The LTTE's ISGA proposals have been declared the first step towards the creation of a separate sovereign territorial entity in Sri Lanka by Indian commentators[21]. This stand has been affirmed by U.S. Government authorities. Yet, the Norwegians had been continuously sponsoring the LTTE's ISGA proposals, that is sponsoring politically a separate State.

Because of the Norwegian sponsored Sri Lanka Monitoring Mission, SLMM, the LTTE has without impunity transported their troops from the Northern Province to the Eastern. As their first sea craft carrying their fighters used this route they released two triumphant photographs to the public[22]. A commentator pointed out that the SLMM had "not only been high-handed, arrogant, partial, prejudiced and haughty but imperious, over bearing and dictatorial and have also been dishonest."[23]

Maj. Gen. (retd.) Teleffsen the Norwegian Head of the Sri Lanka Monitoring Mission had proposed that the Sri Lanka Navy should recognize LTTE's Sea Tigers as "a de facto Naval Unit" and that the LTTE should be excluded from the law concerning limitations on outboard motors horsepower.[24] This very same Teleffsen also sought to confine the Sri Lanka Navy's exercises, to specified areas at sea. He had also marked out in a map the areas in the country's western and eastern seas to be handed out to the LTTE for "training and live firing."[25] He was also found leaking "information to the LTTE concerning a navy operation to track down a suspected LTTE ship smuggling arms into Sri Lanka." The Sri Lanka's navy accused his outfit of jeopardizing its attempt to capture a suspected Tamil Rebel arms shipment. And the President asked the then Government to declare as "persona-non grata", Teleffsen, who allegedly leaked vital military information to the LTTE.

No surprise that the Sri Lankan President denounced the Nordic truce monitors for a "completely unsatisfactory and biased" report on the sinking of a Chinese trawler by the LTTE. The Nordic SLMM said that the attack was not carried out by the LTTE or the Government, but by some other "unidentified armed elements", a clear fabrication[26].

The failure of the current ceasefire is seen most vividly in the human rights field. The European Union severely condemned the LTTE for continuing to engage in political killings, abductions and recruitment of children for its ranks.[27] Human Rights Watch in a special report mentioned that "Many Tamil families who expected a 'peace dividend' now expect an unwelcome visit from armed Tamil Tiger recruiters."[28] The University Teachers for Human Rights, UTHR, the Jaffna university based group noted that the

Norway backed Sri Lanka monitoring mission had miserably failed and was biased. And in spite of its bias SLMM issued a report which shows that there were 2, 491 proved violations by the LTTE compared to only 113 by the Government.[29] The Norwegians were rewarding LTTE tyranny and undermining the democratic potential[30]. The Norwegian brand of "human rights" is illustrated by the fact that according to their own sources, Prabhakaran has the power to change verdicts of the "Eelam Courts" and so intervene in the judicial process and even change the law itself as the need arises.[31]

In spite of LTTE terror, the people in the affected areas continue to protest. At Trincomalee public and private transport services were stopped and all shops kept closed as more than five thousand Tamils, Sinhalese and Muslims demonstrated against LTTE atrocities on unarmed civilians. They demanded action by the Norway backed Sri Lanka Monitoring Mission to prevent this[32]. Tamil residents have fled to save their children from being rounded up for forcible conscription.[33] School children at a Valaichenai Hindu school demonstrate against abductions of children by the LTTE.[34]

One of the biggest insults to this country has been the imposition of Eric Solheim. An insignificant adventurer from an insignificant party in Norway, Solheim has imposed himself as a negotiator.[35] His ideas and actions as recorded in the public sphere are revealing and I have summarized them elsewhere. Let me recap them.

Solheim has brought in many other conditionalities into Sri Lanka which he would not have entertained elsewhere. Let us enumerate them. Solheim has admitted that his very small political party *Sosialistik Venstreparti* inflates the number of its members, so as to get extra subsidies from the Government. This "honest" act in Sri Lanka will bring in severe punishment.

He had supported the bombing of Serbia by NATO to eliminate

Slobodan Milosevic - guilty, among others, of ethnic cleansing. Yet, Milosevic's cruelties do not match those of Prabhakaran. Milosevic did not attack ancient religious institutions and did not indulge in terrorist bombings like those of the Central Bank. There was no recruitment of child soldiers and no use of suicide bombers. Milosevic has been charged for crimes against humanity. Solheim instead of supporting Prabhakaran and the LTTE should be suing them for two easily provable crimes against humanity. They are the ethnic cleansing of Jaffna of all Muslims and Sinhalese and the killing of 600 policemen who surrendered to them, as well as the killing after their surrender of all the armed personnel at Mullativu. Yet Solheim embraces Prabhakaran while he wanted the elimination of Milosevic.

Solheim has publicly called Kissinger a terrorist for his actions in Chile and Vietnam and says Kissinger should be charged as a war criminal. But Kissinger's role in Chile led to the death of only a relative few in comparison with the very much larger number of deaths due to Prabhakaran. Prabhakaran is guilty of far more horrendous crimes than Pinochet's Chile. Solheim is said to be concerned about the spread of a racist party in Norway and wants to isolate it. But in Sri Lanka he befriends the most racist party, the LTTE.

Solheim bemoans that membership of political parties is coming down in Norway and so is bad for democracy. Yet in Sri Lanka Solheim has promoted the LTTE which describes itself as the sole representative of the Tamils. Consequently all Tamil members of the current parliament from the North and East are those who have not been elected under free and fair conditions but under the scepter of LTTE guns and terror. Solheim and Norway also recognize unrepresentative foreign funded NGOs that go against both truth and popular will. This is a sneaky attack against both truth and democracy. It appears that under Solheim truth and democracy is only for Norwegians while only varieties of fiction and a brutal dictatorship are good for Sri Lankans. And even a group whose members had taken public stands against Sri Lanka sovereignty, the Centre for Policy Alternatives (CPA) was soon reporting that in spite of massive propaganda including by the CPA, only less than 20% of Sri Lankans were supporting the Norwegian initiative[36]. Indo-Asian News Service summed up in November 24, 2004 "The Norway-brokered truce of February 2002 between the LTTE and the Government has boosted Prabhakaran politically, militarily and diplomatically."[37] It concluded that nearly three years after the ceasefire Prabhakaran "remains firmly committed to his dream of breaking up Sri Lanka to carve out a Tamil Eelam State."

Indirect Intrusion Means

If the above are the direct means of Norwegian intrusion through her Government, what are the indirect means? The Norwegian Government helps brainwash the Sri Lankan population through unrepresentative NGOs and journalists they fund. Foreign funded NGOs are a new phenomenon of the last 25 years. Earlier we had local voluntary organizations. Now increasingly through foreign funds small unrepresentative groups can influence the country.

Some foreign funded NGOs in fact do perform good functions, for example in such fields as health, education, family planning etc. But often they do not have democratic structures. This new private sector, the NGOs, is accountable only to themselves and to their donors. Such foreign funded NGOs with their access to resources and local and foreign media publicity marginalize real local initiatives. This has resulted in a new NGO colonialism and the creation of a new dependent local class. Especially in the cultural, ideological and political sphere, they have become an insidious force, virtually a fifth column for western interests albeit sometimes from the western left.

This is precisely what Norwegian funded NGOs have done. "Their" NGOs have stood against the sovereignty of this country such as welcoming Indian troops, and asking for foreign intervention.

Norway has become a proxy ruler through such NGO fronts.

Two Norwegian funded organizations "International Alert" (IA) operating internationally and the "National Peace Council" (NPC) operating locally, provide revealing dimensions of how the subversion of Sri Lanka by Norwegian funds has been carefully coordinated and carried out leading in effect to the subversion of the elected representatives of the country.

International Alert (IA)

The IA was formed in the 1980s specifically targeted on Sri Lanka. Its beginnings were as its publications reveal "in the conflict within Sri Lanka between Singhalese and Tamils". But this beginning was very much partial to the separatist cause. Thus, IA's charter was to make "widely known", "the present condition of the Tamil people and their genuine demands" as IA then stated. In keeping with these partisan aims, IA also published an alleged map on the ethnic issue which showed over half of Sri Lanka as Tamil. These alleged Tamil areas included the central highlands as well as substantial sections of the South, including Hambantota. This area was much bigger than that given in the fictitious maps created on the alleged Tamil traditional homelands by the LTTE itself. IA's publications also give as one of its objectives alerting the world on "mass killings and genocide" allegedly of Sri Lankan Tamils. IA also said that it was making a "major effort" internationally on several fronts on Sri Lanka, including "UN interventions."

Some of IA's activities in Sri Lanka have been covered by an international committee that enquired into IA after it was accused of staging a coup in Sierra Leone (to which event we shall later return).[38] It is useful to go to this report. The report says "IA's first initiative [in Sri Lanka] was to form a committee of experts in an attempt to resolve the protracted armed conflict in Sri Lanka; initially, the intelligentsia, the military, the business community, press and other media, religious organizations, politicians ....

were all designated strategic sectors to work with."[39] This was a cross section of the entire Sri Lankan political structure. So, a comprehensive infiltration of the entire power structure was being attempted from the point of view of IA's already published ideology, namely a pro separatist agenda.

IA in its Sri Lankan activities had sent "journalists and "peace activists" to other conflict-torn societies (South Africa and Northern Ireland)", produced TV programmes with the Sri Lanka State owned Broadcasting Corporation, had a workshop "Covering Conflict" organized in conjunction with the Sri Lanka Television Training Institute and the Media Peace Centre (South Africa); and a seminar with The Free Media Movement on responsibility of the press. In December 1996, this was followed by a similar event focusing on human rights and conflict resolution (under the aegis of the Sasakawa Media Project).[40] It sent parliamentarians on trips to other conflict ridden areas "identified with the assistance of the National Peace Council (NPC)."[41] These, all sounded very noble.

They had also assisted the Centre for Policy Research and Analysis (CEPRA) at the University of Colombo, in order to establish a post -graduate course in conflict resolution and supported the National Peace Council (NPC) that was launched in February 1995. In October 1995 IA's programmed director had also met with representatives of the military and the negotiating team with the Tigers with the explicit aim of "influencing the talks" between the Government and rebels.[42]

IA also contributed funds for the activities of the Tamil International Centre (TIC). The principal activities of the TIC based in London and linked to many separatist groups was to provide a forum for the exchange of views and information on the problems of Sri Lanka Tamils by organizing conferences, seminars, consultation meeting and workshops.[43] And when Sri Lankan troops were about to take back Jaffna from the LTTE, Kumar Rupasinghe, Director of IA came on the BBC Sinhala service (28th November1995) and called for UN intervention.

The real workings of IA are found in tracing its controversial activities not in Sri Lanka but in the other country it was as equally involved in. This was in Sierra Leone and typifies particular modes available to unaccountable NGOs. This case is extremely revealing as IA had to face a string of accusations that went up to the UN and the Organization of African Unity. In parts of official Africa, IA's name turned black with allegations of diamond smuggling, arming of illegal groups and supporting a coup under the cover of "conflict resolution".

The events center around a coup in which the elected President of Sierra Leone Dr. Ahmad Tejan Kabbah was overthrown. The best summary of these events was in the American Sunday Talk Show on ABC "Like it is" of October 5, 1997, where the deposed President Ahmed Tejan Kabbah was interviewed for one hour about the coup that overthrew him.

He said (and I quote below directly from the transcript of the program) "for the past six years, we've had a rebel movement in the country. ... The rebels were being sponsored by a third party ... called International Alert... they have as their secretary general someone from Sri Lanka ." [The IA secretary was a Sri Lankan Kumar Rupasinghe to whom we shall later turn.] Dr. Ahmad Tejan Kabbah charged publicly "we have evidence to show that they [meaning IA] were very much interested in smuggling out diamonds and gold and that was how they got associated with the rebels [the RUF] and they were able to really control the rebel leader to virtually do whatever they wanted him to do."[44]

He went on further,

"This group that call themselves International Alert... got hooked onto the rebels and I think they were looking for a way to have a foothold into, our mining possibilities in Sierra Leone... [They were giving money] to the rebels. ... They started out by giving them all forms of equipment, arming them and providing communication equipment, satellites and so on. And so, encouraged them that these people can use, [to] fight their way to the statehouse in Freetown [Sierra Leone's capital] through the barrel of the gun or whatever weaponry they can supply to them."

Ahmed Tejan Kabbah then mentions that previously there were also attempts by the IA supported groups to "derail ... the introduction of democracy into the country" and that these people who "didn't want any formal democracy decided to derail that process through political maneuvering. And then after that ... tried to prevent the election itself from taking place. They would cut off the hands of people [to prevent this]. ... They did all sorts of really inhuman things that I don't think I can describe on the television ... to prevent people from going to the polls. But in the end, the people defied all this and decided to go to the polls and then they decided also to elect the candidate that they thought would help the country get it forward."

But after having "exhausted all these... political maneuvering to stop the election process itself, they decided that perhaps the best way to stop it would be through violence and that's why the rebels came together with ... a faction of the military. ... The rebels were dealing with this International Alert and they and a faction of the military decided to come together and organize a coup."

Before this public TV airing, Ahmed Tejan Kabbah had addressed a strong letter, (a copy of which I have obtained through UN sources), to Kofi Annan, UN Secretary General dated 3 April 1997 where he made very pointed allegations at Kumar Rupasinghe, the Sri Lankan head of AI[45]. He stated that he was "gravely concerned... by the continuing ... activities of... International Alert (IA)... Two of its officials Mr. Kumar Rupasinghe and Mr. Addal Sebo in particular... started interfering in our internal affairs in violation of the principles guiding the conduct of NGOs when Mr. Sebo surreptitiously entered our territory on more than one occasion and stayed with Corporal Sankoh [the head of RUF, the rebel group] for weeks at a time in 1995. During these illegal visits, IA did everything to gain propaganda advantage for the RUF and to raise money for its war efforts in several capitals around the world... Joining forces with the erstwhile military junta, the National Provisional Ruling Council (NPRC) and the RUF, IA fought tooth and nail against the process of democratization, especially the presidential and parliamentary Elections ... IA's role was one of advocacy on behalf of the RUF and not that of a facilitator as it often claimed... In the period since the signing of the Abidjan Accord, IA through its representatives, Kumar Rupasinghe and Addal Sebo, embarked upon sabotaging all efforts at implementing the peace agreement in good faith. [Later,] Rupasinghe and Sebo left no stone unturned to derail or delay the implementation process."[46]

President Kabbah had now lost patience with "all these machinations of International Alert and its representatives." He further charged the IA for allegedly "engaging in activities that are not only intolerable but down right criminal." Kabbah's letter makes a further strong allegation that his elected Government wa, "in possession of concrete evidence that IA have been engaged in these malicious practices in order to prolong the conflict in my country which they use for soliciting funds from donor agencies and Governments while benefiting personally from the illicit mining and sale of precious minerals and the purchase of weapons by the [rebel group] RUF."

"Consequently" his Government had "now decided to severe all relations with International Alert" and was urging "all Governments and International organizations to refrain from interacting with IA."

These activities of IA also reached the Organization of African Unity (OAU). Its key members had been briefed in a special closed session on IA's activities at a meeting of heads of State in Harare and were told not to have anything to do with. In December 1997

Liberia had rebuffed the offer of any cooperation with IA after three consultants were to go there. Abdul Mohammed, President of the Inter Africa Group, which liaises very closely with the OAU, in a letter dated July 14, 1997 addressed to IA puts these matters in a very strong, anti imperialist manner (I have a copy of the letter). It bluntly says:

> "Let us remind you ... there is nothing that you can do for Africa from Europe that we cannot do. So, as you contemplate your presence in Africa, you should be aware that we lack neither the intellectual nor the practical capacity to respond meaningfully to the challenges of early warning and peace building in Africa."

He adds, warning of these imperialist designs "Please do not make the mistake - made by many NGOs in the West - of thinking that Africans are still incapable of addressing the challenges they face in all areas, without the direct management of their affairs by institutions in the North...We have recently come to realize to our dismay and disappointment that you continue to portray us to the donors as lacking in maturity and capacity as a result of which you are indispensable to us. ... We resent that. This is why we say that there is nothing that you can do that we cannot do."

Abdul Mohammed then adds that "the time is overdue" for IA to stop acting "as a manager of African affairs from London".

As a result of these turn of events, IA's reputation and standing suffered greatly in Africa. One consequence was that IA was not being invited to major conferences where it should have been. It also resulted in problems within IA staff. One of the allegations made by some IA staff was that IA was following a (white) racist policy, implying that African employees were being paid less than whites for doing the same type of work. Eventually the British Industrial Tribunal found IA guilty of discrimination and awarded an aggrieved African employee 250,000 pounds, a large sum of money.

With this collapse of IA's image, the Christian Michelsen Institute of Norway was called in to carry out the evaluation I have already referred to in October 1997 at the request of the donors of IA, Denmark, Norway, Sweden and The Netherlands. This Christian Michelsen report itself has to be seen not as a neutral effort, but about how "good" the interventions on internal affairs of sovereign nations were.

The Christian Michelsen report admits that "IA has been subject to serious allegations ... in Sierra Leone, which the organization itself has celebrated as its main achievement.[47] ... IA's neutrality and transparency was... widely questioned by the Freetown [Sierra Leone] authorities, international organizations and other Governments."[48] ... Many in the international community [believed] that IA was working as an adviser [to the rebels], not a neutral facilitator, in the peace process.[49] .... IA's interventions, in particular it's continued lobbying of senior politicians and international civil servants, despite the Trustees' [of IA] decision to become "non-operational", served to create confusion (and thus suspicion) regarding IA's intentions".[50]

After the coup, which overthrew the elected Government, IA was seen the report goes on "as an advocate of [the rebel movement] RUF's interests rather than a neutral party advocating the achievement of a just and peaceful settlement."[51]

The report criticizes the IA for "lack of clarity and transparency"[52]... Problems of credibility and transparency - contradictions between IA's stated position and its actual interventions. - continued to affect IA ... and led to mistrust and suspicion that the organization was neither neutral nor transparent in its dealing with international organizations".[53] All these actions were now "seriously affecting the organization's reputation, credibility and effectiveness and, therefore, also [the IA] staff morale."[54]

So IA's credibility, transparency, reputation and effectiveness were all in strong doubt as documented by their donors' own consultants at the end of 1997. But IA had their warning already in 1996 in a British Parliament report.

This report said:

"International Alert was, in a sense, the odd man out, being the only NGO amongst Governmental regional organizations. Their presence at the talks was controversial for many reasons. International Alert had made the first contact with the [rebel group] RUF and had been successful in persuading Foday Sankoh to release foreign hostages, which raised suspicion that they were not entirely neutral. This concern was fueled by the fact that International Alert is not seen to be entirely transparent in its actions. This sentiment was expressed.... by members of the Government delegation, the press, many NGOs and the public."[55]

The Christian Michelson report has an annexure by Mark Duffield. It is still in the tone of guarding-the-NGO-community, but notes that in recent years, "conflict resolution has been privatized" [with NGOs being the private sector]. Consequently, this "Western intervention ... has created a major expansion opportunity for both international and local NGOs."[56] Duffield further notes that the growth of these conflict resolution NGOs has been accompanied by "the prior demise of alternative political projects within the regions ... which, in different ways, attempted to maintain national independence and autonomy."[57] Translated, what this meant was that these NGOs actively helped erode national independence and sovereignty.

Duffield observes that through these mechanisms "the ability of the West to directly modify internal political processes ... is greater today than at any time since the colonial period."[58] It also notes that "there are a growing number of critics [in the west] of conflict resolution, ... which interpret increased Western involvement in the crisis regions as a new form of imperialism."[59]

The donors' report finally warned International Alert that it needs to develop "a management style characterized by openness, and a willingness to be actively self-critical if it is to defend its interests. An ability to see oneself as others see us is an elusive, but necessary, skill to develop. Denial of others' perceptions risks reinforcing the impression of organizational insensitivity and lack of analytical capacity."[60]

And on IA's role in Sri Lanka the report was specific. It questioned "the wisdom of the high profile held by IA in Sri Lanka ... The Sri Lankan attitude to NGOs as well as international agencies remains largely ambivalent, particularly when it comes to what is regarded as interference and meddling in internal conflict."[61]

IA's start in the 1980s, as we noted, was with the "Sri Lankan problem" taking a position identical to that of the separatists. So there was no doubt of IA's agenda from its very beginnings, its acceptance of a skewed version of Sri Lankan events, a fictitious Sri Lankan history and its advocacy of intervention in the country's internal affairs.

Kumar Rupasinghe: IA's Prince of Light, Prince of Darkness?

It is now relevant to discuss the published attitudes of its Director, Sri Lankan Kumar Rupasinghe who was accused by many reports as being directly involved in many of IA's unsavory activities.

Kumar Rupesinghe had spelled out already in 1992 the need to essentially privatize foreign policy in conflicts and wars. He had said that one "cannot wait for the United Nations. The non-Governmental communities and other actors must develop their own methods of working and cooperating internationally, and developing greater regional institutions"[62]

IA, we noted, had from the beginning, an explicit pro-Tamil separatist agenda claiming that Sri Lanka was involved in an alleged "genocide" of Tamils. But the question remains how IA appointed Kumar Rupasinghe in the first place who in Sri Lanka had taken positions diametrically opposite to what IA stood for. Separatist ideologues take as a key negative event the 1956 victory of nationalist forces overthrowing the Sri Lankan Anglicized elite. Another key turning point in the separatist description of events was the constitution of 1972. But in all these key events, Rupasinghe had taken stands opposite to what IA claimed allegiance.

Rupasinghe had said that it was only in 1956 that the country was "able to shake the shackles of imperialism in Sri Lanka"[63]. And on the 1972 Constitution he was equally positive saying that the country "achieved full political freedom [only] when [it] became a Republic in 1972."[64] Rupasinghe was also an acknowledged public admirer of the genocidal Pol Pot regime of Cambodia, as well documented in Sri Lankan newspapers[65]. Rupasinghe was also feting other dictators and had praised on record Brezhnev and Kim Il Sung - he was a guest of both.[66]

More significant was that Rupasinghe had in the journal which he ran *Jana Vegaya*, firmly taken the view that Tamil separatists were racists working closely with South Indian groups to subvert Sri Lanka, very much the opposite view of IA. Let me elaborate.

As Rupasinghe and IA was arguing for "a comprehensive political package which meets the 'original' problem" of the ethnic conflict, it is interesting to see what "the problem" was as stated by Rupasinghe himself in his journal *Janavegaya* when he was residing in Sri Lanka. Let me translate and transcribe from several *Janavegaya* articles.[67]

Political classes, said *Janavegaya* were being conducted by the Federal Party (FP – the precursor of the TULF) that exhorted Tamils residing in the South of Sri Lanka to migrate to "Tamil Lanka", the North and East. *Janavegaya* warned against this stirring of communal feelings. Power hungry Tamil capitalists, it said were trying to divide the country in order to please foreign masters. Tamil newspapers were publicly engaged in carrying out communal propaganda and *Janavegaya* urged the Government to curb such propaganda. The people, *Janavegaya* warned, should be vigilant of the activities of the Tamil United Front, the immediate precursor of the present TULF.

It further warned that it was important that the country understands the character of the various activities of the FP leaders who, having begun with the 50-50 demand, then demanded parity of status for Sinhala and Tamil, progressed into a demand for Provincial Councils, wanted to go to the UN to demand splitting the country into two through an invasion and are now organizing a military struggle against the Government. They were mobilizing the Tamil speaking youth using racist language. The FP was an agent of national and international reaction, imperialism and neo-colonialism. The efforts to promote an armed struggle *Janavegaya* stated was "supposed to have the support of Mr. M. Sivasitthamparam" the TULF leader.

South Indian newspapers *Janavegaya* said were feeding this Tamil racism in Sri Lanka . Indian Tamil leaders and politicians had claimed a countless number of times that Sri Lanka was a part of Tamil Nadu. The DMK leaders and the leaders of TULF were bosom buddies. *Janavegaya* described how South Indian organizations and newspapers supported the Federal Party to break Sri Lanka in two and establish a separate Tamil State in the North and the East. It also warned that Madras racists were demanding that Indira Gandhi (then Indian Prime Minister) teach Sri Lanka a lesson in the same manner with which India dealt with Bangladesh.

Rupasinghe's *Janavegaya* prescriptions for the problem were simple and straightforward:

> As a first step, all arms should be put down. The so-called Tamil leaders should be isolated... They are just a set of people who are misleading the Tamil people. Therefore, this Government should not have anything to do with these people.

This was a position diametrically opposite to IA's position from the latter's beginnings.

The Christian Michelson evaluation of IA correctly questioned "the wisdom of the high profile held by IA in Sri Lanka at the present time"[68]. The report noted correctly that in Sri Lanka "particularly following the largely negative press coverage of IA's activities, there are worries that a close association with IA may be considered a possible liability."[69] But all these negative activities of IA in support of Tamil separatists was because of Rupasinghe as he switched diametrically from showing Tamil separatism as a racist plot supported by South Indians to advocate the opposite and support Tamil separatism. IA in its publications had shown the Northern and Eastern Provinces as exclusively Tamil. It is based on this that Muslims were driven out of the North and were now under threat in the East. But by the early 2000s Rupasinghe had turned sides again!

Rupasinghe was now sponsoring the Muslim cause and writing about "Regaining Muslim lands in the East".[70] These lands were lost precisely because of the exclusive Tamil zones demarcated by IA. He now states further that the "The politics of information, or rather disinformation, play a critical role in deeply divided societies."[71] He had been in the forefront of politics of information as he had switched ideological sides several times.

What Rupasinghe should be doing now is what International Alert did in Sierra Leone as it attempted to reenter that country n 2001. Its spokesman admitted that its interference in Sierra

Leone brought the organization under international condemnation, "the condemnation and allegation made IA staff [cringe] as many workers left the organizations." He added, "though I was not an employee of IA by then, I on behalf of the organization am asking for forgiveness. We want to win the trust and confidence of Sierra Leoneans." He added that to prevent future disasters [as had happened under Rupasinghe], a new dispensation framework called the "code of conduct for conflict transformation work" has adopted.[72] Rupasinghe instead of apologizing and asking for forgiveness is now opportunistically switching sides.

National Peace Council: A War Front for LTTE Propaganda

A central instrument of International Alert's (IA) presence in Sri Lanka has been another Norwegian funded outfit the National Peace Council (NPC). The latter was one of the organizations IA supported and helped the parliamentarians who went on the trips sponsored by IA to Ireland, Philippines and Geneva (as pointed out by the investigating report on IA).[73]

The National Peace Council's key members have stood for some very interesting stands on peace and war. It is instructive to recall these positions of their key personnel, some of which we have noted earlier. Thus they had recognized the traditional homelands of Tamils hoax as valid and stated so explicitly (as published in *Tamil Voice* the US Tiger organ).

Hot Spring the Tiger outlet in Britain throws light on the organizer of the National Peace Council, Ajith Rupasinghe, the brother of IA's Kumar Rupasinghe[74]. *Hot Spring* records that he participated in a march and rally of the Tigers in Geneva. He also spoke at the rally. The other speakers were strong Tiger sympathizers Rev. Daniel Thiyagarajah "from the Vanni", Ms. Karen Parker, the pro LTTE lawyer from the U.S., Mr. James Karan, President of the International Federation of Tamils, a Tiger front organization, Ms.

Eliza Mann, of the Tamil Centre for Human Rights, U.K. and LTTE representative in Switzerland, Nadarajah Muralitharan. *Hot Spring* noteds that the rally ended with the LTTE liberation song sung in chorus.

Hot Spring also reproduced a "picture taken at a Press Conference elsewhere, [which] shows Ajith Rupasinghe, Ms. Karen Parker, James Karan, Sivaji of the Swiss Federation of Tamil Associations, and Rev. Daniel Thiyagarajah". The NPC national organizer Ajit Rupasinghe was hardly a neutral peacekeeper as he marched and sang in chorus with the LTTE.

The Media Director of the National Peace Council, Jehan Perera, has also taken very "peaceful" positions. At the time of the Indian incursion we noted how he threatened Sri Lanka with dire consequences through the Indian forces on the Island saying that it was time for Sri Lankans to know some hard truths about their weakness vis-à-vis the large neighbour who was then wielding a big stick. Jehan Perera had also questioned the need for sovereignty and had called for "shared sovereignty" and two near-states.[75]

If the above indicates the ideology of the NPC at its highest levels, how does it reach into the Sri Lankan citizenry to give its message? The NPC media director, Jehan Perera has spelled out the NPC strategy of going to the Sri Lankan population for their particular brand of "peace". This strategy is ambitious, targeting the total population of the country through a societal pyramid from the top political hierarchy to the grass roots for a comprehensive propaganda campaign on their brand of peace. It is described explicitly in their literature.

The NPC says:

> that their "… main targets... are grassroots organizations, NGO networks and sectoral organizations, political elites, religious leaders and communities and cultural agents. ... The people's

organizations are the base of this NPC's strategic pyramid. ... At the middle are the various sectoral networks of professional associations, trade unions, peasant organizations, and women and youth organizations. At the very top are the political, cultural and religious elites and power structure primarily in Sri Lanka but also internationally."

Theirs is a carefully laid out propaganda action strategically aimed at different strata in the country.

In addition to these top to bottom workshops, their "peace education" is also provided, the NPC states, to:

"... people on a mass scale through high visibility and high impact multi-media campaigns, utilizing television, radio, newspaper and wall posters which have supported the peace process and opposed the use of violence at crucial moments. Some examples of the themes that have been publicized are, "Divided by war, united by the cry don't wage war on my behalf", "Give a hand to peace", and "Bullets don't give a people's mandate."

These slogans, one should note in parenthesis, imply equating the LTTE with the Government and further do not take place in a Tamil dominated areas, but in Sinhala majority areas.

As NPC influence on part of the top of the pyramid, MPs from the two leading parties, for example were sent on International Alert trips associated with the NPC. At the middle level, the NPC operates through partner organizations. These include workshops held with several other smaller forcign funded NGOs, for example at Ampara with Seva Lanka , Polonnaruwa with INSHA, Nuwara Eliya with the Sinhala-Tamil Women's Forum, Puttalam with the Rural Development Foundation, and Galle with the Marga Institute.

Other foreign funded organizations that have collaborated with the NPC include the Dharmavedi Institute, Plantation Forum, Muslim Refugee Organizations, Rural Development Foundation, Samaseveya, Students' Front for Freedom, Dimbulagala Foundation, Nirmana Institute, INSHA, Wellassa Govi Kantha Sanvidanaya, Fisheries Workers' Cooperative, Hill Country People's Assembly, People's Coalition for Peace and Democracy, Movement for Constitutional Reform and the Sarvodaya Legal Aid Movement. All are foreign funded.[76]

It should be noted that all these activities are not to be confused with the voluntary peace movements in the West. The participants are "targets", they are selected, "educated" in the ideology and then paid to attend these meetings. They are not motivated through their voluntary will. It is basic anti-democratic authoritarianism.

By targeting the so-called border areas (that is where the Tigers are active) and the soldiers, the NPC propaganda was targeting the major victims of the Tigers and in effect psychologically disarming them. By getting to stop the war against the Tigers, they were in reality inviting these groups own death because LTTE supporters or LTTE held areas were not part of the NPC "targets".

But the NPC in their publication says that their ideas was "formulated after extensive discussion at workshops held ... at the district level with the delegates and their communities." It is interesting to trace the message that is made through this sophisticated propaganda machine. At the grass roots it is given by a Mr. S. Balakrishnan of MIRJE, an organization singled out by separatists as unquestionably accepting the traditional homelands fiction and in fact endorsing ethnic cleansing of non Tamils under the guise of removing existing settlements in hitherto jungle lands.

Balakrishnan's version of history is divided into three phases. They are 1930-1956, 1956-1973 and since 1978. In the process Balakrishnan distorts well-known history. He deliberately misleads on the "50-50" demand in the pre Independence period rejected by the British. This was the demand for the 12% Jaffna Tamil population to have the same number of parliamentary seats as the 72% Sinhalese. Balakrishnan explains away this preposterous demand saying that its point "was to avoid passing any bill that was unfair to minorities without getting their consent." He completely ignores the connections of Sri Lankan Tamil separatism to South Indian Tamil separatism with its beginnings in the 19th century through pre and post Independence periods till Indian Tamil separatism was banned by the 6th amendment to the Indian constitution. The 50-50 demand was made, it should be noted, in Sri Lanka in tandem with the growth of the Indian separatist Tamil Justice Party under Ramasamy Naicker. Balakrishnan also ignores the Indian proxy invasion of the country.

The Newsletter of the National Peace Council also reports of a "bipartisan consensus of PA and UNP politicians" in a NPC program in the Southern city of Matara and again propagates their biased views. This was through a workshop that among others had the NPC versions of "historical analyses" on the ethnic issue. As part of an NPC effort Dulles Alahapperuma and Lakshman Yapa Abeywardena, respectively PA and UNP politicians had been sent by IA on NPC's suggestions to IA trips abroad. They now spoke on "peace" at Matara. Alahapperuma, NPC informs us "explained the futility of trying to weaken LTTE by providing more Government support to the other Tamil parties". He said "it simply would not work". He explained the repeated failure of peace talks, not on the LTTE but because "the Government had missed an opportunity for peace by sending persons who were not experienced in political negotiations to discuss the problem with the Tigers. Also the Government had made a mistake by nurturing the other Tamil parties at the same time as the peace talks were going on". This was the standard LTTE position on the breakdown of repeated peace talks during which the LTTE rearmed and suddenly without notice, resumed hostilities, facts that are well recognized.

These biased views of history are challenged even in the

NPC propaganda meetings. Thus a so called "conflict resolution workshop" of the NPC in the Puttalam District for about 20 community leaders consisting of school teachers, Government servants, Buddhist monks and village notables aroused keen dissent. The first was the NPC version of "History of the conflict" presented by the NPC's program officer, S. P. Nathan, which gave a breakdown of the various acts of the Sri Lankan Government that allegedly had led to the progressive alienation of the Tamil Community.

But participants had according to the NPC's own publications objected to this NPC version of history, as it did not contain the acts of the Tamil political parties and militant organizations.

The most far reaching to accommodate LTTE perspectives was the NPC resolution at their 1998 convention of essentially its paid employees around the country. It "called for a radical restructuring of the State along lines that could permit a form of self-Government for all "nationalities and communities" within one country. The NPC propagandist position that the civil war was "a result of a majoritarian State structure which has given rise to a demand for self-determination by the Tamil people" was accepted by this meeting. The resolution also called for "a just and honorable peace" and urged that negotiations between the Government and LTTE should be conducted with parity of status and without preconditions on either side. The central point was that the separatist view of history was accepted and Tigers given equality of status with the State. A complex history and complicated situation was simplified into a Tiger perspective.

Let me give you one more illustrative example of unrepresentative NGOs from a conference on Sri Lanka's "peace process" held in Oslo on 17 June 2003 sponsored by the Norwegian authorities. The speakers were Eric Solheim (from the Norway Perspective) and Rajah Balasingham (from the LTTE Perspective) and one H. Podinilame, Centre for Human Development. The last presumably represented Sinhala interests or at least Sri Lankan interests.

The key points emphasized by this Podi Nilame were:[77] there is no adequate flow of information about the NGO so-called peace process to the people. He claims that nationally nearly two-thirds (65.8%) of the population are not adequately informed about this so-called peace process and so are not sympathetic to it. Yet three types of "anti-peace" (that is anti NGO "peace") groups are active. They are the JVP, the Sihala Urumaya and groups of Buddhist monks. The activities of the few NGO organizations "promoting peace" such as Podi Nilame's Centre for Human Development are not sufficient to counteract the "anti-peace" message.

In order to ensure what he calls "sustainable peace" Podi Nilame wants to increase power to self styled "civil society" (that is to foreign funded NGOs). This implies that the JVP, the Sihala Urumaya and groups of Buddhist monks do not constitute civil society but the artificial creations of foreign money like, his own organization are. He also wants increased education and awareness-raising at community level. These are code words for brain washing the people. He sees also a need to "increase partnership between local and international NGOs", which would imply a transfer of more international funds to local NGOs. He requests greater coordination among international donors. This translates to intensification of the re-colonization process. And, Podi Nilame wants to "bring grassroots voices to the top" which again implies foreign funding for groups like him.

Who then is this Podi Nilame? I know Podi Nilame. His case is very illustrative. About five years ago he invited me as Chief Speaker for the Annual Meeting of local NGOs getting Canadian funds. In my speech I emphasized the need for fund recipients to think independently and not just be Canadian puppets. I added that Canada was a liberal country and would appreciate open thought. After my speech Podi Nilame lost his Canadian funding.

He has now become a Norwegian funded "peace activist". Podi

Nilame clearly has retooled himself and sought Norwegian funds. Now with foreign money, he arrogates to himself ambitions of brainwashing the country.

Norwegian money has created artificial NGO personalities out of hitherto no-bodies. Only Norwegian and other foreign money sustain them in their re-colonization agenda. One of these unrepresentative and artificial NGO groups and personnel spawned through foreign funds, have demanded, among others, the restructuring of the Sri Lankan State under foreign guidance, demilitarization and de-mobilization of the country's armed forces[78]. This is again a clear agenda for re-colonization.

These are only a few examples of NGOs going against the country's sovereign interests. Their agendas are against popular feeling and to undemocratically control the masses. They could go against popular opinion because they have access to foreign – including Norwegian - funding.

In the US, the Logan Act prohibits U.S. private citizens from interfering with foreign policy, which is the prerogative of the Government. After the Indian proxy invasion of Sri Lanka culminating in the Accord, the American Ambassador to Sri Lanka, James Spain told a reporter on the issue of the Indian forces in Sri Lanka "We [meaning Americans]`still blame the Japanese, but ironically in Sri Lanka, the people do not blame India."[79] One does not have to go far to seek for possible reasons. The Sri Lankan public has been continuously brain washed to accept a loss of sovereignty by Norwegian and other foreign funded NGOs.

Norway thus intrudes on Sri Lanka directly and indirectly. But what are Norway's own political arrangements in comparison with Sri Lanka?

Norway: Norge Über Alles?

Norway's Constitution[80] says that the "Evangelical-Lutheran religion" is its "official religion" and that "inhabitants professing it are bound to bring up their children in the same". So it forbids their citizens to change their religion from that particular Christian sect Lutheranism. The Executive Power is vested in the King, who *must* be a member of the official religion and must "uphold and protect the same". The King's Council itself should have a majority of this sect. Senior State officials must speak Norwegian; and an international body can exercise on internal affairs on the country only with a *prior* "three-fourths majority" of parliament, but will "*not*" have the "power to alter the Constitution". Sri Lanka has no equivalent for such discriminatory acts.

If that were Norwegian State theory, let us see her practices.

Norway put the Nazis' theory of selective breeding into practice, and like the Nazis sterilized people as racial policy[81], these experiments actually continued up to 1994. These racist ideas gave rise to Quisling, the Norwegian leader under the Nazis. Even now, minority Lapps – Samis - suffer. Young Sami children were encouraged to ignore their heritage and until very recently, were forbidden to learn their language at school. The use of the Sami language in the Church was banned. In 2,000, the Norwegian Government ordered arbitrary reductions, up to 10% of reindeer herds - the livelihood of the Samis.

Translating this and other relevant Norwegian theory and practice to Sri Lanka is educational.

Unlike today, Buddhism would be the State religion (now given only "foremost position"); there will be a ban on conversions; Chandrika Kumaratunga the present President will be barred from baptizing her children; State officials must speak Sinhala (Sinhala, Tamil and English are all official languages in Sri Lanka); foreign "mediation" on the country's affairs will only be allowed *after* three-fourths of the parliament's approval (the NGOs have been regularly inviting foreign intervention); and will *not* be allowed for *any* discussion to alter the Constitution (interventions have been called by NGOs to alter the Sri Lankan constitution); Tamil children will not be allowed to pray in Tamil (all children in Sri Lanka are educated in their own mother tongues whether it be Tamil or Sinhala, and each child is compulsorily taught her own religion in school on State money, and there are absolutely no language or other restrictions on worship); and agriculture in Jaffna which is their main livelihood would be reduced by 10%. If all these conditions were imposed on Sri Lanka all her communities Sinhala, Tamil, Muslim, Buddhist, Hindu and Christian would rightly object. But not this self righteous and pretentious successor to the Viking hordes.

Sri Lanka in some writings associated with NGOs has been called a failed State. This push to failure was ably aided by the NGOs and their sponsors like Norway. But Sri Lanka is a very much older civilization than Norway. It has a long historical memory.

In the last 500 years of full or partial subjugation by foreign powers we learnt the art of resistance. And maybe now we have to think the not so unthinkable.

Thinking the Thinkable?

Taking into account cost-benefit criteria of the war and Norway's pro-separatist bias, we have to pose the question: in Sri Lanka's aim of building a secure, multi-ethnic and multi-cultural democratic society, would she be better off rejecting all Norwegian development aid and temporarily suspending diplomatic relations with Norway until quieter times emerge?

The cost of the war is far greater than the aid Norway gives us. And this war has been fuelled by the ideological and other help given directly and indirectly by Norway to the LTTE and anti-sovereignty NGOs. This has been a significant factor in prolonging the war and eroding sovereignty. We will indeed be better off rejecting all Norwegian development aid and temporarily suspending diplomatic relations with Norway until quieter times emerge. Would not Norway have done the same under similar conditions of erosion of sovereignty and humiliation? I may not agree with her policies in Sri Lanka, but Norway is a country with self respect.

End notes

1."News from Sri Lanka 21-24 April 2002" SPUR on Line http://www.spur.asn.au/News0204E.htm

2. February 22, Indo-Asian News Service 2002

3. "Norwegian with peace plan for the Tamil tigers" The *Norway Post* 28. Juni 2000

4. *Island* "The Norwegians exposed"

5. "Kumaratunga slams Norway, wants truce reviewed" March 1, 2002 Reuters

6. "Helgesen talks about Norway's role and assesses peace prospects" ***Helgesen in Sunday Island, March 17, 2002***

7. The *Economist* March 2, 2002

8. "Kumaratunga slams Norway, wants truce reviewed" By Dayan Candappa March 1, 2002 Reuters report.

9. Features *Island* "The Norwegians exposed"

10. Helgesen in *Sunday Island*, March 17, 2002

11. *Island* "The Norwegians exposed"

12. Features *Island* "The Norwegians exposed

13. *Daily Mirror* 16th August 2004

14. IPS News Service November 12,2003

15. Features *Island* "The Norwegians exposed"

16. Personal communication by F.R.Rovik

17. Helgesen in *Sunday Island*, March 17, 2002

18. Helgesen in *Sunday Island*, March 17, 2002

19. Helgesen in *Sunday Island*, March 17, 2002

20. Helgesen in *Sunday Island*, March 17, 2002

21. *The Hindustan Times* November 7 2003

22. Walter Jayawardhana reporting from Los Angeles

23. Features *Island* "The Norwegians exposed"

24. Situation Report - April 20

25. On April 24, 2002

26. *The Hindu* of 09/04/2003

27. 16 August 2004 Daily News

28. *Living in Fear: Child Soldiers and the Tamil Tigers in Sri Lanka* Human Rights Watch New York, 2004

29. *Complaints and Violations* SLMM Colombo, 11.08.2004, SLMM website http://www.slmm.lk/

30. University Teachers for Human Rights, Special Report No: 17
7th October 2003

31. S. Pararajasingham, legal advisor to the LTTE in an interview with the BBC's Sinhala language service

32. Walter Jayawardhana reporting from Los Angeles

33. *Island* Thursday, January 31, 2002You

34. Walter Jayawardhana reporting from Los Angeles

35. "Former Socialist Left leader leaves party politics" *The Norway Post* - 15.11.2000

36. "Sri Lankans losing faith in LTTE and facilitator Norway" *Hindustan Times* June 4, 2003

37. "Prabhakaran turns 50, but will he change?" M.R. Narayan Swamy, Indo-Asian News Service November 24, 2004

38. Serbe G, Macrae J. and Wohlgemuth L, *NGOs in Conflict - An Evaluation of International Alert.* Fantoft-Bergen, Norway: Christian Michelsen Institute 1997

39. Serbe, Macrae and Wohlgemuth 1997 p.42.

40. ibid p. 45

41. ibid p. 47

42. ibid p. 46

43. "International Alert gave 3,000 Pound for Singapore Tamil conference" The *Island,* Sunday Edition. February 23, 1997

44. Transcript of the program ABC "Like it is" of October 5, 1997,

45. "International Alert: The True story!" The *Island* - March 29, 1998

46. Ahmed Tejan Kabbah letter addressed to Kofi Annan, UN Secretary General dated 3 April 1997 reproduced in "***International Alert: The True story***!" The Island - March 29, 1998

47. Serbe, Macrae and Wohlgemuth 1997 p1

48. ibid p.58

49. ibid p. 60

50. ibid p61

51. ibid p61

52. ibid p x

53. ibid p. 62

54. ibid p. 63

55. *The Conflict in Sierra Leone* September 1996, Parliamentary Human Rights Group, p 30

56. Duffield, M. 1997. "Evaluating conflict resolution" In Serbe G, Macrae J. and Wohlgemuth L, *NGO's in Conflict - An Evaluation of International Alert.* Fantoft-Bergen, Norway: Christian Michelsen Institute, p.84

57. ibid p. 82

58. ibid p 98

59. ibid p 98

60. ibid p 224

61. ibid p ix

62. Kumar Rupesinghe, "The role of the U.N. and NGO's, CONFLICT RESOLUTION" (2), *Lanka Guardian*, Sep. 1, 1992

63. Kumar Rupasinghe, "Fascist threat unless capitalist ventures are nationalized" Daily News 11. 6. 75

64. "US trying other tactics in S.E Asia" Daily News 15. 5. 75.

65. *The Ceylon Daily* News August 21, 1976

66. "The great Forum" Kumar Rupasinghe Daily, News 2, 11, 73

67. "*Jatibheda Avisseemata Ida Nodenu*" ("Communalism Should Not Be Allowed")., Editorial, *Janavegaya*, Nov. 5, 1976;"*Lankavata Padam Uganvanna Madurasi Jativadihu Indirata Bala Karathi*" ("Madras racists demand that Indira teach Sri Lanka a lesson") Janavegaya, V. 1. No 21 Saturday 4 August 1973; "*Murasoli, Sengal, Thinath Thandi, Dravida Nadu, Vidu Thaley, Lankave Jativadayata Atha Dena Dakunu Indiyanu Pattara*" ("South Indian newspapers that feed racism in Sri Lanka") by H.M.P.Mohideen *Janavegaya* Saturday 2 June 1973; "*Federal Pasala*" ("Federal School"), *Janavegaya* Saturday 21 April 1973;

"*Dravida Janathavage Mithuro Kavarahuda*?" ("Who are the friends of the Tamil people?") *Janavegaya* Saturday 9 June 1973 ; "*Madurasiye Sahayen Satanata Ara Anditi*" ("Getting ready for a struggle with the support of Madras"), *Janavegaya* Saturday 9 June 1973

68. ibid p ix

69. ibidp. 70

70. "Regaining Muslim lands in the East" Kumar Rupesinghe Sunday Times - April 13, 2003

71. "The Stakeholder factor in the peace process ". Kumar Rupasinghe
Ceylon Daily News - March 28, 2003

72. "International Alert Disowns Omrie Golley" *Salone Times* 22 October 2001

73. Serbe, Macrae, Wohlgemuth 1997 p. 47

74. *Hot Spring* Vol: 2 No. 7 August 1997

75. January 12, 1997, The *Island*; May 1998 *Sunday Observer*

76. "Peace rally" The *Sunday Times* PLUS, Sunday, January 5, 1997.

77. I have taken this material from a CD issued by the conference

78. Proposal for workshop for Air Force personnel by the Berghoff Foundation submitted to Sri Lanka Foundation August 2004

79. Gunaratna Rohan I*ndian Intervention In Sri Lanka: The role of India's intelligence agencies* South Asian Network on Conflict Research 1993 Colombo
P 210

80. The Constitution of the Kingdom of Norway :The Constitution, as laid down on 17 May 1814 by the Constituent Assembly at Eidsvoll (with subsequent amendments, the most recent being of 23 July 1995, Oslo.

81. Roll-Hansen, Nils. Eugenics Before World War II: The Case of Norway. Pubblicazioni della Stazzioni Zoologica di Napoli 2 (2): 269-98, 1980. Brobert, Gunnar, and Roll-Hansen, Nils, eds. *Eugenics and the Welfare State*: *Sterilization Policy in Denmark, Sweden, Norway, and Finland.* East Lansing, MI: Michigan State University Press, 1996. 294 p.

Origins of the North-South Conflict

H. L. D. Mahindapala

Tracing the origins of any violent conflict can run in diverse directions withemphasis on one or the other cause that contributed to its growth andmomentum. But of all the approaches to any crisis the most misleading path is to rely on any single cause. In every historical process that leads to crises there are multiple factors that crisscross and interweave, twisting round the core issues and consolidating the thrust of the events culminating in violence. It is, therefore, obvious that any mono-causal interpretation or theory advanced to explain the historical events that led to the current north-south conflict in Sri Lanka will be inadequate to grasp either the essence or its rounded totality.

Invariably, it is politicized history that would tend to focus on mono-causal interpretations. It is virtually a sine qua non for partisan projection of the complex issues (the simplified "them" vs. "us" approach) because a mono-causal interpretation lends itself readily to distort the realities and serve political ends.

This school of mono-causal interpretation of Sri Lankan actions and reactions in the pit of politics had gained ascendancy, particularly with the new school of rewriting the history emerging as one of the growth industries. The impact of this mono-causal interpretation, which blames only the Sinhala-Buddhists, has been to exacerbate the prevailing political climate by polarizing the two communities.

A holistic approach, taking into consideration all the operative factors, is more likely to eliminate emotions and introduce a more balanced view of the evolving chain of events. It is also important that events should be placed in the proper sequence, without omitting one or the other factor to tilt the perspectives favourable to any one side. This is a prime necessity to construct a reasonable historical composition that includes the multi-factorial causes. Equally important is the starting point of the seemingly insignificant events (example: the launching of the *Illankai Thamil Arasu Kachci* (Tamil State Party) on December 18, 1949) that gathered momentum by veering away from the democratic and nonviolent path until it exploded into a violent crisis. In most instances the starting points are selected arbitrarily to suit partisan theories – a common practice that is not conducive for rational analysis or a balanced understanding of the related issues.

In the final analysis, all these factors must be woven into the interconnected flow of events to unravel a discernible pattern from a reasonable distance, away from the emotional impact of exploding events. It is human that events exploding in your face must necessarily colour the perspectives and even distort the realities.

Therefore any meaningful analysis must necessarily step back from the immediacy of events and take a dispassionate view of the totality of forces that led to the crisis. For instance, the grassroots forces breaking out of the old mould crumbling with the antiquated colonial empires fading into oblivion; the rough and tough transition from semi-feudalism to modernity; the caste-based ancient regimes resisting change in the hope of clinging on to their feudal and /or colonial privileges, powers and positions; the historical necessity of redressing imbalances of colonial legacies; the local leadership grabbing and diverting the internal forces to extremities; the stagnant economies that frustrated the hopes of youth looking for social mobility; the rewriting of old histories to justify new ideological claims to exclusive territories; the importing of new ideologies and political vocabularies from the West to rationalize extreme demands and violence; the dynamic interconnectedness of evolving events; the chance happenings and the actions and reactions are some of the key factors that need to be addressed before passing judgments that are neither helpful to understand the crisis nor to find a solution. It must be noted that it is not possible within the short essay to deal with all these factors. Only some factors will be highlighted to question the mono-causal theory and explore the route to the origins of the north-south crisis.

It is also apparent that, as in every other crisis, the north-south conflict produced a plethora of interpreters, theorists, paradigmists, exponents, propagandists and schools of thoughts with each individual or school of thought focusing one or the other cause. By and large, these diverse opinions converged and narrowed down to only one single cause: Sinhala-Buddhism. This mono-causal view turned into a popular and orthodox reference point for the ideologues heading towards the creation of a mono-ethnic enclave as a solution to rival regional claims. In time it gained the sanctity of approved ideological correctness for the interpretation of events that flowed from "1956" – a common starting point for those who advocate the mono-causal view.

As in all other historical movements, the events rolling down the turbulent years collided with each other and exploded with a violent and unmanageable fury -- particularly the events originating in the post-1983 phase. One of the principal victims of this violent process was history. Like the human actors trapped in the cycle of violence history too got politicized and polarized. While bullets waged a relentless war on the ground to grab territory, books and publications were launched at a higher level to win the hearts and minds for one or the other side.

To escape this poisoned atmosphere it is necessary to go to a more neutral period where history unraveling in tortuous paths was interpreted with dispassionate analysis, giving weight to the prevailing facts and not to constructed theories.

History can be written in two main ways: 1) by picking the relevant and available facts from the ground that could lead, by the force of its own logic, to a comprehensive pattern that explains the past or 2) by constructing a theoretical formula at the top from selected facts to fit a preconceived pattern. The first tends to be a broader and more humane view drawn from existential realities.

The second is a narrow theoretical construction imposed by paradigmists and high-flying fashionable schools of expensive ideologues sitting at the top, with a plausible degree of sophistication. The more durable one is the first and the second, like all fashions, tend to fade away with time.

There are two scholarly historians who belong to the pre-1983 neutral period: 1) Dr. G. C. Mendis, one of the pioneering historians of Peradeniya University and 2) Prof. K. M. de Silva, arguably the foremost historian of our time. The disarmingly simple voice of Dr. Mendis has been drowned by the noisy school of re-writers who dominate the current climate of opinion. Prof. de Silva's authority continues undiminished by the partisan or self-serving theories by new inventors of history. Both historians have delved into the origins of the communal rift and though they focus on two different decades their evaluations are not contradictory.

Dr. Mendis, writing in 1963, trace the beginnings of communalism to 1943.[2] "Communalism," he wrote, "was a factor which divided the body politic in Ceylon in the early forties of the century.....This communalism seen in 1943 was undoubtedly a new development. European writers such as the Portuguese Jesuit Fernao de Queyroz and the Englishman Robert Knox of the seventeenth century and James Cordiner and other English writers of the nineteenth century have left us pictures of Ceylon with its various divisions of society but in none of their works does one come across communal conflicts of the type we saw then.

"The Sinhalese-Tamil problem, which was the most acute in 1943, could hardly be traced back even to the last century. Before the tenth century A. D. there is no evidence of any serious antagonism between the Sinhalese and the Tamils. Up to that time the Tamil immigrants seem to have inter-married with the Sinhalese, as they do today in the coastal districts of Negombo and Chilaw, and gradually merged themselves into the Sinhalese population….."[3]

`This conclusion based on a researched survey of the past challenges two fashionable theories. First, it questions whether the starting point of the northsouth was "1956". Second, and more importantly, it challenges the other unsubstantiated theory that the Sinhalese and the Tamils were two hostile communities at each others throat from the year dot. Picking the hard facts from the ground Dr. Mendis emphasizes that communal animosities have not been a feature of both cultures. He argues that it is a new phenomenon caused by the competition of the middle-classes in the two communities to grab the limited amount of jobs in the government service – the only stable and growth industry under the British regime. As a rule colonial regimes did not pursue policies of encouraging indigenous entrepreneurs to compete with the overarching imperial interests.

The Tamils of Jaffna held a disproportionate share of jobs in the government service[4] and it has dawned on them, says Dr. Mendis, that "they cannot expect to hold any longer the same proportion of post as well as the same number of key-posts in the Government as they did in the past…." He sees the roots of the crisis in the stagnant economy. He sees the two middle classes of the two communities trapped inside a stagnant economy without any new space opening up in the economy to absorb the new generations into the system. This is a more reasonable historical setting to explain the sudden explosion of communalism, and also the violence of youth, of the two communities. Down the ages, as pointed out by Dr. Mendis, the two communities had co-existed peacefully at all levels – from the arid dry zone villages to the highest rungs of society. If so how could "1956" – the year of resurgence of the suppressed grassroot forces of nearly five centuries of colonialism

– be categorized as the starting point of all evils in the Sri Lanka polity? It will be argued later that "1956" became the symbolic year for the Tamil leadership to scapegoat the Sinhalese as their enemies. They demonized them as the primary cause of their social and personal problems. Since language was also the vehicle of upward social mobility under colonial and post-colonial times the Tamil leadership focused on the Sinhala Only Act of 1956 as the main instrument of discrimination.

However, Dr. Mendis and Prof. De Silva went beyond "1956" to trace the origins of the communal rift. Dr. Mendis demarcated the forties as the period when communalism raised its ugly head. It was the time when G. G. Ponnambalam raised the divisive cry of 50-50. Prof. de Silva, however, focused sharply on the twenties when Sir. Ponnambalam Arunachalam broke away from the Ceylon National Congress and retired into the womb of Jaffna on the demand for an additional seat for the Tamils in the Western province. (More of this later.) Though Dr. Mendis points to the forties as the time when the communal issues took an acute turn he recognizes that there was a concerted move from the twenties by the Tamils to block any attempt of the Sinhalese to gain their due share of power as the majority community under proposed constitutional reforms. "In 1921 when representative government was about to be granted," wrote Dr. Mendis, "the Ceylon Tamils who comprised eleven per cent of population asked for half the number of seats which the Sinhalese who comprised sixty-nine percent, were to get, and succeeded."[5] In this statement Dr. Mendis reveals the central thrust of Jaffna-centric politics: their demand for parity of status with themajority.

Clearly, both historians emphasize two different decades as the starting point of the north-south divisions. The difference, however, is only in the emphasis and not in the historical flow of events that nudge each other and connect one decade to another. It is quite visible that the core issues of the Tamils that originated in the twenties gathered a new momentum and reincarnated in a more virulent manifestation in the forties and in the subsequent decades. What began as an additional seat for the Tamils in the Western Province in the twenties escalated into 50-50 in the mid-forties and separatism (in the guise of federalism) in the mid-fifties, until it climaxed in the Vaddukoddai Resolution of 1976.

The trajectory of northern events that escalated over the decades, gathering a mono-ethnic virulence and ended in violence, date back to the pre-independence period. The Vaddukoddai Resolution of 1976 was the inevitable outcome of the events that originated in the twenties. This is a defining moment not only in peninsular politics but also in the nation because in 1976, for the first time, the leadership of a community decided consciously and deliberately to abandon the age-old principle of non-violent co-existence among all communities and declared war on another community.

Here a distinction should be made between the unorganized, sporadic mob violence that bursts from time to time and fizzles out and the violence officially adopted, endorsed, organized, financed and promoted by a leadership of a community. Neither individually nor collectively has any leadership of other communities ever encouraged or urged their communities to wage a war against another community. The Vaddukoddai Resolution will stand as an indelible black mark on the conscience and the politics of the Jaffna Tamil leadership that was wont to pose as pious Gandhians in Sri Lankan politics.

Prof. A. J. Wilson confirms that S. J. V. Chelvanayakam, the father of the separatist movement, personally checked and approved the wording of the Vaddukoddai Resolution. In his biography of Chelvanayakam, his father-in-law, Prof. Wilson recorded: "Apart from this (Vaddukodddai Resolution) being a collective decision of the main Ceylon Tamil components of the TULF (Tamil United Liberation Front), that is the Federal Party and the ACTC, (All Ceylon Tamil Congress) Chelvanayakam approved the choice of words."[6]

The Tamil leadership never expected the violence endorsed by the leadership to boomerang on them or their community. They embraced and endorsed violence solely to target the Sinhalese. But the children of the Vaddukoddai Resolution did not hesitate to turn their guns and liquidate the fathers who passed it triumphantly on May 14, 1976. Ironically, the children of the Resolution considered their political fathers to be greater enemies of their cause than the perceived demons of the south. Chelvanayakam escaped assassination by the LTTE only because he died shortly after passing the Resolution. Those who stepped into his shoes, starting from Appapillai Amirthalingam, were gunned down in broad daylight.

In other words, they fell into the grave they dug for their enemies. Today the Tamil community is facing from all quarters the inhuman consequences of the violence unleashed by their political fathers against the south. When the Tamil political elite opted to step out of the democratic framework and pursue their goal of separatism through violence they hardly realized that they were releasing a genie out of the bottle. They believed that the ideology of a separate state they invented in the fifties and climaxed in the call to arms in the concluding clauses of the Vaddukoddai Resolution would help them to ride on the backs of the youth to power.[7]

The Tamil leadership, drawn mainly from the dominant vellahla caste, failed to recognize that violence, once unleashed, would turn into an unmanageable force and assert itself as an independent force with power to remove them from their cherished and established positions. In passing the Vaddukoddai Resolution the dominant vellahla caste literally transferred the power they held for centuries into unknown or hostile forces they trusted initially to do their dirty work. The vellahla caste held sway as long as they remained within the democratic framework. They did not foresee that the Vaddukoddai Resolution would bring down just not themselves individually but the entire vellahla caste that had ruled Jaffna during feudal and colonial times. The only positive feature of the

Tamil violence that flowed from the Vaddukoddai Resolution was to radicalize the calcified Jaffna society structured on inflexible caste lines. Nothing short of violence could have changed that rigid ancient regime of the vellahla high-caste. In hindsight it is apparent that in passing the Vaddukoddai Resolution the vellahla caste dug their own grave.

As "1976" marks the abandonment of democratic and non-violent politics and opens up a new phase in north-south relations the events leading up to it need to be traced, even sketchily, to grasp the impact of the northern politics on the south. This Resolution raises some key questions: Why did the north alone resort to confrontational, aggressive and violent politics? Why did the other Tamilspeaking minorities refuse to join the bandwagon of the northern politics despite overtures made by the Jaffna Tamil leadership?[8] If the claim of discrimination against the Tamil-speaking people is valid then why didn't all the Tamil-speaking join in a common front against the Sinhala majority? How did the Tamil-speaking Muslims and Indian Tamils succeed in settling their differences and grievances non-violently and co-exist in relatively harmony with the Sinhala majority?

Even on the sensitive and explosive language issue it is clear that only the Jaffna Tamil leadership raised a storm over it. This significant feature confirms that the Sri Lankan crisis is not an ethnic issue, with all the Tamil-speaking ganging up against the majority Sinhalese, but a regional issue confined only to the north and the south. If the east and the central hills joined the north against the majority then it would have been unquestionably an ethnic issue of gigantic and unmanageable proportions. A common front of all Tamil-speaking peoples would have been an overwhelming justification of the cries of discrimination against the Tamil-speaking minorities. The refusal of the other two Tamil-speaking communities to join the juggernaut of Jaffna rolling down from the north questions the validity of demonizing the Sinhala majority as anti-Tamil racists. One swallow does not make a summer. Nor does the aggressive campaign of one Tamil-speaking community make the Sinhala majority evil racists.

If conventional wisdom had probed deeper and taken into consideration the relationships of the Sinhala majority with all three Tamil-speaking communities in historical times, and particularly in the post-independence phase, it would have been possible to arrive at a more balanced assessment rather than escape into a mono-causal theory. For instance, if the Sinhala majority is confronted with the violence of only the Tamil-speaking community of the north, then questions must be asked and answers given to explain why violence was confined to only one region and not to all the other Tamil-speaking regions in the island.

Perhaps, the answer could be found in one of two things or both: (1) either there must have been something right that the majority was doing to maintain easy, non-confrontational relations with relations with the minorities or (2) there must some structural faults in the foundations of northern society to adhere to their boast of non-violence and pursue unrelenting violence. If in a multi-cultural society like Sri Lanka the northern community fails to take the east and the centre sharing common ethnic and linguistic interests/values then, in terms of simple arithmetic, it adds up to 3: 1. If two Tamil-speaking communities coexisted, maintaining friendly relations with the majority, then could it be that the north took the wrong turn? Did the Vaddukoddai Resolution – the ultimate expression of antagonism to the south -- came out internal compulsions seeded in the northern political culture? If these questions are not asked then the researcher will be facing a monumental vacuum which can be filled by the facile mono-causal theory of blaming the south..

To arrive at a comprehensive appreciation of the evolving events attempts should be made to go beyond the popular perceptions. The popular starting point for justifying northern violence is, of course, "1956" which has been projected as an anti-Tamil move, particularly the Sinhala Only Act of 1956. But the other starting point is to go beyond "1956" to the roots of peninsular politics that gave birth to the Vaddukoddai Resolution – the final expression of Jaffna-centric politics to prevent the Sinhalese to rule as a majority.

Before going any further it is necessary to draw attention to an over-determining force that governed Jaffna-centric political culture. Ever since the first signs of decolonization emerged in the twenties, peninsular politics was obsessed with the single objective of blocking the evolving democratic process of empowering the electorate with universal franchise, territorial electorates (as opposed to communal representation) and rule by the majority based on the free will expressed by the people. No other community pursued this political objective with such doggedness. The Muslim and the Indian Tamils showed a willingness to coexist in harmony as long as their issues were handled with care.

But in the peninsula an anti-Sinhala thrust was fostered and developed as an intransigent force in its political culture. Consequently, the Jaffna became the home of anti-Sinhala extremism. The opposition to the Sinhala community as an organized force originated and subsequently emerged as a violent force only in Jaffna. They opposed tooth and nail the slightest tendency for democratizing the political process in the dying days of British colonial rule knowing that it would empower the majority. Dr. Mendis wrote: "From 1920, whenever constitutional reforms were about to be made, they have pressed for a solution that would prevent the Sinhalese acquiring a dominant position over the rest. Having failed in their objective they now want to be supreme at least in two provinces……."[9]

It is intellectual suicide to ignore this factor that came down from the north and impacted on national politics. Denying it or ignoring it would leave open for acceptance, as a valid explanation of the crisis, only the mono-causal theory that blames the Sinhala community exclusively. The reality, however, is that the overriding force of confrontation and conflict with the Sinhala majority came only from the north. The northern antagonism to the Sinhala community and its refusal to co-exist like the other Tamil-speaking communities was the over-determining force the exacerbated the north-south relations. There was no room in the monoethnic extremism of the northern politics for compromises to accommodate the aspirations of all communities. Northern politics was designed to pursue only their mono-ethnic ends.

Considering the regional dimensions of this conflict, where neither the east nor the central hills joined the northern forces, it is logical to categorize the current crisis as a north-south conflict. Besides, the demonizing of the Sinhala south was a logical concomitant of the in-built ideological antagonism embedded in peninsular politics. For the anti-Sinhala political culture to thrive and yield results the Sinhala community had to projected as the "other", the hated object that must be destroyed with violence, if necessary. They consistently targeted the Sinhala south from colonial times, long before the Sinhala majority had any role to determine national politics. Rival Tamil political parties in the north, vying for electoral gains, demonized the south and their Tamil rivals who dared to cooperate with the centre. The Tamils who joined the centre either as ministers, or those who allied themselves to national parties (i.e. UNP or SLFP) were branded as "collaborators". The mild-mannered Alfred Duraiyappah, the SLFP Mayor of Jaffna, was the first victim of Velupillai Prabhakaran when the latter began his career of political crimes. Destroying their perceived enemies elevated them to the rank of heroes. The electoral rhetoric of the north overflows with anti-Sinhala rhetoric. Chief Justice Sansoni's report on the violence of seventies records the rhetoric and the actions of the northern leadership that targeted the Sinhala south and its Tamil allies.[10] Inherent in the vocabulary of the so-called liberation politics of the north was an imperative to denigrate the Sinhala community and hail the anti-Sinhala forces as the saviours.

Whipping up anti-Sinhala extremism was a common ploy adopted to defeat rival candidates in the Tamil-speaking north. As this mono-ethnic extremism gathered momentum and hardened in the north it was inevitable that Tamils would willynilly move away from democratic politics into violence. It should also be noted that separatism and violence are inseparable. They go hand in hand as no state is willing to divide a nation by yielding to the extremist demands of one minority at the expense of all other communities.

The incremental growth of extremism in the north pushed it into the Vaddukoddai Resolution – the farthest point the leadership could take peninsular politics to prevent the majority from exercising their democratic right to govern. It was also a Resolution that was born out of the other internal imperatives of the Jaffna political culture which, incidentally, had a long history of violence, oppression and denial of fundamental human rights to a significant segment of its own disempowered people who, from birth, were destined to serve as virtual slaves to the vellahla high-caste. Parenthetically, it must be stated that one of the main contributory factors was the role of the vellahla high-caste who were in command of peninsular politics and directed it to serve their ends exclusively. Separatism, it also could be argued, is direct manifestation of vellahlaism and this aspect needs another chapter at least to deal with the intricacies of the caste factors that governed and directed peninsular politics.

As the foregoing factors point to the crisis as an exclusive conflict of northern and southern forces there is an overwhelming compulsion to probe the inner political culture of Jaffna, more so because practically every nook and corner of the southern culture (from the Kalutrara Bo Tree to Vihara Maha Devi park) have been explored exhaustively by anti-Sinhala-Buddhist ideologues. The northern culture has escaped the attention of sociological, anthropological, political social scientists. Historians generally tend to complain about the lack of evidence on this darker side of the Sri Lankan moon.[11]

The absence of knowledge about the forces that flowed from the north and collided head-on with the south has provided the mono-causal theorists the opportunity to exonerate the north and blame only the Sinhala south. None of these theorists has given due weightage to the north that was generating, on its own steam and without any provocation from the south (as seen during the colonial and pre-1956 phase), political forces constructed and manipulated deliberately to confront and resist liberal, modernizing, democratizing forces penetrating the secluded casteist and feudal fortress of Jaffna.

For instance, the Prevention of Social Disabilities Act of 1957 – the first and the only legislative attack to dismantle the entrenched vellahla caste grip on Jaffna – was resisted with all its might by some of the casteist extremists like Prof. C. Suntheralingam while the other vellahla leaders stood with folded hands, giving their silent nod to the likes of Suntheralingam. The connection between vellahlaism – the dominant political force in the peninsula – and the separatist movement was drawn by Prof. Bryan Pfaffenberger. Pointing out that the Tamil identity was a modern construction he wrote: "Tamil-Sinhalese ethnic conflict in its modern form, moreover, was unknown during the colonial period. The politics of ethnic confrontation in Sri Lanka is a contemporary artifact, one that has been deliberately and politically constructed……What is striking about this case is that all three of the actors on the stage of this drama (of constructing a Tamil identity) – caste, temple religion and Tamil separatism – are of demonstrably modern genesis; if they draw on tradition, it is a tradition that is transformed beyond recognition."[12] He argues that the vellahla casteists who regarded Jaffna as their exclusive preserve found it necessary to resist invasions of advancing modernization, liberalism, capitalism etc that were threatening the old feudal fortress of the vellahlas in Jaffna.

Separatism, therefore, emerged as the last refuge of vellahla caste threatened with extinction by modernity. It was perceived as the viable political formula that could preserve the outdated casteist structures from succumbing to the hostile forces invading the peninsula. The vellahlas were fighting two forces simultaneously: 1) the internal revolts from the low-castes breaking out of the age-old fetters of the oppressive vellahla rule and 2) the external forces of liberalism and market economies that were undermining the feudal land-based economy on which the vellahlas thrived.

The establishment of a separate state was conceived as an effective political instrument to combat the internal and external forces. During the feudal and colonial periods they justified oppression of the people of Jaffna under religious sanctions. Hinduism sanctified the oppression of the low-caste by down-grading the non-vellahlas virtually as non-humans. To avert the external and internal threats to their safe haven in the peninsula they invented the theory of a "homeland". Under colonialism, as revealed in the reports of the successive government agents, the vellahlas were waging a brutal war against the lowcastes who were threatening their supremacy and way of life. But in the dying days of the British Empire they down-graded the internal enemy and turned against the Sinhalese, the external "other". Raising the bogey of the Sinhala enemies was also the prime means of unifying the divided peninsula on caste lines. The "homeland" theory, or Eelam, was manufactured, propagated and developed as a political tool of the vellahlas, by the vellahlas, for the vellahlas.

Any threat to the established feudal and colonial powers of the vellahla regime was met with unremitting violence. The history of vellahlas of the north is one of cruel suppression of the low-caste slaves to keep them in submission under the supremacy of the vellahlas who ruled Jaffna with the casteist ideology derived from Hinduism. Among numerous inhuman cruelties, the vellahlas did not permit the low-castes to step even into the seventh outermost court of their sacred temples, nor did they allow them to bury their dead according to Hindu rituals reserved only for the high-caste. They enforced the rule that the turumbas should not walk in daylight as any sighting of this low-caste would pollute the vision of the pure vellahlas. Throughout the feudal and colonial times, and even into the late seventies, the vellahlas maintained their hegemony in Jaffna through violence. The Vaddukoddai Resolution is a natural extension of vellahla violence to protect their inherited power and privileges. Though the fathers of the 1976 Vaddukoddai Resolution attribute the political source of it to the "aggressive Sinhala nationalism", referring in particular to "1956", a closer scrutiny of the Jaffna culture will indicate that the origins of violence can be traced directly to the inner compulsions of the Jaffna political culture

Despite these glaring factors that bedeviled north-south relations, when it comes to choosing between "1956" and "1976", it is predictable that political or ethnic sympathies would normally tend to determine the preference between the two dates. Nevertheless, it is appropriate to revive the question: Was "1956" really the cause of separatist politics or was it a definite example of poking the eye of the baby who was about to cry, as the Sinhala saying goes? Perhaps, the answer could be found by looking deeper into "1956" and to consider to what extent it was anti-Tamil, if at all. It was, no doubt, a watershed in the post-independence period. It was basically a grassroot movement to restore the traditional culture of the Sinhala-Buddhists who were denied their heritage under nearly five centuries of colonialism. In other post-colonial cultures a renaissance of this magnitude would have been hailed as a commendable legitimate process of redressing the historical imbalances.

Restoring the lost rights of the oppressed people under various regimes were embraced with benign terms like "affirmative action", "positive discrimination" etc. Rawlsian principles insist that advantages should be offered to the disadvantaged. At the end of colonial period Jaffna was on top of the People's Quality of Life Index (PQLI) with advanced infrastructure, schools, hospitals and longer life span. A developing society had to distribute similar resources to the rest of the nation. Allocating resources to build up the neglected areas in the south was perceived as acts of discrimination. But even in the post-independence period Jaffna Tamil leaders participating in the government took substantial resources to develop Jaffna. For instance, G. G. Ponnambalam, who was the minister of industries in the post-independence government of D. S. Senanayake, took all the new industrial projects (example: cement factor in Paranthan) to Jaffna.

But restoring the right of 70% of the population to communicate with their elected government was branded as "communalism", "Sinhala chauvinism", "racism", "hegemonism", "majoritarianism" etc. Implied in these condemnatory terms was the notion that only minorities had rights, aspirations, grievances and needs and the role of the majority was to accede to the "aspirations", "grievances", "demands" of the minorities promptly at the time these issues were raised, irrespective of their merits or their impact on the "aspirations" of the other communities.

At the time of independence the ruling class consisted mainly of the leftovers of the British raj competent only in the English language. This class, drawn from all three communities and nestling in the transplanted Anglicized culture, shared the legacy of common elitist values left behind by the departing British and any deviation to accommodate a native culture was seen as a threat to their dominant position of the administrative overclass and professionals. Hence their resistance to "1956" was instant and instinctive. The Westernized Sinhala elite too joined hands with the Tamils to anathematize the grassroot movement of "1956".

While the Westernized elite of the south sneered at it the Tamil of the north exploited it as an anti-Tamil measure to undermine the identity and the rights of their community. Only those who viewed it as a movement that sprang naturally from nearly five centuries of colonial oppression and suppression grasped the underlying meaning of this historical force. Dr. Mendis wrote: "...(T)he

Sinhalese- Buddhist resurgence is a logical outcome of modern developments, and the attempt to make Sinhalese the only official language did not arise from a desire to destroy the Ceylon Tamil community in the Island. Its chief object was to replace English in the sphere of Government, and the opposition to Tamil was, therefore, really incidental."[13]

Only a few had grasped the significance of this aspect of the Sinhala Only Act of 1956. It is against all common sense to view it as an act against the Tamils because it was a piece of legislation designed specifically to replace English – the language that was imposed as the official language in 1833. After enforcing it for over 100 years only 6 % of the population were competent to use the language. Unmistakably, the Sinhala Only Act was aimed at dethroning the English-speaking minority and not the Tamil-speaking minority. Besides, neither the Sinhalaspeaking majority nor the Tamil-speaking minority benefited from English being enthroned as the official language. In numerical terms 94% of the population was dependent entirely on the 6% of the English speaking elite. How fair was that?

Of course, the Tamil too had the right to communicate with their administration and elected representatives in their mother tongue. In 1958 the Tamil Language (Special Provisions Act) No. 28 was passed to grant the Tamils their right to do so. But the Tamils, who were determined to prevent the Sinhala majority from regaining their historical rights as pioneers that created a new culture, a new civilization and a new identity, distorted the realities and raised the cry of racial discrimination with each move designed to redress historical imbalances. The irony is that despite both languages receiving official status it is English that rules the nation to this day. Furthermore, raising the cry of discrimination was a habitual tendency of the Jaffna Tamils – the most privileged community in Sri Lanka from colonial times. On the eve of independence, they lodged this complaint of discrimination officially with the Soulbury Commissioners in 1945. After a through examination of the facts presented to them they dismissed it as unsubstantiated irrelevance. [14] Though the Sinhalese were accused of majoritarianism at every critical turn it was the dictatorship of the minority that exacerbated the north-south relations. Furthermore, the dilatory process inherent in any democracy, or for that matter, in any political process, was dismissed as giving "too little too late".

Besides, the rise of militant minoritarianism in Sri Lanka tended to exaggerate the missed opportunities and failures of "majoritarianism" despite the successive gains of the minorities which should have paved the way for peaceful coexistence. The historical reality is that the largely tolerant policy of co-existence with minority communities enabled the state to maintain non-violent settlements with the other two Tamil-speaking minorities – i.e. the Muslims and the Indian Tamils. But the Jaffna-centric Tamil leadership alone took to militant minoritarianism refusing to co-exist with the other communities by escalating their demands and resorting to confrontational politics. As pointed out by Ms. Radhika Coomaraswamy and Ms. Malini Parasarathy of The Hindu in Chennai, the southern electorate had shifted significantly to accommodate the Tamilspeaking minorities since "1956" without any corresponding response from the Jaffna-centric leadership to co-exist with the other communities.

They stuck to intransigent politics pushing the Tamil electorates to extremism. While the other two Tamil-speaking minorities settled down to co-exist peacefully with the majority Sinhalese the Jaffna Tamil leadership alone pursued a calculated policy of escalating demands that were designed to create a separate mono-ethnic enclave in the north and the east. More importantly, a characteristic of peninsular politics was that when one Tamil party moves to cooperate with the state the other party would invariably condemn it as "collaboration" with the enemy. Any compromise with the centre would be rejected as capitulation, forcing rivals into inevitable extremism.

A notable characteristic of the immediate aftermath of independence was that the transfer of power had no visible or palpable impact on the lives of the indigenous people. As far as they were concerned, freedom was handed over to the Brown Sahibs by the White Sahibs whose primary role was essentially to imitate and follow the Englishman to the last hole in golf. In other words, the marginalized masses were left stranded at the outer fringes of society – a place they occupied even during the colonial period.

Nor did independence which came virtually on a platter in 1948 catch the imagination of the masses as in India, for instance, where there was an aggressive movement to throw the British out. Nor did independence have any significant impact on the cultural, social, economic or political lives of the vast majority who lived in the villages. They were even deprived of their legitimate right to communicate with their elected government in their own language – a right granted to the Germans, French, Spanish, English and other leading democracies. English continued to be the powerful tool of the exclusive ruling class. The combined Sinhala, Tamil and Muslim elite was comfortable with English as it was not only a status symbol that separated them from the vulgar Sinhalaspeaking and Tamil-speaking masses but also because it armed them with the manipulative means and skills to press the right buttons of power to preserve and promote their exclusive privileges and place in society inherited from colonial rule.

Language thus became a source of power and it was not surprising to find this issue taking centre stage in the post-independence period. In fact, language played a central part in the political violence that erupted in the post-1956 period. When S. W. R. D. Bandaranaike launched the Sinhala Only Act of 1956 it became the most explosive issue dividing the nation on ethnic lines. In particular, the Tamil leadership of the north interpreted the Sinhala Only Act on ethnic lines. But the Sinhala youth, who took up arms against the establishment before the Tamil youth, (i.e. in 1970) also cried discrimination on the language issue. They interpreted the language issue on class lines. They argued that the ruling class continued to retain English, despite the introduction of the Sinhala Only Act in 1956, as a prime tool to oppress the masses. While the Sinhala youth cried discrimination on Marxist lines the Tamil youth were made to believe by the Jaffna-centric leadership that the Sinhala language was imposed on them to deny opportunities for advancement in education, and employment because they were Tamils.

The fact is that neither the Sinhala-speaking people nor the Tamil-speaking Jaffna Tamils were happy with the introduction of the indigenous languages – both Sinhala and Tamil – as the official and national languages. The Tamil Language (Special Provisions Act) No. 28 of 1958 recognised the Tamil language as the medium of the Tamil population to conduct their affairs with the elected government of the day. The Sixteenth Amendment went further and made it the national language. Despite these legal, constitutional and administrative provisions the Jaffna Tamil leadership cried discrimination because it was not given parity of status with Sinhala language.

Total denial by the state to recognize Tamil as a language of a section of its people would undoubtedly have justified accusations of discrimination. Moreover, denying the right of the Tamil-speaking communities to communicate with the state in their own mother tongue would have been an unacceptable violation of their basic human right. However, after the incremental changes to the language provisions, starting from the Tamil Language (Special Provisions Act) No. 28 of 1958 the Jaffna-centric leadership could not justify the accusation of discrimination on the grounds that the "Sinhala-dominated" state had denied the right of the Tamils to use their mother tongue. So they focused on the issue of not giving parity of status to Tamil. They argued that the denial of parity of status as an act of discrimination.

The issue, therefore, was not one of denying the Tamils their right to conduct their courts, administration and communication with the state in the predominantly Tamil areas but one of a minority claiming parity of status with the majority – a common political obsession with the Jaffna Tamil elite. The deteriorating north-south conflict was exacerbated at each critical turn by this claim of parity of status with the majority. This unsubstantiated notion of a minority claiming to be a majority was inherited from colonial times. "The Tamils had for a decade or more laid claim to the status of a majority community…" observed Prof. K. M. de Silva in analyzing the events that unraveled from 1920.[15] Oddly enough, Gov. William Manning, (1921 – 24) one of most manipulative governors, accepted and promoted the view that the Jaffna Tamils constituted a majority despite the fact that the numbers did not stack up to justify this claim.

It was this political ambition of a minority to maintain parity of status with the majority that is at the centre of the deteriorating north-south conflict. The original claim of maintaining parity of status with claims to a special seat Tamils in the Western Province in the twenties or 50-50 in the forties was not based on discrimination, or on a homeland theory, or any of the other complaints that the Jaffna Tamil leadership raised in the fifties. Under constitutional changed introduced in British times the claim of the Tamil leadership to parity of status was rejected. When they failed to achieve this objective in colonial they started the movement for a separate in the post-independence period. It should be noted that the current political arguments raised by the Jaffna Tamil leadership to establish a separate state were deliberately constructed and introduced in the fifties. Initially, in the twenties when the Jaffna-centric leadership launched their agitation for parity of status under the British regime, they did not peddle theories about a homeland, self-determination, discrimination and the usual litany of complaints that are hurled at the majority.

Of all the possible reasons they could think of, they came up with the idea of the minority being a majority community in the twenties. The Tamil proponents of this claim were encouraged by the support of Gov. Manning " for his own political ends of dividing and ruling. ......(T)he Tamils were regarded, not the least by Manning himself, as a majority community," Prof. K. M. de Silva, in his exploratory study of the historical events of this critical period .[16]

Even Sir Ponnambalam Arunachalam, perhaps the first and the last liberal of Jaffna-centric politics, did not advance any realistic or mythical political argument in defence of the special treatment of the Tamils. It is surprising that even a learned leader like Arunachalam believed that the Tamils (meaning only the Jaffna Tamils) were a majority community. "Arunachalam's use of the term "minorities' in his speeches before his departure from the Congress in 1921.... didnot include the Tamils which is not surprising since Arunachalam shared the prevailing opinion that the Tamils were not a minority but were one of two majority communities (p 115)...... There was besides the fact that the Tamils were regarded, not least by Manning himself, as a majority community." (P 107). In particular he focuses on how Gov. Manning manipulated events, through Ponnambalam Ramanathan who "was subordinate always to that master political manipulator, Sri William Manning."[17]

When the Tamil leadership of Jaffna talked themselves into the category of a majority under the British administration it had serious political implications which rolled down the decades leading to extremist claims. The first move to claim parity of status was when the Jaffna-centric leadership claimed a special seat, in addition to the seats given in the north, to the Tamils in the Western Province, a predominantly Sinhala area. Their close links with the British regime and the pre-eminent place they held in the political domain, with the consent of the majority who elected Sir, Ponnambalam Arunachalam as the first president of the Ceylon National Congress, confirmed their sense of superiority.

Besides, under the British colonial regime they were in a commanding position having acquired a disproportionate share of administrative and political power through which they siphoned off the resources of the state to the north.[18] Their drive to maintain parity of status began with the myth of being a majority community along with the Sinhalese. But the process of decolonization and representative government would undermine this unsustainable claim. When Gov. Manning was manoeuvering to juggle the numbers in the Legislative Council he found that communal representation (demanded by the Tamils) would give him a better handle on the affairs of the Council than territorial representation (demanded by the Sinhalese).

"A rift between the Sinhalese and Tamils had emerged after the election to the reformed Legislative Council in early 1921," wrote Prof. K. M. de Silva. "The question of territorial representation became the focal point of the growing controversy. The first elections under the new system had returned 13 Sinhalese to territorial constituencies as against 3 Tamils. In the old Legislative Council there had been a near equality in representation between the Sinhalese and Tamil un-official members. Soon after the new Legislative Council met influential Tamils began to campaign for the restoration of the proportion of Tamil to Sinhalese representations that existed prior to 1920."[19]

Gov. Sir. William Manning (1921 -24), "the master political manipulator", arrived on the shores of Sri Lanka at the critical point when constitutional changes were to introduce, for the first time, a majority of unofficial members in the Legislative Council. In 1920 the official members representing the British imperial throne were in a majority and the governor had no difficulty in obtaining consent from the Legislative Council. But the democratizing of the legislature by increasing the number of elected representatives would strengthen the ranks of the unofficial members, or the opposition to the British administration. The increase in the numbers of the unofficial members, based on territorial elections (as opposed to communal representation) was on the cards under the proposed constitutional reforms. This meant that the Tamils would lose their pre-1920 parity of status in Legislature. Predictably, the Jaffna Tamils moved to increase their numbers by claiming an extra in the predominantly Sinhala Western Province. ".... (T)he rift between the Sinhalese and the Tamils had ......assumed the level of a serious political crisis," wrote Prof. de Silva. "At the centre of the crisis, and assuming a significance out of all proportion to its intricate worth, was the special seat for the Tamils of the Western Province."[20]

This was the first of the many objections and obstructions to come from Jaffna at the mention of any constitutional reforms. This claim for a special seat for the Tamils in the Western Province, in addition to the seats allotted to them in the north, was the first major step in their subsequent campaigns to prevent the majority from inheriting their legitimate position enshrined in any democracy. It was an issue that originated and was confined only to the north. Since 1920s the main thrust of Jaffna-centric politics was to maintain parity of status at the political and administrative levels. Objecting to constitutional reforms that would democratize the legislature was the only tool available to them under colonial rule to block the legitimate aspirations of the majority.

At the core of the cry of discrimination was the failure of a minority to gain parity of status with the majority. Any critical examination of the accusation of discrimination will establish that the Tamils had not experienced any Oslo conference 2004 .no 67 Road Maps to Peace in Sri Lanka discrimination that was not common to the Sinhalese or the Muslims, or the Indian Tamils. Discrimination was endemic and experienced universally by all communities, including the Sinhala majority.[21] Basically, the cry of discrimination was raised partly as political ploy to divert attention from their privileged position and partly to restrain the majority from redressing historical injustices that was inevitable in the process of democratizing and liberalizing a colonized society.

Also at the very base of their cry of discrimination was the perennial obsession to maintain parity of status with the majority. Anything short of that was perceived and broadcast as discrimination. For instance, though the Tamil language was given a special place in the administration through various constitutional and legislative procedures they cried discrimination because it was not given parity of status.

What was uppermost in their political agenda was the ambition to gain parity of status with the majority. In 1921, 1924, 1931, and finally in 1945 when the Soulbury Commissioners were agreed on handing over power to the people of Sri Lanka they cried foul and raised the cry of discrimination to prevent the majority from gaining their rightful place in history. But the Colonial Office dismissed their objections on the basis of constructing a united nation of all communities. When the Tamils demanded a special seat in the Western Province on the basis of communal representation the Colonial Office too agreed that "....the demands of the Tamils.... are somewhat excessive..." and that it would be "a doubtful measure to agree to communal representation for the Tamils who are a numerous and progressive class."[22] Prof. de Silva added: "As for the reserved seat for the Tamils, the point was made that "the Secretary of State would naturally be somewhat reluctant to extend the communal principle of election any further than at present if it can be avoided."[23]

Jaffna-centric politics refused to accept the democratic principles of territorial representation. They were bent on carving out ethnic enclaves based on communal representation. This was the consistent political behaviour of the Jaffna Tamils even during colonial times. They showed a distinct aversion to compromise and coexist peacefully with their neighbours. Running through the last decades of the colonial regime, and throughout the rest of the post-independence period, is the unyielding political thrust of the Jaffna Tamil leadership to prevent the majority from gaining its rightful place in a democracy. Unable to stop the process of democratization the Jaffna political class, represented by G. G. Ponnambalam who headed the All Ceylon Tamil Congress, raised the mathematically unrealistic claim of the minority sharing power with the majority on a 50-50 basis.

This proposal of "balanced representation" was a continuation of the policy of the Tamils to claim an extra seat in the Western Province and the formation of the first communal political organisation, the Tamil Mahajana Sabhai in 1921. Tamil communalism began to organize itself into a formidable political force in colonial times. The successors to the leadership of the Tamil Mahajana Sabhai followed the founders of Tamil communalism to the letter. "The Tamil Congress, under its leader G. G. Ponnambalam," wrote Prof. S. Arasaratnam, the Tamil historian, "took off from the old controversy on which the Ceylon National Congress had split up and over which the Tamils had unsuccessfully boycotted the Donoughmore Constitution. It took as its central issue the question of numbers in the Legislature and asked for a balanced representation or 'fifty-fifty' as it popularly came to be known. Under this scheme the Sinhalese as the majority community, would not hold more than 50% of the seats in the Legislature and the other communities would, in sum, share the remaining 50% of seats." [24]

However, it is the response of the majority Sinhalese that is revealing and cuts into the accusations of the Sinhalese being historically antagonistic to the Tamil minority. Citing Session Paper XIV of 1944, "The Reform of the Constitution" Prof. Arasaratnam wrote: "Without being able to concede the extravagant demand for a perfect balance in representation between the Sinhalese and the minorities, as put forward by G. G. Ponnambalam, they (the Sinhalese) conceded a relationship of 57% to 43% as between Sinhalese and others in the legislature. It was, as it appears now, a tactical error that the Tamil leaders did not grasp this offer at that time, but stuck to their extreme demands."[25]

Clearly, no compromise, however generous, was going to appease the Jaffna Tamils. Their intransigence illustrates their anti-Sinhala stance designed mainly to prevent the majority from obtaining their share of power due to them under accepted democratic principles. Does this unprecedented offer by a majority to a minority confirm the popular accusation that the Sinhala political class comes from an inveterate and intransigent bunch of racists, chauvinists etc? Does this offer indicate an unwillingness to accommodate even the excessive demands of the minorities? Isn't this an exemplary example of a majority bending over backwards to build a new nation on communal harmony and unity? Does this reality substantiate the myths propagandized to denigrate the Sinhala-Buddhists? Or should the finger be pointed to the blind obsession of the Tamil leadership to obstruct the majority from exercising their legitimate rights enshrined in any respected democracy?

There was more than a touch of Tamil arrogance in this offhanded rejection of the offer made by the Sinhalese who were accused of never willing to compromise. No other majority in a commanding position like the Sinhalese is known to have made such a generous offer to a minority of 12 per cent of the Jaffna Tamils or, if taken collectively, a minority of 25 per cent. Commenting on this Prof. Wilson states: "Ponnambalam overreached himself by remaining inflexible on his formula when a group of Sinhalese State Councillors favoured a compromise in the ratio of 60 - 40, or even 55 - 45."[26]

This arrogance of the Tamil leadership was echoed by Chelvanayakam when he said that the Sinhalese are not fit to rule the Tamils. A comparative study of both political cultures will reveal that the "sole representatives of the Tamils" have never shown any signs of generosity, liberalism, tolerance or compromise as the democratic south. Whether it is the caste system or the political system, the southern culture has tended to be more humane than the northern culture. Whether it is Sankili who marched down to Mannar and massacred over 600 Catholics on Christmas eve because they owed allegiance to a foreign ruler and not to him or to his modern avatar, Velupillai Prabhakaran, the Jaffna political culture has shown ingrained tendencies of a closed society governed by authoritarianism, intolerance, and unmitigated violence against their own people, let alone outsiders. Shocked by ferocity of violence Tamil intellectuals have openly wondered how such inhuman brutalities can come out of the womb of Jaffna.[27]

A political culture driven by anti-liberal, anti-democratic and anti-people forces will find it difficult to co-exist with its neighbours. Time and time again, from 1920s, the peninsular culture threw up extremists (example: 50-50 was an extremist demand) whose intransigence exacerbated north-south relations. At each critical point in the north-south relations the tendency of the Jaffna politicalleadership was to insist on settling differences only on their terms. Alternatively, they adopted the policy of "little now and more later" – a policy that was bound to keep the north-south relations simmering or at boiling point. Northern extremist demands reduced the chances of any peaceful co-existence to a zero. This intransigence has not changed to this day.

The Jaffna Tamil argument is that there was no room for them within the Sinhaladominated polity to maintain their identity or to co-exist as equals in a democratic society. Is this a valid argument? If so, how did the other Tamilspeaking communities co-exist and resolve their differences through the nonviolent process? No doubt, Sri Lanka is not a five-star democracy. But the litmus test is to consider whether there was liberal space within the Sri Lankan polity for minorities to co-exist with dignity and respect. As a developing country, did the national leaders take meaningful steps to lay the foundations to build a nation of equals? As pointed out earlier, the main grievance of the Jaffna Tamils was that they were discriminated on the grounds of ethnicity. The fundamental flaw in this statement is that ONLY the Jaffna leadership interpreted the defects in the system as a racist attack on their right to exist as a minority. The reality, however, is that discrimination was a common factor shared by all communities, including the Sinhalese. In fact, it was the Sinhala youth who took up arms – long before the Tamil youth – on grounds of inequalities and discrimination.[28]

The other side of the coin is that the Jaffna Tamils were given equality at all levels, starting from national symbols to ministerial, judicial, administrative and professional ranks. Take, for instance, the example of the national flag. There are nearly 75 million Tamils in the far-flung Tamil diaspora, including nearly 55 million in Tamil Nadu, the historical homeland of the Tamils. The Tamils have no representation in any of these flags – including the Indian or in the other 191 flags flying at the UN – except in the Sri Lankan flag. The green strip represents the Tamil and the orange strip represents the Muslims. Shortly after independence a committee selected from the community leaders sat, designed and agreed on the final format of the flag and put their signatures of approval. G. G. Ponnambalam singed on behalf of the Tamils. T. B. Jayah the Muslim leader put his signature on behalf of the Muslims.

Consider also the currency, the stamps and the aerogrammes. All three represent the Tamil identity at the highest level, giving it a dignity not found in any other nation. It needs to be reiterated that no other nation had given the Tamils in the diaspora, including India, this honoured place. Then there is the vexed issue of Indian indentured labour brought to Sri Lanka by the British to work on their plantations in the 19th century. The argument is that they were denied citizenship because they were Tamils. First significant point to note is that it was passed with the consent of G. G. Ponnambalam, the acknowledged leader of the Tamils, who was a member of the first Cabinet of independent Sri Lanka. If the Citizenship Bill is categorized as a racist act then the leadership of the Jaffna Tamils too is equally guilty of it.

Second, the defining of citizenship is the bounden duty of any independent nation. The first independent government was exercising its birth right, as it were, after the British had inundated the nation with aliens imported as cheap labour to serve their imperial interests. The new independent was within its right to define who its citizens were going to be. Third, not all Indians were denied their citizenship. Those that could prove a longer period of stay, going back to their grandparents, were recognized as citizens. They were asked to apply within a given period. The then leader of the plantation workers, S. Thondaman, boycotted the registration of his people as a mark of protest. At the last minute, however, he realized he would lose his numerical strength and, consequently his political clout and finances derived from membership in his union, he decided to register those qualified.

This last minute move caused utter confusion as there was hardly any time for thousands to lodge their applications. This bungling prevented his people from qualifying under the regulations of the Act. Fourth, in subsequent negotiations with the Indian government they accepted that a substantial residue could be absorbed as citizens of India and under the Sirima-Shastri Pact India agreed to repatriate those who qualified under the Pact. Ignoring all these factors, it is the Sinhala-Buddhists who are accused of being racist or discriminatory. On the surface it is a plausible accusation because victimology reduces issues to blackand- white simplicity without any grey areas. Victimology is so very easy to understand. But the reality is complex and invariably contradicts simplistic presentations.

Perhaps, the notion propagated by the Tamil lobby that they could not find reasonable accommodation for their grievances could be tested with the achievements of the Illankai Thamil Arasu Kachchi (ITAK -Tamil State Party) when it cooperated with the Dudley Senanayake government between 1965 - 1970. This period was considered to be the "golden years" of Tamil achievements.[29] The President of ITAK announced at their annual convention that the Tamils have achieved all what they wanted to achieve by cooperating with the Sinhalese.[30] But in the preamble to the Vaddukoddai Resolution ITAK denigrated the Sinhalese and declaimed that the Tamils had been reduced to a "subject people". It said that "successive Sinhalese Governments since Independence have always encouraged and fostered the aggressive nationalism of the Sinhalese people and used their political power to the detriment of the Tamils…."

This claim of Sinhalese targeting only the Tamils has been questioned and challenged by analysts who have asked the Tamil lobbyists to prove whether they had ever experienced any inequalities, discrimination, oppression, state-directed brutalities etc that were not common to other communities, particularly the Sinhalese. As stated earlier, it was the Sinhala youth who took up arms against the so-called Sinhala-governments precisely on these issues. But the Tamil lobbyists were adepts in focusing only on them as the victims of Sinhala domination. The Sinhalese, no doubt, fuelled the fires of this political line by their aberrations and, more so, by the violence initiated by the lower-level leadership.

Here too it is sad to say that the Tamil leadership exploited this weakness and deliberately provoked the lower-level Sinhala leadership to go on the rampage against the Tamils. In plain words, the Tamil leadership was strategizing to gain political mileage by provoking the Sinhala mobs to attack the Tamils. It is a grim story of a blood-thirsty Tamil leadership planning to thrive on the carnage of their own Tamil people. This chilling tactic would be indeed incredible if it was not documented by the leading Tamil political academic, Prof. Wilson. He wrote: "A second tactic is to destabilize the political situation. Political murders, acts of sabotage, and inflammatory and provocative speeches are the established forms, and these have been tried. The Sinhalese masses and their lower-level ethnic leadership are needled by such acts and urge their rank and file to take retaliatory action. Nothing is more satisfying to the Tamil militants." [31]

Presenting the hidden side, or the darker side of the Sri Lanka moon should not be interpreted as an attempt to exonerate the Sinhala leadership from blame, or to white-wash the sporadic violence led mostly by the unorganized Sinhala mobs. Their biggest folly was in playing into the hands of the Tamil leadership who were waiting on the sidelines to exploit every mistake. Both sides are guilty of missed opportunities and serious political blunders. The interaction of the north-south forces played a key role in exacerbating the crisis. But if the available evidence is placed on a fair and balanced scale on it is quite apparent that the Tamil leadership alone, deliberately and consciously, knowing the consequences constructing a "nationalism" that was never there in history before the forties, took to confrontational and violent politics when the option was there for them to settle their grievances within the non-violent and democratic process like the other two Tamil-speaking communities. The morality of their political behaviour, particularly in resorting to violence, cannot be justified in the light of the nonviolent political conduct of the other two Tamil-speaking communities.

Their "little now and more later" agenda was not designed to co-exist with the majority. Their agenda, starting from the twenties when they pushed for an extras seat in the Western Province and ended in a separate state, would drive them ineluctably to the explosive Vaddukoddai Resolution. Their insatiable political appetites, based on exaggerated claims of victimology, led the politics of the post-independence phase from one crisis to another. When they cooperated with the centre they bargained and gained advantages to their community. Having advanced they would then moved to the next stage of bargaining on their calculated tactic of "little now and more later". The "more later" has nothing to do with "1956". All the issues that were raised as grievances in the post-1956 have been settled. Furthermore, the south has moved taking gigantic steps to address even the "aspirations". But there is no end in sight to the "more later". The nation continues to be brutalized by the violence unleashed in "1976".

Pro-separatist ideologues tend to blame the Sinhala nationalism as the root of all evil in the post-independence phase. The orthodox view promoted by these ideologues emphasize that the "nationalism" constructed by the Tamil leadership of Jaffna has either been fathered by the Sinhalese provocations or went berserk because the Tamil-speaking people have been victims of illiberal Sinhala nationalism. However, these ideologues go along, without any qualms, with the "nationalism" floated in the Vaddukoddai Resolution that dehumanised the political culture of Sri Lanka. Their declaration that "the Tamils of Ceylon…..are a nation distinct and apart from the Sinhalese…." left no room for reconciliation or negotiations expect on the terms dictated by them. The ideological construction of a new "nationalism" by re-writing history can be accepted only by those who deny the hard reality that Sinhala nationalism had co-existed in the past with all the minorities without irredeemable antagonisms or prolonged violence organized by communities refusing to co-exist.

It can be argued that if Tamil "nationalism" was not constructed by the Jaffna elite in the forties on their own initiative, without any provocation from any community, neither the aggressive confrontations nor the unremitting violence would have plagued the nation. The artificially induced birth of Tamil "nationalism" in the forties turned into a ferocious Hanuman running into the four corners of the nation, destroying everything in its wake. As opposed to the mob violence of the lower-level ethnic leadership – and that too provoked by the Tamil instigators, as stated by Prof. Wilson – the north adopted, initiated, organized, propagated financed and totally endorsed violence as the prime tool of advancing their newly constructed "nationalism". It stands out as the only community that declared war on another community in Sri Lanka. So which of the two nationalisms – the natural and the artificial – should accept the greater responsibility for exacerbating the north-south relations that led to this carnage?

Consider briefly, the two political systems that emerged from the two nationalisms. With all its defects the Sinhala nationalism has maintained a democratic system "which speaks for the essentially flexible, plastic nature of Sri Lanka society," wrote Jane Russell. She added: "From a sociological point of view, the major reason for this continuing commitment to democratic norms has been the tolerant nature of the Theravada Buddhist rubric. The traditions of the Buddhist belief system are anti-doctrinaire. Smith (D. E. Smith, Religion and Political Development) notes again that "Buddhist authority patterns are highly incongruent with an authoritarian political system and are supportive of systems encouraging broad areas of individual freedom", a view supported by Bechert and Martin Wickremasinghe. A. J. Wilson goes further. He has argued that the "ethos of tolerance" encouraged by Buddhism has provided solutions to vexed problems" thereby serving a "prime factor" in the maintenance of parliamentary system.".[32]

Jane Russell was quoting A. J. Wilson's writing of 1974. Before the decade was out Wilson was describing Sinhala-Buddhists as chauvinists oppressing the Tamils peaking people by denying them their rights. In his biography of his father-in-law (published in 1993) he portrayed him as the sole hero who was destined to fight the oppressive Sinhala nationalism. Later, without any explanations he did an intellectual somersault and blamed the Sinhala-Buddhists for not letting his father-in-law establish the Tamil State. Prof. S. J. Tambiah, a fellow Tamil at Harvard, too singled out only the Sinhala-Buddhism as the source of political evil in Sri Lanka. Both academics come from Jaffna and both denied the intermeshing forces that collided after the northern elite constructed their Tamil "nationalism" in the forties and handed over the Vaddukoddai Resolution (1976), after stepping out of the democratic framework, for their "boys" to finish the job they had begun. If there was communal harmony before the forties and if communal tensions and confrontations reared its ugly head after the construction of "Tamil nationalism" then it is not difficult to find the source of this crisis.

Geographically, the two communities were destined to coexist. Historically, as stated by Dr. Mendis, this destiny was fulfilled down the ages until the last days of the British raj. Politically, the ruling elite of Jaffna took to mono-ethnic extremism (e.g.: 50-50) or separatism in the forties -- long before Sinhala nationalism caused any provocation to the Tamils. Ethnically, two other Tamilspeaking communities – the Muslims of the east and the Indian Tamils of the central hills -- refused to join hands with the confrontational politics of the northern Tamils. They opted for consensual politics. Regionally, the issue began in the north and continues to be in the north with the east linked to it tangentially. Militarily, too the violence was initiated, organized and driven by the north. Out of these bare facts came the Vaddukoddai Resolution. And that is where the nation is stuck today.

End notes

1. The orthodox version categorizes the current crisis as an "ethnic conflict" in which the majority Sinhalese is accused of discriminating against the Tamil-speaking minorities. It should be noted that there are three Tamil-speaking minorities: 1) the Jaffna Tamils of the north; (2) The Tamil-speaking Muslims of the east and (3) the Tamil-speaking Indian Tamils of the central hills. Of these only the leadership of Jaffna Tamils organized and led aggressive and confrontational political campaign against the majority, escalating their demands over the decades until they took up arms to pursue their agenda of establishing a separate state. It is, therefore, not consistent with the visible realities to categorize the current crisis as an ethnic issue in which all the Tamil-speaking ethnic minorities have collectively formed a common front against the majority. Historically, politically, geographically and even militarily (especially with the breakaway of Karuna from the east) it has been a conflict confined essentially to the north and the south with the east being dragged into it tangentially. For an understanding of the evolving crisis in its proper historical setting, it is best described in geographical terms because the ethnic dimensions are confined to only the northern regions and two ethnic communities in the eastern and central regions have not joined the north in either their demands or violence launched against the majority

2. With the prospects of independence increasing after World War II, the Jaffna Tamils, led by G. G. Ponnambalam, raised the cry

of 50-50 – a political formula to give 50% of seats to the minorities and 50% to the majority. In 1943 the Board of Ministers was asked to draft a constitution for self-government after the War. In 1944 Ponnambalam formed the All Ceylon Tamil Congress and waged the 50-50 campaign to prevent the Sinhalese from obtaining their legitimate and democratic right to a major share in the government. Dr. Mendis wrote: "From 1920, whenever constitutional reforms were about to be made, they have pressed for a solution that would prevent the Sinhalese acquiring a dominant position over the rest." – p.208,Ceylon Today and Yesterday, Main Current of Ceylon History, Second Edition, 1967, Associated Newspapers of Ceylon Ltd.

3. p.127 – Ceylon Today and Yesterday, Main currents of Ceylon History, Dr. G. C. Mendis, 1967, Associated Newspapers of Ceylon Ltd.

4. "thirty per cent of the jobs or more," – p.209, Ibid.

5. Ibid – p. 217

6. p. 128 - – S. J. V. Chelvanayakam and the Crisis of Sri Lankan Tamil Nationalism, 1947 – 1977, A Political Biography, A. J. Wilson, 1994, Lake House Bookshop

7. Clause (f) of the Resolution passed at a Convention of the Tamil United Liberation Front (TULF) held at Pannakam, Vaddukoddai, 14 May 1976: "This Convention directs the Action Committee of the TAMIL UNITED LIBERATION FRONT to formulate a plan of action and launch without delay the struggle for winning the sovereignty and freedom of the Tamil Nation. "And this convention calls upon the Tamil Nation in general and the Tamil youth in particular to come forward to throw themselves fully into the sacred fight for freedom and to flinch not till the goal of a sovereign socialist State of Eelam is reached." Ironically, the youth obeyed their call to arms and turned the guns on those who worded it and passed it

8. Chelvanayakam launched the iyakkum (movement) of Thamil Payasoom Makkal (the Tamil-speaking people) "to create a unity of all Tamil-speaking people in the whole island inclusive of the Tamil-speaking Muslim." – p.70. S. J. V. Chelvanayakam

and the Crisis of Sri Lankan Tamil Nationalism, 1947 – 1977, A Political Biography, A. J. Wilson, 1994, Lake House Bookshop. Obviously, this **iyakkum** was to be a united front of all Tamil-speaking people against the Sinhalaspeaking people. Neither the Muslims of the east nor the Indian Tamils of the central hills joined this movement, confirming the fact that language was whipped up into a political issue only by the Jaffna Tamils. The other Tamil-speaking communities were content to resolve their differences with the majority through non-violent negotiations as they did with all their grievances, including the citizenship rights of the Indians.

9. Ibid – p. 208

10. Justice Sansoni wrote: " On the evidence I have already set out, and further evidence which I shall set out, what right has Mr. Amirthalingam (the Deputy leader of the TULF) to claim, when questioned about the usual day of morning on 22nd May 1973, 'Our action was essentially and fully peaceful, and to the best of my knowledge there was no violence. Our actions did not involve violence anywhere'. Does he wish me to believe that in the face of the prolonged and almost continuous campaign of civil disobedience carried on by the TULF and its associated youth movements which involved murders, acts of arson, attempted murders, bombing, acts of mischief done against public property, forcible prevention of children attending school on the so-called days of mourning and hartals, forcible closing of shops, intimidation of witnesses who could have spoken to various crimes, killing of persons who were brave enough to give information to the Police regarding breaches of the laws of the land, ...and, most regrettable of all, the failure of his party members to openly condemn the commission of such crimes or to express their sympathy towards the victims, be believed it was all done peacefully and without violence?" Report of the Sansoni Commission, p.52 -53

11. "......The northern regions of Ceylon directly exposed to the western impact since the second quarter of the sixteenth century has failed to attract modern historians....." – p.57, History of Ceylon (circa 1500 – 1658), A historiographical and bibliographical survey, C. R. de Silva and D. de Silva., The Ceylon Journal of Historical

and Social Studies, Vol III, No. 1 January June, 1973

12. p.163 The Political Construction of Defensive Nationalism: The 1968 Temple Enrty Crisis in Sri Lanka. The Sri Lankan Tamils, Ethnicity & Identity, edited by Chelvadurai Manogaram and Bryan Pfaffenberger.

13. Op sit, Wilson – p.217

14. See (in the attached Appendix) extracts of Chapter 8 of the Soulbury Commission Report that dealt exclusively with this complaint of discrimination raised by the Tamil representatives

15. p.117, The Ceylon Journal of Historical and Social Studies, The Ceylon National Congress in Disarray, 1920-1; Sir Ponnambalam Arunachalam leaves the Congress, Prof. K. M. de Silva, Vol II, No.2, July-December, 1971

16. Ibid – p.107

17. p.17, The Ceylon Journal of Historical and Social Studies, The Ceylon National Congress in Disarray II: The Triumph of Sir William Manning, 1921 -1924, Vol III, January-June, 1973, No.1.

18. Jane Russell, Communal Politics Under the Donoughmore Constitution 1931 -1947: "In 1929, there existed in the peninsula, 65 English schools, ten of them being first-class collegiate schools, twelve Anglo-Vernacular schools, and 426 Vernacular schools... The Ceylon Tamils constituted 20% of all pupils in schools, and the percentage was considerably higher in English schools."- p.23. She added later: "From 1900 to 1931 the Northern and Eastern Province had received almost 50% of the total government expenditure on major irrigation works – p.170"

19. p. 106, The Ceylon Journal of Historical and Social Studies, The Ceylon National Congress in Disarray, 1920-1; Sir Ponnambalam Arunachalam leaves the Congress, Prof. K. M. de Silva, Vol II, No.2, July-December

20. Ibid. Vol III – p.26

21. For instance, more Sinhalese have been killed by the state than members of any other community. In JVP insurrection of 1971 it is estimated that 20,000 Sinhala youth were killed. In the next uprising of 1989 -90 it is estimated that over 60,000 were killed. But in the morality of partisan political pundits only the deaths

of the Tamils have been allotted a sanctity not granted to others. Second, the persecution of party rivals at the end of each election is a common practice. Transfers, denial of promotions and other punitive action by the party in power against rival supporters in the public and private sectors are quite common. But only those acts that affected the Tamils were rated as being more immoral than the others. Third, the mass migration of the Sinhalese took place after Badi-ud-din Mahamoud, the Minister of Education under the SLFP-Marxist coalition government, introduced standardization of marks to enable students in disadvantaged areas to gain easy access to tertiary education. Before the standardization of marks mainly the coastal belt in the south and Jaffna – two advantaged areas – benefited. Both areas were affected by the new system but only the failure of the Tamils to maintain their high proportion of entrants was highlighted as acts of racist discrimination. Fourth, despite the allegations of discrimination on the basis of language there is room at the top only for those competent in English. The English –speaking elite still rule the nation and the JVP youth cried discrimination because they were not armed with the "kaduwa" (sword) – i.e. the English language. Clearly the cry of discrimination on the basis of language was not applicable only to the Tamils of the north. Fifth, it was the Sinhala youth who rose up in rebellion alleging discrimination, long before the Tamil youth. The reality, however, is that to this day, despite the allegations of discrimination on the basis of language, there is room at the top only for those competent in English. The English–speaking elite still rule the nation and the JVP youth cried discrimination because they were not armed with the "kaduwa" (sword) – i.e. the English language. Besides, the Sinhala Only Act was introduced to dethrone English and not Tamil. Though no community gained upward social mobility through the Sinhala Only Act or from the Tamil Language (Special Provisions) Act it was the cry of language discrimination raised by the Tamils that drew the attention of the anti-majority lobby. The cry of the most privileged community was heard above all the other communities, even though they experienced iniquity more than the Tamils of the north.

22. Ibid – p. 30

23. Ibid – p.30, footnote quoting "CO. 54/854. H. R. Cowell's memorandum of 16 May 1921."

24. p.504 – Nationalism in Sri Lanka and the Tamils, S. Arasaratnam in Collective Identities: Nationalism and Protest in Modern Sri Lanka, MARGA Institute, 1979

25. Ibid – pp. 505 -506

26. p.13 – S. J. V. Chelvanayakam and the Crisis of Sri Lankan Tamil Nationalism, 1947 – 1977, A Political Biography, A. J. Wilson, 1994, Lake House Bookshop

27. Rajan Hoole, Wake UP Tamils, Sunday Times......

28. The Jathika Vimukthi Peramuna, a Marxist-oriented youth movement, rose up in rebellion twice – 1) in 1971 and 2) 1988-90. Among other accusations of inequalities and discrimination they too took up the issue of language – meaning the English language – as a tool of oppression used by the ruling class. Wilson: "...the period of Dudley Senanayake's National Government', 1965-70,marked the golden years of Sinhala-Tamil reconciliation."

30. Wilson: "The President of the FP, S. M. Rasamanickam, in his presidential address to the annual convention of 1969, spoke of the rewarding relationship: "During the last four years we were able to gain some rights, if not all of what we expected, through the method of cooperation."

31. A. Jeyaratnam Wilson, Sri Lanka and its Future: Sinhalese versus Tamils – p.301

32. Jane Russell. Op cit – pp. xiv – xv

The Impact of LTTE Terrorism on Sri Lankan Society

Shantha K. Hennayake

Introduction

"War is a game in which princes seldom win, the people never"

(Charles Caleb Colton, Lacon, 1825, 1:534)

To suit the contemporary Sri Lankan context we could paraphrase the above as 'War is a game in which terrorists seldom win, the people never'.

Terrorism can be simply defined as "the use of force or threat to demoralize; intimidate and subjugate especially such use as a political weapon or policy" (Websters Electronic Dictionary). Terrorism is now adopted in many parts of the world as a political strategy as became clearly evident from the 9/11 incident, the destruction of the World Trade Center in New York.

Terrorism today is a household word internationally but its vernacular equivalent – *thrasthvaadaya* – had been in common parlance in Sri Lanka since 1971 when the exclusively Sinhala dominated JVP first resorted to terror and repeated the terror campaign with more vigor in 1989. Although the JVP organization has now embraced democratic politics, they are responsible for the introduction of terrorism to achieve political objectives in Sri Lanka.

Terrorist tradition of Sri Lankan politics was raised to new heights by the now world famous LTTE of which Norway is very familiar in more than one way. The LTTE arose from the youth groups who were frustrated by the unattainable promises made by the extremist leaders of the TULF. The LTTE was then trained and supported by India in its efforts to pressurize the pro-west Sri Lankan policy. LTTE, better trained and armed, quickly liquidated all other rival guerrilla groups. By the late 1980s, the LTTE became the most powerful terrorist group and by 1990s, it had developed into a formidable terrorist outfit with international links. The LTTE continued its terror against both the Sri Lankan State and its citizens, Sinhalese and Muslims in particular also the Tamils. By the late 1990s, the LTTE was proscribed by the United States, India, England and a few other countries and the 9/11 incident put LTTE into a tight corner. However, the MOU brokered by Norway treated the LTTE terrorist organization as an equal partner with the legitimate Sri Lankan Government, giving the former a new lease of life.

What is the LTTE?

The LTTE is a perceived differently by different people. The LTTE at its early days was intimately identified as "boys" by the extremist Tamil politicians who themselves were eventually gunned down by the LTTE itself. The LTTE labeled itself as a "liberation organization". Many have labeled the LTTE as a "guerrilla movement". The Sri Lankan government and the Sinhalese have defined it as a terrorist organization and this was endorsed by the world community when a number of states (e.g. USA, India, UK) proscribed it as a terrorist organization and was considered threatening even beyond the shores of Sri Lanka.

The LTTE is not just a terrorist organization on the run like Al Qaeda. It is more dangerously stable with some parts of the Sri Lankan territory under its control with the help of a conventional armed cadre and an administrative structure. To make matters worse, the LTTE collect taxes within areas under its control. Three processes were responsible for the "success" of the LTTE. First is that the Indian Government in its misguided policy of trying to change the Sri Lankan pro west policy during the height of the Cold War, trained and supported the LTTE. In fact, India is primarily responsible for turning a bunch of lawbreakers in Sri Lanka into a formidable terrorist organization. Second, the short sighted policies or more correctly lack of a consistent policy of the successive Sri Lankan governments since mid 1980s allowed the LTTE to strengthen itself as a military organization. The UNP and SLFP governments in their bitter political rivalry failed to agree on an effective national strategy against LTTE terrorism so much so both parties when in government provided financial, material support and even military hardware to the LTTE! Third the tactical, combat and intelligence failure of Sri Lankan armed forces led the LTTE to secure more and more territory. The corruption in the military and the rivalry at the top level has also prevented the armed forces becoming an effective and successful anti-LTTE force protecting the security and sovereignty of the Sri Lankan state. The forth factor is the extreme violence and brutality directed by the LTTE against the Tamils who challenge or question its ideology or strategy. The LTTE has been able to bring the entire Tamil community into total submission through intimidation and terror that LTTE has a free run on the Tamil society. Unfortunately, the Sri Lankan governments have not taken any effective measure to extricate the Tamil people from LTTE brutality.

The LTTE has effectively internationalized itself using four discourses; civil right discourse' nationalist discourse, Marxist discourse and the liberal discourse. Thus, LTTE hiding that it is a terrorist organization, yet engaging in terrorism against the Sri Lankan state and its people all the time, projected in the international scene that they represent fighting against discrimination, that they are fighting for self determination of Tamils, that they are oppressed and finally that their human rights have been violated. What is ironic about these claims is that the truth is exactly the opposite. The LTTE has been able to successfully deceive the democratic yet politically ignorant citizens in many western countries including Norway to support an essentially a terrorist organization. The lethargy and the ineffectiveness of Sri Lankan diplomatic mission was an asset to the LTTE as there was hardly any rebuttal of the false LTTE propaganda in these countries. LTTE was also successful in utilizing the Tamil academics to intellectually legitimize them and many Tamils who sought political refugee status although in reality to take advantage of the greener pastures in many western countries eventually became strong blocks of votes and thus an internal voice for the LTTE in these countries.

LTTE in Action

The LTTE's terrorist activities can be classified into firstly direct or crude terrorism targeted primarily against its "enemies" i.e. the Sri Lankan State and the Sinhalese, non Tamils living in the "Tamil homeland" and Tamils opposing the LTTE. Secondly indirect terrorism applied through fear, intimidation and threat against potential challenges and alternatives both in thinking and practice. The indirect terrorism is mostly directed against the Tamils themselves and it has effectively silenced the Tamil community except perhaps a very brave few who are identified as traitors to the Tamil cause by the LTTE. To save space I am compelled only to give a single example for each of the most destructive terrorist activities of LTTE[1].

1. Assassination of a foreign leaders by a suicide women bomber. (e.g Rajiv Gandhi, Prime Minister of India).

2. Assassination of Sri Lanka President (e.g. R. Premadasa; the attempt on President Chandrika Kumaratunge failed).

3. Assassination of Presidential Candidates (Gamini Dissanayake)

4. Assassination of Tamil Politicians (TULF Founder President, A. Amirthalingam)

5. Assassination of Tamil Intellectuals (Prof. Mrs. Rajani Tiranagama and Dr. Neelam Tiruchelvam)

6. Cultural terrorism (Bombing of the Sacred Temple of Tooth, which is a UNESCO recognized World Heritage site and the killing of devotees) by a suicide lorry bomber.

7. Genocide (massacre of Sinhalese in Dollar Farm, Kent Farm, Kebitigollewa and Massacre of Muslims at prayer at a Mosque in Kattankudi, and of surrendered policemen numbering over 600)

8. Ethnic Cleansing (chasing Muslims and Sinhalese out of Jaffna and Mannar)

9. Fratricide (killing of cardres belong to rival groups such as PLOTE, EPDP)

10. Massacre of Buddhist Monks (over 60 Buddhist monks were killed in Eastern Sri Lanka)

11. Mass destruction of infrastructure and property (Bombing of World Trade Center, Central Bank of Ceylon, International Airport, Petroleum Storage Depot. Etc.)

12. Killing of innocent civilians including women and children including school children (Series of Suicide Bombings in Colombo)

13. Extortion, torture and killing of Tamil civilians who oppose LTTE (Farmers, government servants and businessmen in Batticaloa, Jaffna and Colombo)

14 Silencing opposition through threat and intimidation and fear (all over Sri Lanka and in the West)

15. Confiscating land and property that belonged to the Sinhalese

and Tamils who lived in areas presently under LTTE control.
16 International terrorism (sinking a Chinese fishing trawler, and sinking of ships exporting minerals)

Impacts on Society

The direct and indirect impact of LTTE terrorism on the Sri Lankan society since mid 1970s in general and more intensively since mid 1980s is immense and far reaching that no aspect of life and no inch of land is spared. Destruction and the lost opportunities due to terrorism is so vast that the economic development and social and cultural life of the country is permanently damaged. Although a rupee estimate of impact of terrorism has never been done it has come out in disguise as the cost of war in a study by Institute of Policy Studies (see appendix 1). As IPS (2000) stated, "The human and social costs of death, disability, dispossession, and the psychological trauma associated with violence and terror are not really quantifiable. On the other hand, at least in principle, the "purely economic costs" are amenable to quantitative measurement". According to this study, although limited and simplistic, the cost of war between 1984-1996 is Rs. 1,429,144 million ($ 14,290 million at today's exchange rates) or 1.7 times Sri Lanka's 1996 GDP. The actual cost of the terrorism in Sri Lanka would be much higher than this. The Sri Lanka Monitor of the British Refugee Council (September 1996) referring to another NGO study says that it "estimates the total LTTE Attack on a skyscraper in Colombo annual cost of the war at Rs. 110 billion ($ 1.1 billion)"[2]. This was 16.7 per cent of Sri Lanka's GNP in 1995. Ross and Samaranayake (1988) point out that in the 1980s that the civil war resulted in GDP loosing 1% of growth. They further argue that this resulted in "a loss of between 10% and 15% of the country's real growth potential" (p. 1241)

What is generally unsaid is the impact of terrorism on Tamil society which is far greater than that on the other communities in Sri Lanka. It is extremely sad that in the name of an elusive future

Tamil state, almost an entire generation of Sri Lankans have lost so much including thousands of lives. It is almost impossible to put a dollar value to the destruction and loss due to terrorism except perhaps to say that Sri Lanka will not be able to overcome this loss for a few generations.

Economic Impact: Destruction of Infrastructure and Production

LTTE Terrorist attack on Colombo Oil Storage Facility
LTTE Terrorist Attack on the Colombo International Airport
LTTE Terroist attck on the Central Bank

The Economic impact is the most direct and visible among all terrorism impacts. The biggest economic impact of terrorism is the direct destruction of economic infrastructure and productive systems. Destruction of infrastructure has been one of the terrorist strategies to deny the government access to the LTTE controlled regions on the one hand and to cripple the Sri Lankan economy on the other. Destruction caused to the International Airport, the Central Bank of Ceylon, the oil Storage facilities in Colombo created not only immediate draw backs to the economy but also long term impacts. The international community, including the US, until 9/11 readily imposed punitive action against Sri Lanka arguing that Sri Lanka is unsafe for international commerce thus raising insurance premium on shipping.

The destruction of infrastructure such as the railroads and highways, the electricity grid and the schools, hospitals, and other government service institutions caused by the anti-terrorist war has totally crippled ordinary life in LTTE controlled areas. The terrorism induced war also crippled agricultural production in the North to a large extent with large tracts of farms abandoned. The Central Bank of Sri Lanka estimates the reduction of paddy production in the North and East to be as high as 18% in 1987. The trend would have continued unchanged into the late 1990s. The fish production had declined significantly and many fishermen completely lost their livelihood due to restriction of fishing in some parts of the

Northern Province. Jaffna which was one of the most productive agricultural centers became an importer of agricultural produce as a result of the war. The LTTE also destroyed the industrial base in Jaffna by totally vandalizing chemical, cement, salt, mineral sands production facilities thus making many Tamils to loose their means of income. The once vibrant Jaffna economy which was second in GRP (gross regional production) only to Colombo became almost a poor and backward region.

Severance of the Link between LTTE Areas and the Rest of the Island

During the pre-terrorist era, the Northern and Eastern parts of Sri Lanka including the areas controlled by LTTE was an integral part of the national economic system of Sri Lanka. These areas produced many agricultural products such as tobacco, vegetables, fruits, paddy, marine products such as fish, dry fish and industrial products such as cement, chemicals, salt and paper. These areas in turn depended on the rest of the country for other essential food and consumer items. At one point Jaffna supplied over 50% of all cement and chemicals and over 40% of fish to the rest of the country. This commercial inter-linkage sustained the economy of Jaffna and other Tamil areas in the Northern and Eastern Provinces.

The delinking of Jaffna with the rest of the country led to the loss of market for the Jaffna producers and the scarcity of many consumer products led to high inflation. The scarcity of food including the basic essentials such as food and medicine exerted severe hardships on the people living under LTTE controlled areas. Travel and trade between LTTE areas and the rest of the country had come to a complete halt preventing the inflow of money into the regions as it was the case before 1980s. The Jaffna economy was once known as the postal order economy due to the large monthly remittances to Jaffna from the rest of the country by the Tamil government servants and businessmen. With the self isolationist policy of the LTTE, the number of Tamils working in other areas of the country has declined and many Tamils who are in the working age group sought refugee status in many western countries alleging insecurity and prosecution in Sri Lanka. Most of these post 1980s Tamil refugees in the West have become a new source of money for Jaffna. Thus the new economy in Jaffna can be described as an international money order economy in which money transfer is almost completely controlled by the LTTE directly and indirectly.

Economic Impact: Non-Development of the North and East

One of the most significant impacts of terrorism is the non-development of the North and East in general and LTTE controlled areas in particular. As a result 2/3 of the coast line and about 1/3 of the land area with its rich natural resource base remained out of reach of development process during last 20 years. The eastern coast being one of the most picturesque in the country could have developed into a booming tourist attraction; rather, it became a killing field. The access roads from Colombo to Jaffna, Batticaloa, Trincomalee and Mannar could have become development corridors with vibrant service centers. Instead many of these roads were destroyed and were converted to death traps by the LTTE.

Sarvananthan (2002) may be not too far off in arguing that the Northern and Eastern Provinces "would have experienced negative growth since 1990 when the civil war intensified".

Economic Impact: Lost Opportunities in Development

Terrorism brings terror and repel potential development opportunities. The last 20 years of economic history of Sri Lanka is one of missing and loosing opportunities. By 1983, when terrorism began to intensify, the Sri Lankan economy was moving ahead at over 6% with direct and indirect foreign investment freely flowing into the country.

However, since then the country's economy grew at a more sluggish rate largely due to the reduced or lack of inflow of foreign investment into the country which is affected by terrorism. The tourism potential in the country at large and in the North and Eastern coastal region remain underdeveloped and undeveloped. The prevalence of underdevelopment if not poverty in Sri Lanka today in large measure is a result of LTTE terrorism. The Budget Speech of November 1996 neatly summarized how terrorism is affecting Sri Lankan economy.

> "The tourist industry which provides nearly 90,000 employment and over US$200 million foreign exchange earnings and its great potential to expand are severely constrained by a sharp fall in tourist arrivals. It (continued violence) depresses economic activities through dislocation of trade and business, the production of vegetables, fruits, rice and fish, affecting the cost of living and the overall quality of social welfare. The security risk results in high risk premium and [rise in] cost of international trade and finance. It deprives [us of] the full utilization of investor interest in Sri Lanka's economy. It is this reality that should bring all of us together to reach a peaceful solution to the ethnic problem and end the war, as a national priority."

Economic Impact: Government Expenditure on anti-Terrorist war and LTTE expenditure on Terrorism

Intensification of LTTE terrorism against the state, its people and properties has compelled the Government to channel a significant share of its income to defend the country, its people and the properties against terrorism. In 1990 the total security expenditure was consistently higher than 5% of the GDP (Annual Report, Central Bank, 1997 p. 2). In terms of government expenditure the defense component was as high as 6.5 % in the early 1980s and it reached almost the 20% level in the early 1990s. The annual budget of the armed forces today is the largest single item of expenditure.

According to Wijemanne (2000)

> For the last 17 years the war was waged without any serious financial or economic sacrifices by the Sinhala people. The annual budgetary provision for the war ran at less than the annual cost of servicing the public debt both local and foreign. But now for the first time this has changed. The massive military defeats since November 1999 have led to huge increases in war expenditure. Already the pain is beginning to be felt. Cuts in subsidies, increases in the charges for public utilities, widening of the GST net to catch the tourist industry are all but the first steps of far more pain to come.

What is most often not said about LTTE terrorism is that the LTTE itself is spending millions of dollars to sustain itself and its terror machinery. This was estimated at about US$ 2 million a month. In either case, it is the money that could have been spent on the productive development of this country and improving the quality of life of its citizens.

Wijemanne (2000) makes a very revealing analysis on the military expenditure by the Government in fighting LTTE terrorism.

> The paucity of financial resources is clearly seen if the country's finances are looked at from an international perspective. The government's annual expenditure budget plus the extra budgetary costs of servicing the public debt (foreign as well as local – they are about evenly balanced) come to a total of SL Rs. 320 billion for this year. At current exchange rates (i.e. SL Rs. 120=£1 Stg) this comes to £2.7 billion – a piffling sum by international standards. Of this small sum only about SL Rs. 80 billion is for the war effort, mostly local rupee expenditure on local rupee expenses such as salaries, food etc. Of the Rs.80 billion only about Rs.36 billion are for external purchases of all the requirements of modern warfare ranging from armaments (terrestrial, naval and aerial), fuel, medical supplies and communications equipment. This comes to about £300 million per year for a military force of 180,000 men and

women – itself a piffling figure considering the costs of modern armaments. The LTTE, fielding one-twentieth the number of the Sri Lankan Government forces would require for parity one-twentieth of the Sri Lanka government's appropriation, i.e. one-twentieth of £300 million or £15 million per year. Many multiples of that sum are easily within reach for the Eelam Tamil diaspora.

It is important to know that although most studies concentrate only on the government expenditure on curbing terrorism, the LTTE also spend substantial funds to continue its terrorism. Casperz captures both sides of the story in his analysis

> The 1997 Budget figure of the defense expenditure of Rs 47 billion this year means that the country was spending Rs 129 million per day on the military operations and their concomitants. The NGO figure is of Rs 110 billion as the total cost of war, if correct, it would mean that the war costs the country Rs 301 million per day. If the LTTE budget were included, the cost would probably be Rs 400 million per day, more not less. Sri Lanka simply cannot afford expenditure of the magnitude of Rs 129 million, much less Rs 301 million or Rs 400 million per day, on the war. To say it can put one outside the pale of sanity. International capital, led by the TNCs, the World Bank and the IMF, tells Sri Lanka to eliminate or reduce subsidies and imposes on the poor the satanic principle of "cost recovery". If Sri Lanka has Rs 129 million a day, it could tell them to go where they belong, finally and definitively taking development into its own hands.

But unfortunately the LTTE is not willing to give up terrorism, even after the CFA and MOU and as a result, the legitimate government of the state of Sri Lanka is compelled to fight against terrorism. Thus, the military expenditure continues pushing capital away from the productive investments.

Economic Impact: Intensification of Spatial Unevenness

The Physical Quality of Life Index (PQLI) in Jaffna in 1982 was only second to Colombo. However, today it could be one of the lowest in the country. Jaffna used to be the second vibrant economic, commercial, industrial and service center of the island after Colombo. However over 20 years of severance of Jaffna and other LTTE areas from the rest of the island prevented the government from maintaining its services such as education, health, infrastructure facilities in most areas held by the LTTE. Because the LTTE prevented the Government from operating in these areas, it could not initiate any new development activities in the areas held by the LTTE. LTTE terrorism, totalitarian approach, heavy taxation, fear and intimidation also prevented private investment in these areas even by the Tamils themselves. Tamil private investment continued in the direction of Colombo or stayed in Colombo during the last 20 years. There is no foreign private investment of any kind in the LTTE controlled areas during the last 20 years. The destruction of what was there and the lack of infrastructure facilities to start new industries and other development activities increase the disparity between the LTTE held areas and the rest of the country. In fact what has happened in LTTE areas is not simply underdevelopment but de-development.

The 2002 Central Bank of Sri Lanka summarized the economic impact of the anti-terrorist war identifying terrorism and resulting civil disturbances as the primary factor affecting negatively on the Sri Lankan economy.

> The first and the most important factor was the continuation of civil disturbances first started as a guerrilla war, but which soon developed into a conventional civil war in the country threatening political stability, worsening social conditions and hindering economic development. It brought in its own cost to the economy by preventing the economy from operating at full capacity, hindering improvements in productivity, disturbing

> the resource allocation efficiency and interfering with the free mobility of both inputs and finished products throughout the country. Its adverse impact on economic activity was not limited to the North and East, but was also evident in other parts of the country. The resultant deterioration of market confidence constrained investment expansion particularly discouraging much needed foreign investment (p. 27).

Much of what is said in this report is still true even after the CFA and MOU as the behaviour of the LTTE remain fundamentally the same. The failure of the LTTE to publicly denounce terrorism and embrace democracy and frequent threats that it will have to resort to war continue to have the same negative impact on the economy as before.

The Central Bank in its 1991 report points out what the economy lost due to the terrorist war.

> The greatest challenge to the (economy) is the ongoing armed conflict in the North and the East. While some estimates can be made of the direct and as well as some of the indirect costs of the armed conflict, it is not easy to quantify other costs such as the loss of human life and destruction of social fabric. In the absence of the conflict Sri Lanka's annual investment would have been about 2 to 3 percentage points higher due to higher private investment, supported by accelerated foreign direct investment and higher public investment. All sectors in the economy would have grown faster to generate an economic growth about 2-3 percentage points higher. Such higher growth during the last 16 years of conflict would have elevated Sri Lanka from a low income country status to a low middle income country status in 1994 with a per capita annual income of about US $ 800 in that year. The country's per capita income would have reached approximately US $ 1,200 in 1999 instead of US $ 829. This means that the monthly income of an average Sri Lankans would have been Rs. 7040 in 1999 instead of Rs. 4875. These approximate figures underscores the paramount

need to take all steps to end the senseless conflict. If allowed to continue, the conflict could seriously drain the resources and the energies of the people and marginalize the country in the international community (p. 22).

Social Impacts

"As wounded men may limp through life, so our war minds may not regain the balance of their thoughts for decades"
(Frank Moore Colby, "War Minds", The Colby Essays, 1926, V.2)

It is unfortunate that Sri Lankan social science has ignored the area of social impact of terrorism in Sri Lanka. For example, there is hardly any serious scholarly work on the social impact of terrorism on Sri Lankan society in general and Tamil society in particular. While the reasons for the Tamil scholars to be silent on the impact of LTTE terrorism is understandable, I have not been able to fathom the reasons for others indifference to a total social calamity that has befallen on Sri Lankan society due to the war.

A previous study on the War and the Economy lists out a series of impacts under the title of "human cost of the war" while correctly arguing that such impacts cannot be measured in monetary terms (see Appendix two).

Creation of a Hate Culture

One of the most unfortunate developments of LTTE terrorism is the creation of a hate culture in Sri Lanka especially among the Tamils under the hegemonic control of the LTTE. The LTTE version of Tamil nation is fundamentally founded upon hating Sinhalese, Buddhist and the Sri Lankan State. Thus, the core doctrine of Tamil nationalism is the anti-Sinhaleseness and all LTTE political and ideological activities are founded on this premise as amply revealed by fundamental LTTE writing including the most recent ISGA document. The practical manifestation of this hate culture created by the LTTE were the bomb attck on the most sacred temple of Buddhists the world over, the Temple of Tooth in Kandy, a declared World Heritage site, an attempt on an equally sacred ancient Bo tree in Anuradhapura and massacre of over 60 Buddhist monks in Arantalawa.

The LTTE has taken steps to introduce this hate culture into the school curriculum by distributing its version of history to the Tamil school children (Daily Mirror, January 10, 2004). It is extremely sad that the present generation of Tamils living under LTTE ideological control have become extremely hateful beings.

LTTE Assassinated Young Buddhist Monks in Arantalawa

This extreme hate makes it possible for the LTTE cadres to commit the most gruesome killings and other forms of violence. Ladduwahetty in 1996 elaborated on this.

> It is only a fresh approach that will enable the "Tamil Nation" to be saved from the isolation that they have created for themselves, and the "tragic bitterness" that they have brought upon the whole nation. The only hope for the Tamil community is to support the Sinhala people and together build an inclusive "beloved community".

Genocidal Massacre of Sinhalese Villagers by the LTTE

However, given that LTTE's survival depend on hate ideology and that there is no room for or sign of a progressive Tamil political thinking in the horizon "peace and harmony" in its true sense has no opportunity under LTTE.

What is most alarming is the tacit intellectual legitimation of the LTTEs hate culture by Tamil academics and intellectuals and other professionals living both in Sri Lanka and abroad. They have not only affirmed the terrorism of LTTE but have become open collaborators of manufacturing the hate ideology. H.L.D

Mahindapala (2001) captured this intellectually hypocritical phenomenon

> What the intellectuals and the ideologues have begun at the top end is completed and executed by the political manipulators at the bottom. …Having manufactured the ideology of hate, and seeing it in action along with the brutalities that flow from it, the intellectuals sit back and then pontificate on the correctness of their analyses and justifications as if they had nothing to do with the unfolding consequences of their perverse sociology, anthropology and now historiography" (Mahindapala, 2001).

Emergence of a Violent Society

One of the most disastrous outcomes of LTTE terrorism is that it has made violence a normal and acceptable form of social behavior in the country. The JVP terrorism during 1989 also contributed to this immensely in the Sinhalese areas. All forms of physical violence including killings have become common strategies of expressing opposition or disagreement. The society at large has become indifference to violence to such an extent, that people have become numbed and unresponsive even to help a victim of a violent act. Dead and dying bodies were left lying on the streets with no one wanting even to report the incident to the authorities. A murder was headlines in Sri Lankan newspapers in the past, but today daily newspapers are like extended police reports of crimes.

Violence has become the only expression of dissent in the Tamil society. The series of killings of opponents by the LTTE even after the Cease Fire Agreement and Memorandum of Understanding on the one hand and Karuna's violent challenge of LTTE and LTTE's reprisal killings on the other are but a few manifestations of the new violence that has engulfed the Tamil society.

Proliferation of Gun Culture

The violence and especially killing has become so easy not only due to the free availability of guns, hand grenades but also gangs who are ever ready to use them against anybody who their leaders want killed.

According to Martin van Creveld, "Once the legal monopoly of armed force, long claimed by the state, is wrestled out of its hands, existing distinctions between war and crime will break down much as is already the case today in...Lebanon, Sri Lanka, El Salvador, Peru or Colombia." This points to situations where, as "small-scale violence multiplies at home and abroad, state armies will continue to shrink, being gradually replaced by a booming private security business, and by urban mafias, especially in the former communist world, who may be better equipped than municipal police forces to grant physical protection to local inhabitants" (Kaplan, 1994). LTTE pistol gangs are freely operating not only in the LTTE controlled areas but also in the heart of Colombo not too far away from the Norwegian Embassy.

Venerating Death though aggrandizing Suicide

Death is venerated and life has become expendable in Sri Lanka in general and in Tamil society in particular due to 20 years of LTTE terrorism. Cynaide capsule worn around the neck ensure death as a respectable act though it is one of the most inhuman activities of all. Suicide cadres have the pride of place in LTTE terrorism and they are venerated as true martyrs (See *Tamilnation.org* for detailed discussion on the virtues of suicide in the name of Tamil nation). The LTTE and Al Qaeda are the only two international terrorist organizations that has elevated suicide to divine status as long as it lead to killing of "enemies". A life and respect for life is the most fundamental ethics of any society. A society that elevates death over life is not only fundamentally sick and immoral in today's standards: such a society is killing itself. This is what has happened to the Tamil society.

According to Rajan Hoole recently, leading LTTE theoretician Thirunavukkarasu said at the University of Jaffna: "The hour of destiny awaits an accident. Any accident may trigger off war. In that event the Sinhalese State will bear sole responsibility. The Indian Ocean would then be transformed to a gravy of blood. Let not Prime Minister Ranil Wickremasinhghe dilly-dally, using the opposition as an excuse. We have Millar and Thileepan [as monumental examples of suicide]. They are not expended explosives. From time to time, groups from nooks and corners of our movement will emerge as potent incendiary matter". LTTE continues to venerate its former suicide bombers as national heroes in its major annual gatherings.

Fear Psychosis

LTTE has brought fear including primeval fear to the people of Sri Lanka in general and Tamils in particular. At the height of bomb threats the parents feared for the safe return of their school children as over 100 school children died at various bombing by LTTE. Wives and husbands feared for the lives of their spouses as many working men and women were mimed at various bombings in Colombo including the Central Bank. People feared to be in crowds as any potential gathering had become a target of LTTE bombing. Tamil parents feared all the time that their children would be forcibly conscripted to the LTTE.

Carnage created by Terrorist Bombing of a Colombo Railway Station

Ordinary Tamils refrained from carrying out even an ordinary conversation for fear of being spied on and punished for being frank. Tamil society was totally muted by this fear psychosis created by the LTTE terror.

Loss of Youth, Educators, Intellectuals

Terrorism in Sri Lanka and the resultant war has caused over 60,000 deaths and the majority of them are male youths between

12- 50 years. What is lost in the war is the future generation. The loss of this generation to the society is quite significant in terms of social and cultural production and reproduction. The implication of this is felt at family level within the Tamil community; some women remain unmarried and some families have lost continuity. LTTE terrorism has specifically targeted independent voices within the Tamil community. Thus, almost all Tamils with a conscience to speak for what is happening to their society have been eliminated. This includes not only University intellectuals such as Professor Mrs. Rajani Thiranagama but also internationally renowned human rights lawyers such as Dr. Neelan Tiruchelvam. Tamil society has been stripped of its right thinking independent intellectuals and it is becoming an intellectual desert.

The LTTE has been able to transform a once vibrant and critical Tamil scholarship into a totally socially insensitive uncritical enterprise on the one hand and partial and subservient to LTTE on the other. The University Teachers for Human Rights –Jaffna pointed out that "directly and indirectly, the whole arena of public discourse has been monopolized by the LTTE". Except for a handful of individuals (e.g Dr. Rajan Hoole) and organizations (e.g. University Teachers for Human Rights- Jaffna), the vast majority of Tamils academics and intellectuals both in Sri Lanka and abroad have become spokespersons for the extremist nationalist ideology of LTTE and worse, the apologists for LTTE terrorism directly and indirectly. It is sad and ironical, for example, that Jaffna University, instead of becoming a socially responsible center of excellence studying the problems faced by the Tamil society, has been transformed into a political stage and an expression of the LTTE. The inability or the failure of the Tamil intellectuals to be critical and the tacit affirmation of LTTE terrorism either by silence or by endorsement is very largely responsible for the continuation of disastrous impacts of LTTE on the Tamil society. A former Minister of National Security, Mr. Lalith Athulathmudali who himself was assassinated by the LTTE warned of the extremism of the LTTE as early as 1990.

'But let us examine factually the genocide story. Tamil have got killed by various people, various groups and various forces, but if you were to take a count, more Tamils have been killed by the LTTE than by any other militant group or by the Sri Lankan army or by Muslims or by the Sinhalese or by the IPKF even. The LTTE has caused more harm to Tamils than any other force. … these are facts that the Tamils also must think of. Some Tamils are doing that. There is a book called "The Broken Palmyrah written by some academics in the University of Jaffna. I do not know whether they will be able to live in Jaffna after that, but they have pointed out that those who started with a cause have transformed themselves into fascists" (Athulathmudali, 1990:4)

Athulathmudali was correct in his prediction as one of the authors – Prof. Mrs. Rajani Thirangama - was murdered by LTTE.

Creation of a Disabled Population

Terrorism not only kills people: it also cripples the survivors. A large number of people both Tamil and Sinhalese have been crippled as a result of suicide and other bombing by the LTTE: LTTE cadres fighting as terrorists and members of the Sri Lankan armed forces fighting against terrorism. Land mines too have caused many people to lose their limbs. Although no reliable statistics are available, the total number of people who are suffering from various disabilities caused directly and indirectly by LTTE terrorism varies from 50,000 to 100,000. For Sri Lanka, this is a large segment of the population. Unfortunately, the problem is compounded by the fact that Sri Lanka does not have disabled friendly systems.

Refugees

"Refugees" was an alien concept in Sri Lanka prior to mid 1980s. However since then it has become a household word. Refugees were deliberately produced by the LTTE as a part of its terrorist strategy on several occasions. When the LTTE massacred the Sinhalese in a few border villages, others fled their homes and ended up as refugees. When the LTTE engaged in ethnic cleansing in Jaffna and Mannar of the non-Tamils, the Muslims and Sinhalese became ethnic refugees. When the Sri Lankan army took over Jaffna, the LTTE asked millions of Tamils to flee Jaffna and many became refugees. Many who fled Jaffna to Tamil Nadu as a result of the fighting between the LTTE and Sri Lankan army and IPKF ended up in refugee camps. Over a million people in Sri Lanka have become refugees as the direct and indirect result of LTTE terrorism. The standard of living in the refugee camps is not only appalling but also degrading. A new generation is born as refugees and live as refugees. Refugee life has become the *de facto* and *de jure* normal life for these people.

Child Soldiers

LTTE has mastered the conscription of child soldiers and it has been estimated that over 5000 child soldiers have been serving as LTTE cadres. Some of them were as young as 12 years and most of them were forcibly recruited removing them from their schools, thus denying them their right to education as well as their childhood. UNICEF has blamed the LTTE on a number of occasions for continuing the practice of conscripting children even after the CFA and MOU brokered by Norway. These children were then indoctrinated into a hate culture of anti-Sinhaleseness and were mechanistically moulded into terrorists who have no respect for life. The LTTE terrorism has produced 'a lost generation' of Tamils in Sri Lanka.

Frustrated by the inability to change the fate of children, Rajan Hoole, an active member of the University Teachers for Human Rights (Jaffna) wrote

> Tamil children in Sri Lanka have been scarred by these events and deprived of crucial aspects of their childhood in many

> different ways. We averred at the outset that their rehabilitation involves primarily, restoring that lost sense of community. By needlessly compromising on human rights and universal norms in dealing with the LTTE the international community has been driven to acknowledge its powerlessness. However, its potential power is far greater and the LTTE knows it. Unless it challenges the LTTE and enables the people to recapture that moral community with its wholeness, all is lost.

The University Teachers for Human Rights – Jaffna elaborated the continuation of child conscription and the indifference of the major players towards their plight.

> Subsequent to our Bulletin 26 on child conscription in the East, there were news reports on the subject and a press release from Amnesty International. This bulletin updates the earlier one and elucidates how little the LTTE has been constrained by the publicity. We underscore the predicament of children in the rural East and the powerlessness of parents. At present the international community is preoccupied with what the powers-that-be have dubbed a "war on terrorism" and its tragic fallout. The local media and political establishment are playing out their power games with callous disregard for the gaping pitfalls just ahead. The ongoing tragedy in a corner of this island would tend to be therefore passed by with indifference. Being mindful of this, and yet knowing the trauma of the families concerned, and their desperate entreaties, we feel impelled to publish this update. We trust that these victims would be given a hearing, at least by those who understand the gravity of phenomena involving child soldiers. Their outgrowth, we well know, cannot be confined to a time and place (2001)

Rajan Hoole also makes a penetrating yet shocking revelation of how young recruits were used by the LTTE

> The militants turn these children into killers. In the LTTE's unprovoked attacks on Muslim villages in the East, even 12-year-old children were employed in mangling Muslim women and infants as part of a deliberate policy of brutalization. Such

children are frequently handpicked and used secretively by leaders as internal assassins of troublesome elements within the LTTE. Many such children broke down in due course. In a case I am familiar with, a boy who was a 'lamb' at home became a trusted assassin who, on orders, treacherously killed several of his comrades. Shortly before his death, he confessed all this to his aunt. "Every time I see my father," he said, "I feel like plugging a bullet into his brain, just to see him suffer."

The Impact on Women

Women, perhaps even more than children were negatively affected by terrorism. Only a very few attempts have been made to examine this aspect of the impact of terrorism. The number of women who lost their children, parents, husbands runs into tens of thousands and a large number of women remains unmarried simply because of the shortage of males.

The woman in Tamil society is being redefined by the LTTE under the new terror culture. Sornorajah (2004) in an appreciating tone reveal the new image of women under LTTE terrorism

> In recent years Tamil women fighters in Sri Lanka belonging to the Liberation Tigers of Tamil Eelam (LTTE) have burst into our visual horizons insistently demanding our attention, holding up their spectacular feats of commando attacks, sabotage operations , suicide missions and assassinations, as evidence of their proud achievements towards their own emancipation. These `singular achievements' of the women fighters of one of the most terrifyingly efficient guerrilla forces of the world today, have impressed not only military analysts but also the international media, and even academics and feminist activists as evidence of a radical transformation of women's position in a 'traditional' South Asian society.

The LTTE gives privileged positions to women as Adele Ann, the Australian-born wife of Anton Balasingham, LTTE theoretician, argues in her book *Women Fighters of Liberation Tigers* (1989). She says that the decision by Tamil women to join the organization is a message to society "that they are not satisfied with the social status quo; it means they are young women capable of defying authority; it means they are women with independent thoughts; young women prepared to lift up their heads". However, other Sri Lankan Tamil women disagree with her. For example, Radhika Coomaraswamy, United Nations Special Rapporteur on Violence Against Women, and director of the Colombo-based International Centre of Ethnic Studies, has argued that the induction of women into the LTTE has less to do with women's emancipation than with the organisation's need for a constant supply of cadres. Coomaraswamy questions the militarisation of women, pointing out that it flies in the face of the humanism, non-violence and the "celebration of life over death" that are the foundations of the feminist movement the world-over (Hindu, 2002 March 10)

However, the real image of the ordinary Tamil women in LTTE areas is very different. The life of Tamil women has become even more difficult and challenging as the ordinary life in general became difficult and challenging. While a few Tamil women may be celebrated as heroines, a vast number of women live degrading lives in refugee camps located both in Sri Lanka and in Tamilnadu. A large number of Sinhalese and Muslim women too live in similar degrading conditions in refugee camps. It is certainly sad that the situation of women under terrorism is completely overlooked by the sensationalized stories of a few women.

The refugee watch provides a more revealing story of the impact of terrorist war on women.

> Oppressive power relations, sexual assault, attack and disappearance of family members, and the general insecurity on the streets, lead to an overall loss of freedom for women. Women in refugee camps can be particularly exposed to violence, due to the lack of space and security, and their freedom is often confined: "In Refugee Camps due to restricted areas of movement it is difficult to find a place to change clothes, or to have a space to sleep. So their freedom is very restricted in the

camps." Women from all three communities, Sinhalese, Tamil and Muslim have been affected and have their different stories to tell.

(Kate de Rivero, http://www.safhr.org/pdf/srilanka.pdf

Denial and Violation of Human Rights

As LTTE is a totalitarian and authoritarian terrorist organization, it does not allow any room for human rights as most people understand it. The LTTE has redefined human rights in a strange way to confine it to the Tamils who affirm the LTTE version of Tamil politics. Everyone else is considered a lesser Tamil and a traitor to be punished and the LTTE has not hesitated to carry out its punishment including death openly and without even an iota of protest from strangely enough the international community including Norway who are actively involved in reestablishing "peace" and "human rights" in Sri Lanka. The UNHCR and Human Rights Commission of Sri Lanka reports and the University Teachers for Human Rights – Jaffna (UTHR-J reports and the Sri Lanka police reports provide ample evidence of human right violations by the LTTE.

UTHR-J Report No 7 identifies human right violations as a major problem: "We have argued in our reports that at the root of the present political crisis and the spate of human rights violations, lies the degrading feeling of powerlessness which the different communities feel in the face of forces who not just impose upon them, but are often ready to resort to massacres".

Denial of Democracy and Freedom of Expression

Another important impact of LTTE terrorism is the denial of democracy and freedom of expression (except in support of the LTTE) to the Tamil people. The last democratic or for that matter any form of election in Jaffna was held in 1982. The election that was held in 2004 was totally rigged by the LTTE through intimidation, violence and all other malpractices. Thus, the Tamil people who were born since 1964 (as the voting eligibility in Sri Lanka is 18, a person to vote in 1982 has to be born in 1964 or before) have been denied the right to vote. This means that for 40 years Tamil people have been denied the democratic right to elect their own representatives! Yet until about the late 1980s, the Tamils still could speak their conscience and engage in a critical discussion on what is happening to their community. However, since then even that freedom of expression has been denied to them by the LTTE. Only a brave few, at great risk to their normal life and life itself, could be critical of LTTE as revealed by Rajan Hoole:

> There has always been a struggle among the Tamil people to preserve the moral community and many have paid dearly for it. External circumstances have been against us and those who stood up to preserve life and public standards have been the first victims. Norway and the international agencies had the opportunity and the obligation to identify sections of the society that could advance choice and freedom for the people and give priority to their well-being. Instead, they have disregarded them.

Conclusion

It is amply clear that LTTE terrorism has been the most destructive force in post independent Sri Lankan society in general and Sri Lankan Tamil society in particular. It is imperative that LTTE terrorism be eradicated to create a peaceful society where human rights and democracy is upheld and to ensure a decent standard of living. No society can develop and no economy can improve through terrorism and there is no precedence in the world where development and peace is achieved through terrorism. Thus not only terrorism but also the direct and indirect support for terrorism should also stop.

There is no argument that Sri Lankan Tamils are having genuine problems as other communities in Sri Lanka. These problems are created primarily by the political leaders who put their own expedient interest over and above that of the national interest and the welfare and well being of the people who they claim to represent. As became amply evident from the disastrous impacts of the LTTE terrorism in Sri Lanka and Al Qaeda terrorism world wide, terrorism cannot and should not be an excuse to resolve problems in modern civilized society No civilized individual, society, government or state can sanction and endorse LTTE terrorism directly or indirectly in the name of peace. As terrorism has become a global problem, eradicating LTTE terrorism itself has become a global need and a responsibility.

Let me quote from *Lines,* a journal published in the US, looking critically into the Sri Lankan Tamil society

> While there is a diversity of views on the peace process, none of the visions of peace stand for peace with dignity and justice to the peoples of the North and East. This neglect, unfortunately, is not new. We seem to be relying on the same neglect that fueled the crisis to end it! History has shown how costly this neglect can be for the country.

If this is the peace brokered for Sri Lanka by the international community including Norway, someone will have to write an article on the negative or adverse impacts of peace in Sri Lanka in the near future!

However, there can be peace with dignity too. The solution is simple. Request the LTTE to desist from all forms of terrorism and join the mainstream democratic politics, if the request fails, ask and if asking fails, tell and if telling fails demand and if demand fails, use force. A terrorism free environment will be the dawn of a new era not only for Sri Lankan Tamils but for all the people in Sri Lanka.

Acknowledgements

I wish to thank Ms. Chitrangani Ratnayake for collecting background material used in this article and Dr. Nalani Hennayake for editorial help.

APPENDIX 1

Source: The Economic Cost of War in Sri Lanka, Institute of Policy Studies, Jan. 2000, Colombo, Sri Lanka

- Table1: Defense Expenditure 1982 - 1996 (Selected Years)
- Table 2: Effect of Military Expenditure on GDP
- Table 3: Compounded Present Value (1996) of Estimated Cost of the War, 1984 - 1996 (Mn. of 1996 Rs.)1

Table 1

	1982	1983	1985	1988	1990	1993	1994	1995	1996
Defense expenditure as a % of total government expenditure	3.1	4.4	10.2	14.3	14.6	14.7	15.2	18.1	21.6
Defense Budget as a % of GDP	1.1	1.4	3.5	4.8	4.5	4.2	4.4	5.4	6.0

Sources: Central Bank of Sri Lanka. Review of the Economy and Annual Report, various issues.

Table 2

Year	Govt. Military Expenditure (GM) (%GDP)	Effect of GM on Public Investment (% GDP)	Using Marginal Product of Investment on GDP			Using Average Product of Investment on GDP			
			Drop in GDP Growth Rate (%)	Estimated Lost GDP		ICOR	Drop in GDP Growth Rate (%)	Estimated Lost GDP	
				Rs. Mn (1996)	(Per cent GDP)			Rs. Mn (1996)	(Per cent GDP)
1984	1.61	-0.79	0.07	283	0.07	5.11	0.15	615	0.15
1985	3.46	-5.21	0.47	1,956	0.45	4.81	1.08	4,527	1.03
1986	5.41	-9.90	0.89	3,913	0.86	5.53	1.79	7,913	1.73
1987	5.79	-10.81	0.97	4,476	0.97	16.05	0.67	3,125	0.68
1988	4.83	-8.51	0.77	3,579	0.75	8.44	1.01	4,697	0.99
1989	3.49	-5.30	0.48	2,282	0.47	9.65	0.55	2,633	0.54
1990	4.54	-7.81	0.70	3,431	0.67	3.60	2.17	10,607	2.06
1991	4.21	-7.01	0.63	3,279	0.61	4.96	1.41	7,448	1.38
1992	4.23	-7.07	0.64	3,457	0.61	5.67	1.25	6,824	1.21
1993	4.16	-6.90	0.62	3,518	0.58	3.68	1.88	10,687	1.78
1994	4.41	-7.50	0.67	4,086	0.64	4.80	1.56	9,565	1.50
1995	5.24	-9.49	0.85	5,464	0.81	4.72	2.01	12,974	1.94
1996	6.02	-11.37	1.02	6,915	0.99	6.45	1.76	12,045	1.73

Sources: Central Bank of Sri Lanka, Annual Report, various issues, calculated

Table 3[1]

	Interest rate		
	r = 0.00	r = 0.05	r = 0.10
Direct Costs Direct government military expenditure	224,148 32.2%	287,543 41.3%	375,466 54.0%
LTTE military expenditure	22,415 3.2%	28,754 4.1%	37,547 5.4%
Government expenditure on relief services[2]	20,742 3.0%	20,742 3.0%	20,742 3.0%
Cost of lost Infrastructure[2,3]	93,584 13.5%	93,584 13.5%	93,584 13.5%
Indirect Costs Lost income due to foregone public investment	46,639 6.70%	59,884 8.61%	78,263 11.25%
Lost income from reduced tourist arrivals	91,832 13.2%	118,365 17.0%	155,323 22.3%
Lost earning due to lost foreign investment	423,446 60.9%	495,252 71.2%	588,897 84.7%
Lost income due to displacement (up to 1995)	29,784 4.3%	38,219 5.5%	49,417 7.1%
Lost income due to lost human capital of dead or injured persons[4]	14,641 2.1%	17,229 2.5%	20,875 3.0%
Output foregone in the Northern Province in 1996[5]	9,031 1.3%	9,031 1.3%	9,031 1.3%
Total	**976,261** **140.3%**	**1,168,603** **168.0%**	**1,429,144** **205.4%**

Notes:

1. Values as a % of GDP are given in italics

2. Due to lack of yearly data, values given in last two columns are not compounded

3. This includes rehabilitation and reconstruction in the North and

the East up to 1995 (85,034), infrastructure in the greater Colombo area up to 1996 (4,500), damages to houses in Jaffna in 1996 (4,050).

4. Income could also have been lost due to “brain-drain”; however, because of data problems this cost is not included in the calculation.

5. Cost of damages on top of damages to houses.

APPNDIX II

Fatalities

While accurate figures are difficult to ascertain, estimates put the total number of people killed between 50,000 - 60,000 up to 1998. Of these around half are civilians.

The Disabled

The Association of Disabled Ex- Service Personnel puts the number of disabled soldiers at 10,000 - 15,000. Disabled soldiers often experience lack of recognition and a decline in social status.

Female Headed Households

Widows and female-headed households are an ever-growing and vulnerable group. While many widows receive some kind of financial compensation, they are also subject to social exclusion on account of their circumstances.

Displacement and Homelessness

About 800,000 people have been displaced by the conflict, from all communities Tamil, Muslim and Sinhalese. Of those, only 40,000 families are housed in very basic welfare centres.

Children affected by the war

Children are among those most seriously affected by the **war**. These include child combatants, orphans and those traumatised by brutal violence. Around 200,000 of those displaced by the **war** are under 14.

Social and Economic Deprivation

The estimate of loss of output in the north and east indicate that household incomes have probably dropped to a level half that of 1982.Neither the government of in its absence the **LTTE**, have been able to provide adequately for the basic needs of the population in areas such as food supply, health care, education, water and sanitation.

Surveys indicate a decline in nutritional standards and an increase in infant mortality in some areas. Social structures too have been destroyed.

Fear and Insecurity

A pervasive sense of insecurity has become the norm for the entire population. For the 130,000 households who have family members fighting in the **war**, fear is ever present. For others violence and terror is frequent but unpredictable.

(http://www.peace-srilanka.org/MEDIA/WAR%20and%20the%20ECONOMY)

REFERENCES

Casperz, Paul (...) 'Development: the Great Leveller', Opinion, The Daily Mirror.

Central Bank of Sri Lanka (2002) Annual Report

Central Bank of Sri Lanka (1987) Annual Report

Central Bank of Sri Lanka (1997) Annual Report

Central Bank of Sri Lanka (1991) Annual Report

Hennayake, Shantha K. (1997) 'The Civil War: An Impediment to Sustainable Development', *Sri Lanka Journal of Social Science*, 20 (1&2).

http://www.peace-srilanka.org/MEDIA/WAR%20and%20the%20ECONOMY

http://www/uthr.org/Special Reports/sreport13

Institute of Policy Studies, (2000), The Economic Cost of War in Sri Lanka Colombo, Sri Lanka

Kaplan R. "The Coming Anarchy", *Atlantic Monthly* , February 1994, p.74

Ladduwahetty, Neville (1996), 'The polarization of the Tamil community and its impact on a political solution for Sri Lanka' *Lakbima: Sri Lankan Issues* September 12,

Nanthikesan, (2004) 'Sri Lanka Elections: Peace as if People Mattered', *Lines,* February 2(4)

Rajan Hoole, (ud) 'Child Sacrifice: Conscription, Compromise and International Failure', in *The Little Magazine*, 4 (3)

Ross Lee Ann and Tilak Samaranayake (1988) 'The Economic Impact of the Recent Ethnic Disturbances in SRis Lanka', Asian Survey. Vol 56 (11) pp. 1240-1255.

Sarvananthan, M. (2002) 'Economic Imperative for Peace in Sri Lanka', Ceylon Daily News, December 6, 2002

The Little Magazine - Growing up - Rajan Hoole - Child sacrifice 4(3).

UNICEF Sri Lanka Reports.
University Teachers for Human Rights- Jaffna (2001) Report No. 10.

University Teachers for Human Rights- Jaffna (2001) Information Bulletin No. 27
Date of Release : 19th October , *The LTTE, Child Soldiers and Serial Disasters :*
A Challenge Without an Answer?

Wijemanna, Adrian, (2000), War and the New Realities, Courtesy Tamil Circle

End notes

[1] Please see the following for a exhaustive list of LTTE terrorism. The Monthly Emergency Debate since 1983, Hansard, Parliament of Sri Lanka. At the beginning of these debates, the Minister of Defense lists all the terrorist activities of the previous month. Also see the Reports of the University Teachers for Human Rights (Jaffna), Eelam People's Democratic Party's website. Reports of the United Nations High Commissioner for Human Rights. Report of the Human Right Commission in Sri Lanka.

[2] The study estimate takes into account not only government defense costs but also the damage to various sectors, the loss to agriculture and tourism and the cost of rehabilitation" (Casperz, ...)

The Appeasement of Terrorism: Doomed to Failure

Paul Harris

It is a privilege to be speaking to you today. I would like to be able to say it is a pleasure. But it is not. For me, it is a matter for profound regret that I am today talking at a conference which could turn out to be an inquest on the terminal division of the sovereign state of Sri Lanka.

A few brief words as to why I – an Englishman – stand here today. My formal academic qualifications are as a political scientist. But I think on-the-ground experience is of rather more relevance. I have carried out conflict analyses for *Jane's Intelligence Review* in Bosnia, Kosovo, Nepal, North East India, Aceh, East Timor, Uganda, Algeria, Eritrea, Sudan, Nagorno Karabakh, the Saharawi Arab Democratic Republic and, of course, Sri Lanka. It's a tricky job working as a professional prophet of doom. Fortune tellers may be comfortable with predictions in a darkened room, but making them in print is always hazardous. I didn't always get it right, of course. But I did most of the time.

Let me make it clear. I have no personal axe to grind in relation to the future of Sri Lanka. No political interest as a foreigner; no economic interest as a businessman or entrepreneur. I do, however, strongly believe that the country of Sri Lanka should not be offered as some extravagant reward for a bunch of avaricious terrorists. I admit I am prejudiced. I have observed terrorists in more than a dozen countries. I have seen the blood and the misery with my own eyes. I don't like terrorists: I don't like what they stand for and I don't like their methods. And I believe their methods intrinsically deny them the capability of engaging in any *meaningful* peace process.

The crucial question must be: Does the LTTE want peace and, if so, what sort of peace? The answer seems clear to me. Of course, the LTTE wants peace, that is to say, peace on its own terms: the terminal division of the sovereign state of Sri Lanka with two thirds of the coast and half of the landmass ceded to the LTTE in perpetuity.

In the past, I have not been shy about making my views known on what I regard as not just a Sri Lankan issue but a universal moral issue. Curiously, when I addressed the Colombo Rotary Club on April 23 2002 the reaction in the room was, let us just say, a trifle muted. Stunned might be more accurate a description. I suppose I had underestimated the impact of what I said. I termed what was going in Sri Lanka 'the greatest giveaway in history'. This, of course, did not sit well in UNP government circles. I identified then what I personally found most worrying about the peace process and it came as a shock, I realise in retrospect. I averred that the LTTE was implementing,

"A whole series of sophisticated strategies designed to occupy all the political and social space throughout the north and the east of the country . . . The strategies encompass all areas of public life and include:

*Forcing government department heads to work for the LTTE

*Taxing civil servants 8% of salaries

*Controlling business of government cooperatives and thereby obtaining a steady income

*All contracts for government and NGO projects are to be carried out by the LTTE approved contractors and income is thereby derived

*Controlling and using all available government resources

*Demeaning activities of competing political groups

*Sending cadres into government areas in defiance of conditions of the MoU

*Influencing and using teachers, students and labour unions to carry out *hartals*, demonstrations, picketing and protests

*Erection of monuments to martyrs and LTTE figures

*Influencing government servants to use LTTE headquarters in place of government facilities in the eastern province

*Influencing civilians to make legal complaints via the LTTE, rather than to the police

*Organising mass 'Tamil awakening' rallies known as Pongu Tamils

*Classes on Eelam in schools

*Edicts on dress code for women instructing them to dress in traditional clothes.

*Restrictions on businesses involved in private tutoring of schoolchildren.

*The creation of a general psychosis of fear in coveted areas to be included in the State of Tamil Eelam. A psychosis of fear is being brought about by enforced conscription of youth into the LTTE, general coercion and extortion of funds from traders, especially the Muslim community".

"In addition to the undermining of government control and authority, the enhancement of LTTE military capability is being undertaken through reconstruction of defences; accelerated recruitment; reinforcement of command posts and radio rooms with concrete allowed into LTTE areas under the MoU; smuggling of arms and ammunition; building up of arms and ammunition stockpiles in government areas; movement of heavy mortars and machine guns into the east; increased level of training; intensified reconnaissance on army, Special Task Force (STF) and police locations; and the reorganisation of LTTE cadres into regiments. Military cadres are moving into government held areas under the conditions created by the MoU and undertaking their missions with little impediment."

When I said all this 28 months ago in Colombo, large numbers of people thought I was paranoid; some thought I was quite mad;

others, like PM Wickremesinghe, who proceeded to set his goons on me, thought I was dangerous: as the PM described me, I was 'an enemy of the peace process'. Wickremesinghe, instead of occupying himself with the real enemies of Sri Lanka, set up a Prime Ministerial Security Division at Temple Trees to put the enemies of the peace process under surveillance: telephone tapping, physical surveillance and illegal searches were all part and parcel of the work of this new unit. I was one of the first to be subjected to its attentions.

I was even termed a warmonger in the public print. Well, in my view, it is not necessary to blindly support a peace process *per se* without analysing and assessing its implications and making a balanced judgement. If a peace process looks likely to institutionalise political violence; support the abrogation of human rights and intolerance of democracy; and imply approval of a megalomaniac murderer, then I, for one, find myself unable to support it; and I think any rational, fair-minded human being must reject it as a hopeless sham and a fraud upon the very people it is supposed to help.

Also, an inequitable peace agreement which embodies immorality and the reward of terrorism must, in my view, be doomed to failure. As recently as last month, Amnesty International reported on the continuing recruitment drive for child soldiers by the LTTE. I quote from Amnesty, July 7 2004: "Since the beginning of April, 190 children have been recruited to fight, according to information provided by UNICEF. This brings the number of verified cases this year to 330. Many of these children have been forcibly abducted from public places or their homes. Some of the new recruits are as young as fourteen. *The Tamil Tigers are also increasingly re-recruiting former child soldiers by force.*"

There are not many ways to deal with terrorists. And let us be in no doubt whatsoever about this: the LTTE have proved themselves to be, time and again, unreformed and brutal terrorists. Even the distant and remote US government recognises this. On June 22, US Assistant Secretary of State Christine Rocca spoke to the House Committee on International Relations. She told the Committee that the Tigers still "recruit child soldiers, stockpile weapons and conduct extrajudicial assassinations of politicians who disagree with them. We will not remove our designation of the LTTE as a terrorist organisation until it has firmly and decidedly given up terrorism and such policies as the recruitment of children as soldiers."

Remember that the LTTE are the people who actually brought suicide bombing as a tactic to this world long before it was visited upon it by al-Qaeda; the people who traded the suicide jacket technology with Hamas for weapons and conventional training. Within Sri Lanka they have been responsible for the deaths of thousands of people from the Sacred Bo Tree massacre in Anuradhapura on May 14 1985: 146 innocents dead to the Central Bank bombing of January 31 1996: 96 dead and 1400 injured, and the Dehiwala twin train bombs of July 1996 with more than 70 dead. Just three horrific incidents among the 50 devastating attacks which have seen the deaths of more than 260 suicide bombers. For the LTTE, no target is too sacred and, indeed, a hallmark of their activities has been the ingenious range of targets: trains, buses, Colombo airport and harbour, international 5-star hotels, the financial district, fuel tanks and electrical supplies; army headquarters, air force headquarters, the sacred Bo Tree and the Dalada Maligawa Temple in Kandy.

These are the people for whom political assassination is a way of life. Just a random sample of the unfortunate who have suffered at the hands of the LTTE:

May 21 1991 Indian PM Rajiv Gandhi
May 1 1993 President Ranasinghe Premadasa
October 24 1994 Presidential Candidate Gamini Dissanayake
July 29 1999 Leading Tamil politician Neelan Thiruchelvam
June 7 2000 Minister C. V. Gooneratne

And, as if to prove they still represent a potent assassination force even during a peace process, the unsuccessful attempt last month to kill Douglas Devananda in Colombo in which four policemen died at Kollupitiya Police Station.

A state has limited options when dealing with terrorists. It can:

1 Talk to them and sue for peace. There are no examples of success in this strategy in relation to *significant* potent terrorist groups.

2 Adopt a mid-way approach, alternately talking peace and fighting the terrorists. This has effectively been the Sri Lanka strategy. Under this strategy the terrorists' goals remain firmly fixed while those of the state tend to become diffused.

3 Pursue the terrorists remorselessly and kill them in large numbers before they kill you. This implies 100% commitment physically and mentally. This course of action implies the use of special forces, extra-judicial execution and significant loss of human rights for the period in which it is employed. *Intelligence is the key*. There was a glimmer of hope for this strategy three years ago through the activities of the Long Range Patrol Group. This was the first really effective initiative of the Sri Lankan army for many years. Disgracefully, the group was betrayed in its 'safe' house on January 2 2002, its agents compromised and the operation willfully deserted by the Wickremesinghe government. As a result, a whole intelligence network and a most effective organisation were brought down from within. In most countries, treason trials would have followed . . . This strategy has been used successfully by the British in Northern Ireland, by the Omanis and Bahrainis, by the Indonesians and, to a lesser extent, by the Indians in the fractious N and E states. It has, however, also failed, e.g. in Chechnya. Each scenario is different.

BUT SRI LANKA ABANDONED ITS ONLY WINNING STRATEGY AT THE VERY POINT AT WHICH IT WAS

WORKING. Several of Prabhakaran's aides had been taken out by the group working undercover and even Thamil Chelvam only survived by the skin of his teeth. Anecdotal evidence suggests that even Prabhakaran had become paranoid about his own safety.

4. Talk peace whilst actively plotting the downfall of your enemy. This could have been a strategy for the Sri Lankan government. In fact, it was the strategy adopted by the LTTE who used the period of the so-called peace process to re-arm, re-train, re-equip, forcibly recruit new cadres and strengthen their political and terror systems, particularly in the east of the country.

Of course, in their bid for international acceptance and recognition, the terrorist tag has been deeply embarrassing to the LTTE as they jostled, freshly suited and booted, for seats at conference tables from Oslo to Bangkok. Some people have taken what is to me the quite extraordinary view that Prabhakaran is some sort of new, reformed man. One leading member of the last government recounted to me a 'delightful' lunch he had with Mr. P. Apparently, all he talked about was his family life, his son and fervent hopes for his academic success. He even smiled a lot to the amazement of his listeners. These UNP people came away totally charmed . . .

Of course, Mr. P makes very few public appearances. I suspect he finds the forced performances of geniality he is obliged to make in support of the present peace strategy to be, well, a very great strain. We had a brief chance to look at him during his famous press conference. The press conference seriously backfired on the terrorist leader for it clearly indicated he was unreformed, unrepentant and blithely insouciant of world opinion. Given a heaven-sent opportunity to apologise to the Indian people for the assassination of Rajiv Gandhi he peremptorily dismissed the suggestion with a wave of his hand and the averment that it was all 'history' which he no longer wished to discuss.

Of course, Prabhakaran seriously misjudged the deep feelings of the Indian people – and thereby ensured that the LTTE would remain for the foreseeable future on the proscribed list of terrorist organisations, not just in India but also Europe and America. Personally, I was reassured by his making that great error of judgement: it showed that he was not infallible and that his judgement and abilities are, indeed, limited. Responses to other questions represented a curious mixture of wiliness and opportunism. Some appeared to indicate that the LTTE had a very clear appreciation of the then weakness of the Sri Lankan State. "We don't think that Ranil Wickremesinghe is capable of addressing the core issues and is able to offer us a permanent solution at this stage because the executive powers of governance are vested with the President and his powers are limited to parliament. It is because of this that we are suggesting an interim administration in the north east. In the meantime, Ranil Wickremesinghe will have space to build up southern Sri Lanka. So it will be advantageous for the Tamils as well as for the Sinhalese to work out an interim set up for the time being. Once this is set up then we are prepared to discuss the core issues and negotiate for a permanent settlement to the ethnic issue. But now we believe the government is not politically stable or powerful enough to take up the core issues of the Tamils and offer us a permanent solution."

By virtue of his own analysis of the then contorted political scenario, Mr. P should, now, be only too willing to discuss peace with a more powerful President with more extensive parliamentary control . . . but the LTTE gives no sign of returning to the conference table except on its own terms. It was clear he left little room for compromise in the matter of the creation of an independent Tamil Eelam. Prabhakaran is still irrevocably committed to the creation of an independent State.

Most significantly, and to my amazement, at one of the earliest *pongu tamil* celebrations in Batticaloa in March 2002 several speakers told the large audience that 'wherever there are Tamils there is Tamil Eelam'. This inflammatory imprecation was not repeated at later gatherings; it was *also* an error of judgment likely to be alarming to States from India to Malaysia to Canada. Asked about the statement he once made to the effect that his cadres would shoot him if he ever renounced Eelam, Prabhakaran smiled, glanced at his heavily armed bodyguards and observed "that statement still holds". He said that "the right conditions have not arisen for the LTTE to abandon the policy of independent statehood." Asked if he recognised Ranil Wickremesinghe as his Prime Minister, Prabhakaran laughed and Balasingham answered, "Ranil Wickremesinghe is the Prime Minister of those who elected him. Mr Prabhakaran is the President and Prime Minister of Tamil Eelam." It was further averred that armed struggle would only be given up after "three fundamentals" were accepted by the government. "They are Tamil homeland, Tamil nationality and self-determination of the Tamils. If a political solution is put forward recognising these fundamentals then we can consider giving up the demand for Tamil Eelam . . . But if the Sri Lanka Government rejects our demand for autonomy and self governance then – as a last resort – we will opt for secession."

In short, Prabhakaran and the LTTE have not adjusted their demands one iota since those they made at the failed Thimpu talks with the J R Jayawardene Government back in 1985. The demand for territory for the nascent State of Tamil Eelam grows ever more ambitious. Maps of Tamil Eelam put on public display at Pongu Thamil rallies clearly showed two thirds of the coastline of the island and almost a half of the land mass of Sri Lanka within the proposed territory of Tamil Eelam. Such division would deny the Sinhalese majority access to some of the best agricultural land and fishing grounds, as well as the best tourist beaches. Not to mention potential assets in the form of offshore oil and mineral resources which will be available to Sri Lanka under the economic zone. Loss of the hill country would imply the additional loss of most of the lucrative tea estates.

Just over two years ago I said, "There would seem to me to be little doubt that the State of Sri Lanka is headed for early division between a Sinhalese State in the south and the west and the State of Tamil Eelam in the north and the east. This division will likely be *de facto* rather than *de jure*. . . The Sinhalese are exhausted mentally and economically by almost twenty years of war and there is now a widespread sense of resignation about the future, albeit with the implication of their own nation State being much reduced in physical size and financial resources."

And so it came to pass. Will the LTTE return to war? Another large-scale battlefield war seems unlikely, unnecessary indeed. The LTTE has effectively occupied all the social and political space in the north and the east of Sri Lanka. It has gained much ground during the time of the Peace Junket while the Government in Colombo has given in on almost all points whenever it seemed necessary to save the doomed process. The State of Tamil Eelam is in operation: it has set up its border crossing points, its passes, papers, duties and taxes, its police, civil administration, banking and political infrastructure. Even a powerful radio station, obligingly supplied by the Norwegians has been allowed by the Government.

I see no reason to revise my assessment made back in 2004. In so many ways, the *de facto* division of Sri Lanka has already been achieved: the writ of Government in Colombo hardly exists in the north and the east, even in those areas under the nominal control of the state security forces. It is not my brief to discuss here the strategies necessary for the State to re-impose its control over the north and the east of Sri Lanka and secure the Sri Lankan State's territorial, sovereign integrity. It could be done but it would represent an enormous commitment by all those who believe Sri Lanka deserves to survive as a unified State.

I believe that there is a danger little discussed. The ultimate doomsday scenario for Sri Lank would be the imposition of an inequitable ethnic division which would disadvantage the large number of Muslims in the east of the country, claimed by the LTTE as their exclusive ethnic homeland. Their intolerance of the Muslim community has frequently been made clear: significantly in the attack on the mosque at Kattankudy. As LTTE leader Karikalan told me – and he was disgraced within the fortnight: "It is for Tamil youth to repossess the lands stolen by the Muslims".

Al-Qaeda operatives have visited Sri Lanka and travelled to the east. For the moment, Sri Lanka is low on the list of concerns for a revolutionary organization fighting a war on many fronts from Baghdad to Palestine, the US to Europe. However, make no mistake about it, if Muslims are physically threatened in the east of Sri Lanka then al-Qaeda operatives will secure the safety and well being of their Muslim brothers. The plans are already laid. At that point, the LTTE will find themselves more than evenly matched against an enemy which will be contemptuous of their limited nationalism and, ultimately, even more ruthless. Al-Qaeda might be the only organisation in the world that could take down the LTTE with car bombs outside every LTTE police station, barracks and training centre.

Assassinations of LTTE political leaders would soon lead to the collapse of the house of cards that is Prabhakaran's Tamil Eelam. That would be the final battle for supremacy in Sri Lanka which I trust we shall never witness. And that would be the worst possible outcome for the failed politics of appeasement. Meantime, significant evidence has emerged that the LTTE has been actively cooperating with other international terror organisations. I have previously published my findings in regards to the links with the Maoists of Nepal whose military strategies, if not their ideals, appear to be drawn from the LTTE.

The work of Rohan Gunaratna, an expert on Asian terror groups and a Sri Lankan himself, who works at Singapore's Centre for the Study of terrorism and Political Violence, will be well known to most people here. Gunaratna says that 'Asian intelligence agencies had reported before the US attacks [of 9/11] that the LTTE, masters in suicide technology, were involved in training the Moro Islamic Liberation Front (MILF) and the Abu Sayyaf Group (ASG), two groups very close to al-Qaeda, in the second half of the 1990s'. [*The Times of India* July 7 2004].

In May of this year, the LTTE's chief procurement officer, Kumaran, visited Afghanistan from his base in Thailand. As the peace process has dragged on, Western intelligence and law enforcement agencies have taken a relaxed view of LTTE activities. That may soon come to an end: Gunaratna believes 'it is only a matter of time before al-Qaeda fully targets India', probably with the support of its affiliates Harkat-ul-Mujahadeen or Harkat-ul-Jehad.

I hope this short paper has established three things:

1 The LTTE and its leader Prabhakaran remain unreformed terrorists operating internationally.

2 The period of talking peace has been used to rearm, regroup and prepare for another outbreak of war.

3 There can be no future – apart from buying time - in continuing to parley peace with committed terrorists wholly uninterested in compromise.

Peace, Justice and Democracy in Sri Lanka

Asoka Bandarage

PART 1: CURRENT PEACE PROCESS

Practically everyone in Sri Lanka and Sri Lanka's friends abroad desire peace and want the ceasefire to hold. There is a consensus that the solution does not lie in a return to armed conflict. Yet, at the same time, the vast majority of the people in the country, Sinhalese, Tamil and Muslim, do not want appeasement of terrorism in the name of peace. They want a sustainable peace, a peace that upholds human rights, social justice, political pluralism and democracy. Mass discontent with the handling of the peace process was a primary reason for the defeat of the previous UNP led UNF coalition at the April 2 elections in Sri Lanka. Appeasement of terrorism, the partiality of the Norwegian facilitators towards the LTTE and the threats to the country's security and sovereignty were some of the reasons for the opposition to the previous government. The SLFP led UPFA coalition which came to power at the April elections promised to make the peace process transparent and to fine tune the role of the facilitator. The SLFP, like its coalition partner, the JVP, rejected the LTTE's claim to be the 'sole representative' of Tamils as an undemocratic premise and its ISGA proposal as a blue print for a separate state. The Sri Lankan President, Chandrika Kumaratunga, also talked of sending the Norwegian facilitators back home given the public's loss of faith in their neutrality.

Since coming to power, however, Ms. Kumaratunga's UPFA government seems to be following the same path as its predecessor:

the appeasement of LTTE terrorism. The Norwegian facilitators and the Scandinavian Monitoring Mission (SLMM) seem to be doing the same. When the LTTE North moved against renegade leader, Karuna, in the East, violating the MOU, the SLMM and the Sri Lankan government turned a blind eye. The continuing military build-up by the LTTE at the strategic harbour at Trincomalee and growing threats to the country's security have not received much attention either.

The April elections in the North and the were ridden with widespread violence and fraud on the part of the LTTE. Tamil political parties that tried to contest the elections democratically have called for new elections, but, the legal cases to revoke the April 2004 elections have yet to be taken up in the courts. Violation of human rights and democratic norms by the LTTE has increased since the elections. Fratricidal killings between the LTTE Northern and Eastern wings have intensified as have killings of dissident Tamil politicians, intellectuals and Sri Lankan government intelligence operatives in the East and in Colombo. According to some reports, over 100 people from the Tamil political party, the EPDP, have been killed during the course of the cease fire. A suicide bombing which took place in July in Colombo, apparently to assassinate the leader of the EPDP, has been attributed to the LTTE. Forcible child conscription has not ceased either. The University Teachers for Human Rights (Jaffna) has charged the UNICEF for being lax with the LTTE concerning child abduction and conscription, especially in the East.

Notwithstanding their on-going violations of fundamental rights of children, universal human rights and democracy, the LTTE demands that its ISGA proposals be accepted as the basis for continued peace talks with the Sri Lankan government. It has categorically refused to include any proposals from the Sri Lankan government as the basis for talks. At the same time, the LTTE threatens to return to war if its conditions are not met. Fearing the resumption of war, the Norwegian facilitators and donor countries, such as Japan, are putting pressure on the Sri Lankan government to return to peace talks accepting a peace-at-any cost approach on terms laid down by the LTTE.

The current government like the previous one, does not have a clear parliamentary majority. It too is beholden to the TNA (Tamil National Alliance), the political wing of the LTTE that contested the April elections and won 22 seats in the North and the East. In addition, the economy is in dire straits and the government desperately needs the economic aid promised by the international donors on condition that the peace process gets back on track. There is increasing pressure from the international NGO community, the local peace lobby and various think tanks to consider the ISGA proposals in the name of peace. The ISGA would pave the way to a separate, mono-ethnic, totalitarian state in the North and the East of Sri Lanka. The ISGA proposal contains a clause which calls for an absolute majority in the ISGA for the LTTE. It also contains a clause which stipulates that if a final settlement has not been reached and implemented five years after the adoption of the interim agreement, then, the ISGA would appoint an independent election commission to conduct an election. As a comprehensive critique of the ISGA proposal by the SLFP pointed out in November 2003, this clause conceals the right to secede.

A realignment of political forces seems to be taking place now in Sri Lanka to accept the seemingly inevitable reality of secession. The President has abruptly resigned from her chairmanship of the UNFPA coalition which releases her from previous positions of her coalition and, perhaps, also her political party, the SLFP. There is talk of the so-called 'modernist' segments of the SLFP joining with the UNP to save the peace process. If this happens, the JVP, which is opposed to the ISGA and the MOU will be side-lined and the ISGA or something very close to it would possibly be accepted as a political settlement of the conflict.

This may seem like a victory in the short-term. The LTTE will be well on its way to achieving Eelam; Sinhala politicians may be able to maintain their positions and the international community will be able to move in and extract the vast, untapped natural resources of the North and the East and set the economic growth engine rolling.

PART 2: GROUND REALITIES AND FUTURE SCENARIOS

The Sri Lankan situation is interpreted as a primordial conflict between the Sinhala majority and the Tamil minority. The commonality of grievances of underprivileged youth from both communities - lack of educational opportunities and employment-have been overlooked by intellectuals and policymakers promoting the dominant ethno-nationalist interpretation. The 'chauvinism' of the Sinhala Buddhists is identified as the main cause of the Sri Lankan conflict while a host of other factors including the desire of a handful of Tamil elites to maintain privileges gained under British colonialism and the contradictions of globalization are neglected. So are the intra-ethnic conflicts and violence within all groups and the common suffering of ordinary people from all ethnic and religious communities.

The popularization of a limited perspective that singularly focuses on Sinhla-Tamil antagonism has helped exacerbate ethnic polarization, justify Tamil separatism and win sympathy for the LTTE internationally.

The policy prescriptions emanating from the narrow ethno-nationalist perspective call for changes in the historical consciousness of the Sinhala Buddhists and the satisfaction of the aspirations of the Tamil elite including the grant of the ISGA. The transformation of global and local socio-economic structures which underlie the competition between groups for limited resources, is not called for. Lacking choice, a poor country like Sri Lanka is thus compelled to accept externally imposed economic, political and cultural models and institutions. In so doing, the elites of most ethno-religious groups tend to protect their own interests at the expense of the interests of their masses, this of course, is not a situation peculiar to contemporary Sri Lanka.

What, indeed, could be the future for Sri Lanka? Would the current peace process and the possible creation of a separate Tamil totalitarian regime in the North and the East lead to a lasting peace? Or, would it lead to balkanization, increased ethnic cleansing, border wars, population transfers and anarchy? To address this question, we need to look at the social and demographic realities of the island and the North and the East in particular. The regional South Asian context needs also to be considered, although, only a few significant demographic features can be mentioned here.

There is no accurate accounting of the population in the North and the East of Sri Lanka because the LTTE did not allow the Sri Lankan government to carry out the 2001 census in those regions. According to estimates, including those of the Economist, only about 8% of the total population of Sri Lanka live in the North and the East But, the area being demanded by the LTTE constitutes about one third of the land mass and two-thirds of the coastline and is home to some of the most valuable natural resources of the island.. The political myth of the 'Tamil Homelands' aside, the offer of such a vast area to a tiny group, outside the constitutional and legal democratic processes is dangerous and highly unjustifiable. Sri Lanka has been identified as the tenth most densely populated country in the world.

The population density is extremely high in South West while it is very low in the outlying areas such as the Eastern Province and parts of the Northern Province (excepting Jaffna). Peasant resettlement programs begun in the sparsely populated regions of the North, East and North Central Provinces during the British period. These were further extended during the post-colonial period by Sinhala leaders who sought to revive the ancient Sinhala hydraulic civilization in those regions. Tamil nationalists, charge that the settlements were motivated entirely by Sinhala hegemonic interests and this ethno-nationalist interpretation is widely used to legitimate the demand for an exclusive Tamil regime in the North and the East. This limited interpretation, however, overlooks the fact that peasant colonization schemes were largely a response to the demographic and economic problems created by the uneven and unequal nature of colonial development. The acute landlessness and poverty in the densely populated Sinhala areas motivated many Sinhalese to relocate, just as many Tamils from the island's north as well from South India, came to the so-called Sinhala areas during the course of British colonialism and the expansion of plantation agriculture. The freedom that has historically existed for any individual from any ethnic or religious group to obtain land or live anywhere on the island, however, will be terminated with the establishment of an exclusive Tamil region in the North and the East

The injustice and irrationality of the proposed division of the island is compounded by the fact that the majority of Tamils, today, do not live in the North and the East, but, in the so-called South. Many Tamils have fled to the South to live among the Sinhalese during the course of the war. There have not been Sinhala riots against Tamils in the South since the horrific attacks in 1983 which fuelled the Tamil separatist movement.

A further demographic fact that compounds the injustice of the LTTE demand for a separate state in the combined North East is that the Tamils are only a minority in the Eastern Province. The Sinhalese and the Muslims together constitute about 68% of the population and the Sinhalese own about 50% of the land in the region. The North and the East also have hundreds of sacred heritage sites, mostly Buddhist. These sites which represent the world historical heritage, could be lost under a hostile regime which is bent on establishing its exclusive claims to those areas. If the Eastern Province is handed to the LTTE, the ethnic cleansing of the Sinhala and Muslim population there could be complete, as it already has been in the Northern Province. There could be a complete elimination of all Tamil dissidents as well.

It is unlikely, however, that the Sinhalese and the Muslims in the East or other parts of the island, for that matter, would passively accept the usurpation of their land and resources by a racist, totalitarian regime without resistance. The Sinhalese have a very long history of rebellion against many different types of external domination and it is unlikely that that historical legacy could be completely suppressed.

Muslims have engaged in various acts of civil disobedience in recent months. A hartal to mark the LTTE massacre of 103 Muslim civilians worshipping at a mosque in Kattankudy in 1990 paralyzed most parts of the East this month (August 2004).There are signs that the Muslim resistance to the LTTE is being internationalized. If a LTTE regime is hoisted upon the Muslims, the resistance could become much worse. The result could be the creation of a separate Muslim administrative unit in parts of the Eastern Province.

In addition, there could be border wars between the LTTE and the south over access to the water originating in the central hill country. There could also be struggles to annex districts in the hill country where Indian Tamil plantation labourers brought by British colonialists now form a majority. Pro-LTTE political leaders of the Indian Tamils have already alluded to these possibilities. The emergence of a Tamil separatist state in Sri Lanka would, undoubtedly impact on South India where over 60 million Tamils live. There would be serious implications for the security, sovereignty and territorial integrity of India which has been battling her own secessionist movements. It is likely that creation of a terrorist state in the North and East of Sri Lanka would have global repercussions given the LTTE's world wide networks of illegal economic enterprises and military activities, as well as alleged ties to other terrorist organization.

PART 3: THE GLOBAL CONTEXT

It is no mystery that in the current world order, economic interests take precedence over human rights and democracy. W hat is more disheartening, however, is that many intellectuals, the media, local and international NGOs and even so-called peace activists seem also to overlook violations of human rights and democratic principles in their search for quick answers to complex conflicts. These apparent contradictions need to be understood in the context of widening economic inequality and the inter-connections between the increasing wealth and privileges of a global minority and the deepening poverty of the majority. The so-called neo-liberal economic model which promotes corporate led globalization and cultural homogenization contributes to the weakening of local economies, cultures, communities, families and so on. Yet, the resultant conflicts over economic resources are frequently attributed to cultural difference and primordial enmity and are mobilized against cultural others by opportunistic leaders of the local and global status-quo.

There is a close relationship between the concentration of wealth in the rich countries in the North and cultural destruction and political fragmentation in the poor countries of the global South. Privatisation, structural adjustment and other policies have contributed to the dismantling of social welfare services and the weakening of nation states. The international NGOs and internationally funded local NGOs step into fill the vacuum. Similarly, they play a determining role in 'post-conflict reconstruction', which is a fast growing field of employment for the military, private contractors and NGOs. International Christian NGOs, such as, World Vision and Mercy Corps, are among the largest NGOS managing basic social services and civil sectors in so-called post-conflict and transitional societies. Although the creation of new, ethno-nationalist states has become a lucrative enterprise, many 'post-conflict' societies have not achieved lasting peace. In fact, in many contexts, such as the Balkans, the creation of primordial nation states may have exacerbated ethnic polarization and extremism and the institutionalization of political violence and insecurity.

PART 4: TOWARDS A SUSTAINABLE PEACE

Absence of war is not necessarily peace. The peace-at-any-cost approach that seems to be pursued now does not guarantee a lasting peace. To avert a return to war and the emergence of new types of violence and terrorism, a number of important, hitherto neglected issues need to be addressed.

Ultimately all those concerned with peace, justice and democracy, Sri Lankans at home and abroad and our friends around the world including the Norwegians must try to recognize that the Sri Lankan conflict is not simply a primordial conflict that can be resolved by the mere grant of a separate ethno-nationalist administration. We need to develop broader perspectives that can help understand the complexity of the situation and develop more sustainable solutions. While recognizing the specific problems facing the Tamil community, we must also recognize and address the injustices and grievances of the Sinhala, Muslim and other communities. We must recognize the common suffering of all the people and the stresses and challenges faced by them all in the context of rapid socio-economic and cultural changes and the break down of the natural environment. We must be sensitive to the disproportionate burden borne by the poor and the women and children in particular.

To address the complex situation facing the country, we must develop local and international coalitions across ethnic and religious divisions. While recognizing our differences, we must nevertheless come together on a common platform for peace that honors fundamental human rights of all women, men and children, a peace which upholds the long history of political pluralism and mutual coexistence in our country. Instead of leaving the peace process in the hands of just the two parties –the Sri Lankan government and the LTTE- and the facilitators, more civil society actors need to be engaged in the so-called multi-track diplomacy and peace building.

We need the support of the influential Sri Lankan diaspora and the international community to strengthen the emerging international platform for peace and democracy in Sri Lanka . The Sri Lankan Diaspora that has helped perpetuate the conflict needs to make a positive international contribution to the resolution of the conflict, instead. Expatriates can help by engaging in dialogue within and across the ethnic and religious to develop specific strategies for intervention. Instead of promoting the messages of hate and enmity, or sending hard-earned money to buy weapons to continue the killing machine, they can help create a new analysis and message for peace and democracy. They can send money for alternative economic opportunities for the poor and ensure that the children have a future.

The international community, the donors and the Norwegian facilitators in particular must pressure all parties to the Sri Lankan conflict to abide by the rule of law and the international covenants against the conscription of child soldiers, the Universal Declaration of Human Rights and other relevant instruments. The LTTE must be required to uphold paragraph 18 of the Tokyo Declaration which was signed by 51 countries and 22 international organizations as part of the Sri Lankan peace process. This paragraph was introduced to ensure the protection of human rights of all people, the termination of child recruitment, balanced and verifiable de-escalation, demilitarisation and normalisation necessary to arrive at a political settlement.

Norway is a leading democratic and liberal country in the world. We need the Norwegian media, academic and NGO communities to make their officials facilitating the Sri Lankan peace process accountable. We need Norway to play their rightful role rather than capitulating to terrorist threats. They must be required to uphold the norms of neutrality expected of a third party facilitator; they must be required to ensure respect for the ceasefire and human rights b both parties as stipulated in the Tokyo Declaration. If the Norwegian facilitators take a strong and principled stance in the enforcement of the Tokyo principles, then, there is a chance that the LTTE could also be influenced to change their ways and enter the democratic process. The LTTE is a mis-guided organization; but, if the human potential and great talents represented by that organization can be put to positive use, Sri Lanka and the world at large, would undoubtedly be safer and more peaceful.

Norwegian Experiences with Peace Processes and Norway as facilitator in Sri Lanka

Lisa Golden

WAPS note: Lisa Golden's following presentation belies her actual statement in the WAPS conference. WAPS had wanted Eric Solheim to attend the conference as he was the self- appointed chief facilitator, but Solheim declined. Golden came in his stead and made a false statement not carried in this text, hence this explanatory note. She said that all Sri Lankan political parties were having discussions with the Norwegians on the ethnic issue. She went out of the way to mention that this included the JVP. WAPS on subsequent enquiry found this to be a falsehood. In spite of declared Norwegian intention to "hear and gain insight into the range of different points of view in Sri Lankan society" as Golden puts it here, she after the delivery of the text wanted to immediately leave the conference. There was a howl of protest from the audience and she had to stay. There was no better illustration of Norwegian intentions.

I am pleased to be here with you this morning representing the Ministry of Foreign Affairs of Norway, at the "World Alliance for Peace in Sri Lanka's Oslo Conference," at the kind invitation of the organizers.

In the Government of Norway's efforts as impartial facilitator for the peace process between the Government of Sri Lanka and the LTTE, it is important for us to hear and gain insight into the range of different points of view in Sri Lankan society.

We appreciate the chance to hear more today about the views on the peace process represented by those speakers and participants from Sri Lanka and elsewhere who have gathered here in Oslo.

My presentation on behalf of the Norwegian Foreign Ministry this afternoon will focus on Norwegian experiences drawn from facilitating peace and reconciliation processes, on our own and multilaterally, in a number of different contexts, such as Guatemala, the Philippines, Sudan, and the Middle East, and with a particular emphasis on our role as facilitator for the peace process in Sri Lanka.

Norwegian foreign policy embodies a strong commitment to international cooperation that is motivated by universal values of freedom and justice, peace and security, democracy and human rights, the fight against poverty and for sustainable development. Our long standing commitment to multilateral cooperation, in particular the UN, our involvement in support of peace and reconciliation processes, our support for human rights and humanitarian action and our development co-operation should be seen in this light.

As a small country, Norway is not in a position to impose its views on others. The best way for us to meet our foreign policy interests is in fact through international dialogue and partnership.

As a small country, we are committed to a world order based on international co-operation, international law and global stability. While these sound like big words, it is in our concrete interest as a small country to support the building of multilateral institutions and rules, which render states, groups and people so interdependent that it becomes clear to all that war is not an effective solution. Helping to build a world based on these ideals is ultimately in the interest of any small country – and in the wider interest of all states and individuals.

Norway is therefore playing an active role in peace and

reconciliation efforts and in promoting human rights and democracy in parts of the world as far apart as Europe, Asia, the Middle East, Africa and Latin America.

You may ask why, more specifically, has Norway engaged in attempts to facilitate reconciliation internationally. Some key factors may be identified.

Norway has long traditions of being actively involved in humanitarian issues and supporting international structures set up to provide collective security.

Since 1945, few countries have matched Norway's faith and large investments in the UN - not to mention its general enthusiasm for the Organization. Whatever the political color of the Norwegian governments in power, the UN has always been a vital arena and instrument for our foreign policy.

Peace and stability in countries far remote from this corner of the world serve Norway's interests in collective security and economic stability. For example, peace reduces the flow of refugees across international borders, including our own. And peace ensures a smoother international economic exchange, which is beneficial for us all.

In many ways, our involvement in attempts to facilitate peace and reconciliation processes around the world is a continuation of our long-standing commitment to build peace through humanitarian action and development co-operation.

As a relatively wealthy country, Norway is a fairly large provider of humanitarian and development assistance, with the aim of promoting human development and global stability. However, as I have indicated, in certain situations we can be in a position to contribute in a broader sense than simply financially. Economic assistance can never replace political solutions to conflicts that are by their nature political. When we provide political support to efforts to create peace, we are supporting the very same objectives that we are pursuing through our humanitarian assistance, development co-operation, and dialogues on human rights.

No two conflicts are the same, and there are of course different kinds of peace and reconciliation processes. Some require involvement at the political level; some take place at the civil society level. Some seek specific solutions, some simply aim to make space for dialogue. Some are between States, and others are within States and involve non-State actors.

Nonetheless, there are a number of common features of Norway's assistance to the various peace processes in which we have been engaged, including many that are relevant in our role in Sri Lanka. Let me highlight a few features:

First, Norway's ability to play an effective role depends on the willingness and readiness of the parties to a peace process themselves to take responsibility for the process. Though my presentation is supposed to focus on Norway's facilitation, it is important to underscore that peace can only be won or lost by the parties themselves. Truly, sustainable peace cannot be imposed from abroad.

At the request of the parties to the different peace efforts where we have been involved, Norway has therefore played the role of facilitator to assist the parties in their own efforts, rather than to impose any solutions on the parties from outside. It bears repeating that Norway as a small country is not in a position to lean on parties or lock them up in a room until they sign a deal. And even if we were, it would not be advisable, as nearly all imposed peace agreements historically have laid the ground for renewed conflict.

When it comes to what Norway does concretely in facilitation, our main task is to promote understanding between parties by helping the parties to communicate. Parties often request help to build communication in conflict situations, since when trust is low, misunderstandings occur easily.

As an outsider, we can never steer a peace process. Norway as facilitator takes action only at the request of the parties themselves, and the parties themselves have the responsibility and control of the process. However, outsiders can provide useful assistance, in particular with communication. To do this, we need a clear understanding of our role and where responsibility lies. We also need in-depth knowledge of history and a good understanding of the parties' genuine interests. For this, it is essential to maintain good and friendly relations with all parties and to enjoy one another's respect and confidence.

Only if we earn the trust of the parties, can we try to help them understand each other's interests. Only when parties understand each other's interests, can they have successful negotiations. Thus the most important contribution a facilitator can make is to help the parties communicate about their interests and concerns.

Naturally, from the perspective of each party, a third party can seem closer to the other party at times, because the third party is standing in the middle. We have learned to live with the criticism that follows from not taking sides, and the parties themselves appreciate that impartiality is essential for our role.

Norway can never have the depth of knowledge of a situation, such as in Sri Lanka, that the country's own citizens possess. For this reason, it is particularly important for us to consult broadly when in the role of facilitator. In Sri Lanka, we wish to speak with all parties.

Another feature and asset is that, in many cases, Norwegian involvement has started through the long-term commitment of a Norwegian non-governmental organization to development cooperation, or through cooperation between academic institutions.

A common feature is also that Norwegian humanitarian

assistance and development cooperation have supported peace building. Peace processes often rely on international assistance (1) to help bring dividends of peace to populations; (2)to build capacity among parties and civil society for doing politics as an alternative to war; (3) and to promote confidence-building processes and reconciliation between parties and in the population.

We have learned, for example in the Middle East, that mechanisms agreed by the parties to monitor the implementation of their agreements often are important for the success of peace processes. Norway, therefore, has increasingly assisted such mechanisms, such as Sri Lanka Monitoring Mission (SLMM). SLMM is the group observing the Cease Fire Agreement (CFA), at the request of the parties. SLMM consists of civilian monitors from all five Nordic countries. Their mandate is to observe implementation of the CFA and facilitate contact between the parties to help them resolve issues, but not to enforce the CFA. As with the peace process, implementation of the CFA is the responsibility of the parties.

Another important feature has been to understand the limits of our own function as facilitator, and to cooperate well with other actors working for peace, be they international organizations, countries in the region, major powers, or civil society organizations.

An attribute that should not be overlooked is that we have in many cases been able to play a facilitating role, thanks to the fact that Norway is a small country with no colonial past and with few vested interests in regions outside Europe.

Furthermore, we have a level of political stability and consensus that enables us to participate in such processes regardless of which government is in power in Norway. Because of this, we can have a long-term perspective on our involvement. The ability to be a patient partner is often useful, since lasting solutions are generally those that parties themselves have created. Homegrown peace solutions invariably take more time to reach than peace deals imposed from outside.

After the Cold War, most conflicts have been within rather than between States. This has necessitated new approaches for promoting peace and reconciliation between State and non-State actors. One lesson we have drawn from our support for various peace efforts, within and outside the UN, is that the international community needs mechanisms to address the asymmetry between State and non-State parties to peace processes, in order to help them achieve negotiated peace.

The dynamics of a peace process are different from the dynamics of war. In order for parties to bring negotiations to a successful conclusion, each party needs political capacity and other expertise. On one side of the peace table, you may have Governments with well-established institutions, access to expertise and international legitimacy. On the other side, you may have rebel or guerilla organizations with more limited political experience and long battlefield experience. Non-State actors will need to have the opportunity to engage constructively with other actors in society, internationally and domestically, such as experts, academics, and political representatives, in order to engage in the difficult process of transforming into a political organization. If a negotiated solution is the goal, the State actor may choose to accept the need of the non-State actor for assistance with political capacity building and transformation.

Norway's work as the facilitator in the peace process in Sri Lanka illustrates many of the common features that I have mentioned with regard to Norway's work for peace and reconciliation internationally.

Both the Government of Sri Lanka (GOSL) and the Liberation Tigers of Tamil Eelam (LTTE) have stated that they no longer believe in a military solution and are ready for difficult compromises in the pursuit of a negotiated to end a terrible war.

Norway has been formally involved in the peace efforts since 2000, at the parties' request. At that time, President Kumaratunga, as the leading advocate for a negotiated settlement to the conflict on the government side, and LTTE leader Prabhakaran, requested Norway to play the role of impartial third-party facilitator.

Norway's role as facilitator in Sri Lanka as elsewhere is to assist the parties in their own efforts to reach a political solution, not to impose a solution on them. A significant part of Norway's efforts in Sri Lanka have been focused on facilitating understanding between the parties: we have spent much time providing a channel for communication between the parties and helping explore solutions to bridge the gap between their respective positions. In this effort, we take only those actions, such as arranging meetings or supporting projects, that the parties request of us and that are acceptable to both parties. At the parties' request, Norway also has put much time and effort into communicating about the peace process with the international community and encouraging economic assistance to support peace building.

When it comes to the status of the peace process in Sri Lanka, that would be the subject of another presentation. In conclusion, I may mention briefly that the parties have made some significant progress the last few years, although there remains a long way to go. The Ceasefire Agreement between the Government and the LTTE came into force on 23 February 2002 has saved thousands of lives and secured the absence of wide-spread hostilities for a longer period of time than at any previous stage in the armed conflict. However, this does not mean that peace has been won yet.

In the absence of political negotiations, the ceasefire naturally becomes more vulnerable. The killings and bombing that have taken place recently are causing anxiety and if not stopped may have the potential to put the ceasefire at risk. The continued commitment by the parties to uphold the ceasefire is essential. It is therefore positive that both parties have reiterated their full support for the CFA. It is important that all segments of civil society, and political leaders from all sides, contribute to a conducive atmosphere for the peace process.

In turn, it will be important when negotiations eventually resume that the parties find ways to reach out and build understanding, support and ownership for a negotiated solution among all communities.

The parties have also succeeded through the peace process at attracting international attention and pledges of substantial assistance from major donors for rehabilitation and development of the war torn areas of the north and east and for development in the south. International assistance remains important to relieve suffering, promote development, and demonstrate that sustained peace will improve people's lives. It is a reality that renewed progress in the peace process - toward a solution that will protect and respect the human rights of all people in Sri Lanka - is important in order for substantial international aid and investment to flow and to make a difference in people's lives.

At the request of President Kumaratunga and LTTE leader Prabhakaran after the elections this spring, Norway continues to facilitate the peace process. We continue to consult with both parties on the modalities for future negotiations. The Government of Norway is convinced that the Government of Sri Lanka and the LTTE are committed to the peace process, and we hope that direct talks will be resumed as soon as possible. Norway is willing to be a partner for peace, for as long as the parties want our assistance in seeking an agreed political solution and as long as we can make a constructive contribution.

The Snow Tigers: The Canadian Tamil Tigers

A summary of a paper presented by Stewart Bell at the conference

With the bitter experience of separatist movements in Quebec, Canada should have been more sympathetic to other nations like Sri Lanka facing separatist campaigns in their countries. Yet she had not responded convincingly to the global terrorist challenge. Terrorist activity has taken place within Canada and this was done by supporting violence in other countries. And Canadians themselves did not see bloody results in other places.

Although Canada passed an Anti- terrorist law in December 2001 this has not yielded significant results. Thus the Canadian Intelligence knew about many terrorists but up to then only one of them had been charged. Fund raising for terrorism continued apace and according to the government's own financial investigations, Canadians had sent $22million to terrorist groups in 2003 and the figure for the first three Quarters of 2004 was $35M.

There was also a noticeable public and political sympathy for terrorist movements in Canada. Canada had Internet sites devoted to freeing terrorists captured by law enforcement authorities and by the immigration authorities. There were rallies, petitions and lawsuits in support of only the rights of terrorists. The focus in Canada was on rights of terrorists and not on the deep suffering consequences caused by Canada's "lax approaching to fight terrorism".

The free and tolerant immigration and security policy of Canada had made the country vulnerable to exploitation by terror groups. "Terrorists can enter Canada with nothing more than a concocted story of woe". And government-funded institutions for new immigrants were easily co-opted by extremists.

The LTTE expertly exploited the laxity of the immigration policy to bring in large numbers as 'refugees' to strengthen its action base and organization in Canada. Migrants smuggling rings brought in thousands of Tamils into Canada. Although generally law abiding, many of them "have abused the freedom Canada had given to them and used their new found wealth and freedom to bring the Eelam war to Canada". The Canada Police estimated that as many as 8, 000-10,000 trained Tamil guerillas slipped into Canada during this wave of migration.

The LTTE was also getting political support in Canada. LTTE sympathizers were fiercely lobbying politicians promising payback in form of votes at elections and got their support to influence national policy. The LTTE established criminal organizations, front organizations and front companies to encircle the Canadian Tamil community, influence Canadian policy and raise money for the LTTE.

Police and intelligent reports confirm that Canada had become a major base for the LTTE, one of the world's most ruthless guerilla/ terrorist groups. 'Canada had become a safe haven for a terrorist organization that had killed more than one hundred thousand, assassinated the leaders of India and Sri Lanka and carried out more suicide bombing than any other militant group in the world'.

Canada had become the LTTE's largest foreign base of operations. The LTTE raised about $ 1 million a month in Canada and diverted it to LTTE's war effort. According to Canadian Intelligence Reports, the Canadian LTTE bought about $1M worth of explosives in the mid- 1990s and sent it to for violence in Sri Lanka. Trained LTTE fighters were escaping to Canada and going back to Sri Lanka to engage in war. Consequently LTTE cadres with Canadian passports were found in the battlefields of Jaffna and Wanni.

Canadian Police and Intelligence had found that the Canadian LTTE operates in the form of front organizations, front companies and as organized crime gangs. These extensive operations in Canada have allowed the LTTE to gain the money it needed to fight the war for Tamil Eelam and to build world opinion justifying its violence. It was the international support structure in Canada that enabled the Tigers to mount a sustained campaign of violence. "Although few in Canada realize it (or could find Sri Lanka on a map), the Canadian Branch of the LTTE has helped fuel bloodshed in Sri Lanka, sometimes directly".

LTTE Front Organizations in Canada

The first thing that the LTTE did was to seize control of the community institutions- e.g. the World Tamil Movement (WTM), and an umbrella group called the Federation of Associations of Canadian Tamils (FACT). The WTM of Ontario was registered as a non-profit society dedicated to 'destitute refugees' and at one point got grants from the Ontario government. But it was clearly interested in more than refugees.

The WTM held 'cultural events 'in public school auditoriums in Toronto and Montreal but they were nothing more than LTTE events. The LTTE also carried political propaganda and organization and collected money by coercion under cover of religious functions. (Bell cited an experience he had in Toronto). The organization was by the Tamil Rehabilitation Organization of the LTTE. Oblivious to these questionable activities the Canadian Police present in the locality were concerned only with control of crowds (about 10,000, mostly youth participated during the week long function) and vehicle parking. Those events were often attended by Members of

Parliament. (Bell named a few).

The Canadian Tamil community was large enough to attract the attention of politicians, especially those in the ruling Liberal Party that got most of its support from urban areas, especially Toronto where the Tamil population was dense. The LTTE support network was strong and maintained grips on politics and public opinion. With such organized pressure Canadian politicians have 'succumbed to LTTE propaganda. LTTE sympathizers had entered the Canadian political machinery and they were influencing the national policy.

The Police reported that LTTE fronts were involved in taxing the earnings of the Tamil community and according to a survey done it was by extortion. There were many other active groups identified by the Canadian Intelligence as LTTE Fronts. At one point a front by name of Tamil Eelam Society was getting $2million a year from the Government.

There were about six companies in Canada run by those linked to LTTE fund raising Canadian Security Intelligence Service considered them as 'highly lucrative' and their main function was to launder money collected in Canada to the LTTE.

According to the Royal Canadian Mounted police (RCMP) and Toronto Police, "LTTE is involved in almost every facet of organized crime: money laundering, extortion, migrant smuggling, drug smuggling, passport forgery, theft and assault. There is clear evidence, the PCMP sys, that money raised through such crimes is making its way into LTTE coffers. There are also a cluster of violent street gangs loyal to the Tigers which the police say act as enforcers for the LTTE".

According to RCMP reports 'Tamil Tigers control every aspect of Tamil gang life in Toronto.' The main pro- LTTE gang was the VVT led by past and present LTTE fighters and they used violence and intimidation to suppress dissent in the Tamil community. The

VVT supported the LTTE partly by trying to kill a rival gang that was loyal to the PLOTE. Despite their violence they were rarely convicted as few risked testifying in courts against them. One gang circulated a flyer offering reward against a crown witness and at one trial; gangsters sat in a courtroom and held up photos of the children of witnesses who were to testify against the gangs.

Canada's immigration system made it almost impossible to deport suspected terrorists. Although many LTTE were arrested for deportation, virtually none had been sent home.

Despite all these, Canada had not outlawed the Tigers under its Anti Terrorist Act, even though it had banned many similar groups such as the Al-Qaeda, Hamas and the Colombian FARC. Canadian security agencies had repetitively asked the Cabinet to outlaw the LTTE but the Liberal ministers had refused. It was unbelievable that such things took place with complete disregard by the law enforcement officers "in a country that prides itself as a place of law and order and stability and human rights, a world peace keeper…"

Since the Sri Lanka cease-fire many of the key players in the Snow Tigers (Canadian LTTE terrorists) are still in Canada. "The fronts remain in plaçe. Should there be a resumption of violence. The network will be quickly activated to support the LTTE on the frontlines. When LTTE comes looking for money to finance their war, Canadian Intelligence officials know which country they will come to first".

"LTTE Suicide Terrorism: Evolution, Tactics and Execution"

A summary of a paper presented by Peter Chalk

LTTE was originally named Tamil New Tigers and its main aim is to establish a Tamil homeland in the Northern and Eastern Provinces of Sri Lanka. LTTE is generally considered to be one of the most sophisticated and deadly terrorist organizations in the world today. For example it crippled Sri Lankan Armed Forces at one point and today it controls a *de facto* Tamil state covering about 15% of the island.

Suicide terrorism is an integral strategy of the LTTE. It has institutionalized martyrdom as a permanent strategy and suicide or rather the fear of suicide could be the principal factor driving Sri Lankan leaders into the negotiations with the LTTE. Prabhakaran wields a consistent and omnipresent influence within the LTTE. He has managed to obtain unswerving loyalty of its cadres through the cyanide capsule worn around the neck. The command is to kill oneself rather than be taken by the enemy. Parbhakaran is the central factor in legitimating and venerating martyrdom. The emphasis on suicide terrorism has come from practical lessons and experiences of other terrorist groups such as Hezbollah and Parbhakaran's love of films with military, criminal and terrorist exploits such as Death Wish II. Prabahkaran uses suicide as a powerful force equalizer and as the ultimate expression of selflessness and dedication to the Tamil cause.

The Black Tigers is the main suicide squad of the LTTE. There are 350 Black Tigers who are drawn from other LTTE military ranks. Three principle criteria of selection were their ability to blend in to the larger society, capacity to operate independently and their extreme hatred towards the enemy. The suicide cadre is selected in small groups with not more than ten at a time and after specialized training, they are used to carryout three operations against Sri Lankan armed forces, critical national infrastructure such as the airport and World Trade Center and VIPs in the Sri Lankan government.

The Suicide training program last 9 months in two phases; the first developing physical fitness and skills such as bomb construction, vehicular driving, counter-surveillance and the second emphasizing special mission-oriented training developed through simulations and test runs of suicide bombing operations. Suicide bombings are carried out only after extensive prior surveillance of the target lasting over several months or even more. The suicide bomber is always accompanied by specially-designated handlers drawn from the intelligence wing. The attacks are invariablly videotaped for post bombing de-briefings which have been used to guide future suicide bombings. The suicide bombing success in killing the primary target is about 80%.

LTTE has over the years developed many different types of explosive vests all equipped with built-in fail-safe and redundancy systems. There is a claim that children suicide vests too have been developed by the LTTE. The delivery mechanisms vary from cars to bikes to boats.

LTTE suicide bombings have benefited from the behavior of Sri Lankans. These include the use of private security services and the tendency of Sri Lankan armed forces to concentrate on a bombing site. Curtailed police powers too have been exploited by the LTTE in carrying out their suicide bombing operations. In addition, the LTTE have established a number of safe houses in major cities and have deployed cadres to follow VIPs.

Sea Tiger suicide bombings are carried out by explosive-laden boats that are rammed into surface ships of the SL Navy. Sea Tiger suicide bombers typically consist of wounded cadres who perform the suicide as a last service to the LTTE. Sea Tiger attack boats are fiber glass maneuverable crafts with special penetration rods designed to amplify shock-waves by puncturing hulls before the explosives are detonated. The Sea Tigers also known to have experimented with two-man suicide submarines. Over 40 Sea Tiger suicide attacks were launched since 1990 and this has been a major factor discouraging recruitment to the Navy. In 1990 Sea Tiger suicide attack resembled very closely the Al Quaida attack on the USS Cole. The LTTE is at least 10 years ahead of al Qaeda in suicide missions. The LTTE may thus be providing a critical benchmark for general developments in the area of maritime terrorism.

The LTTE has explicitly institutionalized and venerated suicide terrorism. Therefore the LTTE is unlikely to disband their martyr units in the near term. The LTTE doubtless views the Black Tigers s as a de-facto "sword of Damocles" which can be brought into play should the peace process evolve in a direction counter to the interests of the LTTE. Already there was one attack against a police station in Colombo (July 2004) and warnings of a full return to war have been issued periodically. The LTTE has made very clear signals that the group is ready, willing and able to strike out against the Sri Lankan state that it continues to view with antipathy. Finally the LTTE has normalized suicide terrorism as not only "useful" but as the very essence of the LTTE's mission.

PART II

BACKGROUND DOCUMENTATION 1

International and Regional Implications of the Sri Lankan Tamil Insurgency

Rohan Gunaratne

The following article written by Rohan Gunaratne, *one of the world's leading experts on terrorism, is over five years old. It may not take into account all of the recent developments. But as a good summary of the LTTE international network it is still one of the most comprehensive.*

Author's Note

In the eyes of the international community, the conflict in Sri Lanka is developing into a living laboratory to study ethnicity, insurgency and security at the turn of the millennium. What has escaped the attention of the international community is thetransformation of insurgent groups into transnational networks in the last decade of the 20th century. Today, actively or passively, the Liberation Tigers of Tamil Eelam (LTTE) receives or derives, sanctuary, finance, weapons, and training from other governments, non-governmental organizations, and individuals. The traditionally held belief that an external support base is a prerequisite for an insurgency to flourish has been over taken by the recent sweeping changes of the globe. Today, a globe in chaos, a globe without direction, a globe struggling for a new order, is the base. In reality, modern insurgents are no more groups but entities. They have their investments, lawyers, ships, and armies. They tap from the resources and expertise from a range of sources. The saturated arms market and the fledgling arms industry to soldiers of fortune and mercenaries in search of greener pastures have become the center of attraction for groups like the LTTE. Mastery in improvisation of explosives (suicide body suit, land mines, anti-personnel mines), the use of dual-technology (civilian equipment that will enhance the performance of a militancy), and acquisition of area impact munitions (cluster bombs, fuel air explosives, multiple rocket launchers) by subnational groups have added a new dimension to warfare.

Transnational networks cannot be fought by domestic governments without a transnational capability and capacity, both to monitor and operate. For a domestic militarily, it is impossible to meet a threat that has grown into a global network, over two decades. Legal norms of the international system, preclude the expansion of the theater of war beyond the domestic shores of a centralized nation state. It is ironic that a bulk of the war budget of the LTTE is raised from the heartland of continental Europe and North America, the guardians of human rights and the proponents of democracy. It is also a paradox that a bulk of the weapons and explosives used to kill and maim hundreds of thousands of men, women and children of this century is being produced in the West. The West is beginning to experience the implications of this duality. Using the cover of the Muslim émigré, Iran and Libya continues to hunt their opponents down in France and Germany. Governments, with the help of the Diaspora and other armed groups, continue to fight the international infrastructures of the Hezbollah, the PKK and the LTTE, by proxy. Such events have proved that individual governments - whether in the north or the south - cannot sustain and maintain their security in the years ahead. Such trends are indicative that at least the challenges to late 20th and early 21st century security can only be addressed collectively.

These transnational networks are increasingly gathering momentum and generating their own dynamic. By themselves, government bureaucracies, unlike transnational terrorist networks, are not administratively or operationally flexible, to engage and interlock new threats. Similarly, the classical roles of defense and foreign affairs establishments designed for deterrence and bilateral relations respectively do not have the institutional mechanisms or the sophistication to meet such new threats. An integrated, multipronged and a transnational strategy is the key to addressing the political, economic and security delimma confronting Sri Lanka today.

International and Regional Implications of the Sri Lankan Tamil Insurgency

Introduction

The impact of the regional and international activity of the Sri Lankan Tamil insurgents on the national security of Sri Lanka has not received adequate attention by the domestic security, intelligence and foreign service community. The wider threat posed to regional and international security by Tamil insurgents - by the enhanced ideological, technological and financial interaction with overseas insurgent groups - has also escaped their close attention. Therefore, an understanding of the international infrastructure of the Liberation Tigers of Tamil Eelam (LTTE) as well as their relationship with the Tamil Diaspora, is vital for improving Sri Lankan, South Asian and global stability and security. Although, I have been engaged in research and writing on the Sri Lankan Tamil and Sinhala insurgencies during the past decade, I had the opportunity to focus on their international operations, only during the past two years. I conducted most of my research while resident at two research institutions in the US: the Office of Arms Control, Disarmament and International Security at the University of Illinois in 1994 and at the Center for International and Security Studies at the University of Maryland in 1995. At Illinois, I had the opportunity of working with Professor Stephen Cohen, a US expert on South Asian security, and at Maryland, with Admiral

Stansfield Turner, one time head of the US intelligence community. My presentation is organized into three areas:

First, a brief history of the Tamil insurgents and the origins of their international network. Second, a description of the international network and its operation. Third, the impact and the implications of the network, both on the security of Sri Lanka and the world at large.

History of Insurgency

Contrary to popular perception, Tamil insurgency originated in northern Sri Lanka in the early 1970s, during the United Front government, a coalition of the SLFP, LSSP and CP. From 1970 onwards, there were a number of acts of terrorism in the Jaffna peninsula. In February 1971, bombs were thrown at the residence of the Jaffna Mayor Alfred Duraiappah. On March 11, a bomb was placed in his car. On August 27, 1972, Velupillai Prabhakaran, the current leader of the LTTE, who was only 18 years of age, lobbed bombs at a carnival organized by the mayor in the stadium in Jaffna. Once again bombs were thrown at the stadium on September 17, and at the mayor's residence on December 19, 1972. On July 27, 1975, Duraiappah, who visited the Krishnan temple at Ponnalai in his car, was assassinated by Prabhakaran and two others. The mayor was the representative of the then United Front government in Jaffna. His elimination was symbolic of the contempt the Tamil insurgents had over the rule of Jaffna by a representative from Colombo. In their literature, the LTTE, the most formidable of Sri Lankan insurgent groups, claim that they originated in 1972. However, they did not begin to operate as an organization - the Tamil New Tigers (TNT) - until 1974. The leader was Chetti Tanabalasingham, a common criminal. Prabhakaran, who was politically motivated from his younger days, developed the military organization of the TNT and later the LTTE. Three early secretive linkages the LTTE enjoyed with other Tamil political - militant organizations helped the LTTE to develop its international component. They were tactical and not enduring relationships.

Origins of the Network

The LTTE link with the Tamil United Liberation Front (TULF) arose even before the TULF obtained a formal mandate from the Tamil people for a separate Tamil State in 1977. In the mid 1970s, the TULF leader Appapillai Amirthalingam clandestinely supported the LTTE. Amirthalingam believed that his position as the political leader of the Tamil people would be enhanced if he could exercise control over the Tamil insurgent groups. The TULF helped the LTTE to emerge as a powerful force. Two of its prominent youth wing members, Uma Maheswaran, joined the LTTE as its chairman, and Urmila Kandiah, as its first female member. On government stationary, Amirthalingam, as leader of the parliamentary opposition, provided letters of reference to the LTTE and to other Tamil insurgent groups to raise funds. Amirthalingam, also introduced N.S. Krishnan, to Prabhakaran. Prabhakaran, who later became the first LTTE international representative, laid the foundation for LTTE overseas activity ***(note 1)***. Interestingly, it was Krishnan who introduced the current LTTE theoretician and ideologue Anton Balasingham to Prabhakaran. Balasingham, a former Tamil journalist and a translator at the British High Commission in Colombo, was then a Ph.D. candidate writing his dissertation on the psychology of Marxism at the South Bank Polytechnic.

The tutors at the polytechnic, (now known as the South Bank University) still remember him as a bright but unusual student. Balasingham's first Jaffna Tamil wife, whom he loved very much, died of kidney failure in London. Balasingham's current wife Adele, an Australian citizen and a nurse by professional training, is a prominent member of the women's wing of the LTTE. Another TULF parliamentarian that supported the LTTE was the then Chavakachcheri MP V.N. Navaratnam, who was an executive committee member of the Inter Parliamentary Union (IPU). Navaratnam introduced many influential and wealthy Tamils living overseas to Tamil insurgent leaders. In one of the first meetings in

Oslo, Norway, Navaratnam, introduced the Polisario representative to the LTTE. Polisario, a Moroccan insurgent group was ready to cooperate with the LTTE. The second organization that helped the LTTE to develop its international component was the Eelam Revolutionary Organizers (EROS), erroneously and better known as the Eelam Revolutionary Organization of Students founded by Eliyathamby Ratnasabapathy ***(note-2)***. Like most ideologues, Ratnasabapathy too was a Marxist-Leninist. In Sri Lanka, he had lived both in the north and in the plantations of the central hills and was a LSSP supporter and a JVP sympathizer. After taking up residence in London, he also formed the General Union of Eelam Students (GUES), modeled on the General Union of Palestinian Students (GUPS). While GUES was the student wing, EROS was the principal group.

As a supporter of the Palestinian cause, he had developed excellent relations with Sayed Hamami, the PLO representative in London. Before Sayed was assassinated by Israeli operatives, he helped Ratnasabapathy to develop links with Fatah, the military wing of the PLO. Fatah offered a training opportunity to EROS. This was a time when the insurgent groups shared their expertise and resources. EROS shared the training offer with the LTTE. As a result in early 1977, Vichweshwaran alias Visu of EROS (later LTTE) and Uma Maheswaran of LTTE (later PLOTE), traveled to Lebanon and trained with Fatah. The third organization that helped the LTTE to develop its international component was the Tamil Liberation Front, the precursor of the Tamil Liberation Organization (TLO) ***(note-3)***. The TLO, distinct from the Tamil Eelam Liberation Organization (TELO), originated in London in the mid-1970s. The dynamic leadership of TLO made it a powerful organization within a short period of time. TLO organized a number of demonstrations, rallies and protest marches opposing the Government of Sri Lanka. During the second half of the 1970s, TLO was gradually absorbed by the LTTE. TLO began to function as the international arm of the LTTE.

Rationale for the Network

The powerful presence of an international link was a major morale boost for the Tamil insurgents in Sri Lanka. It was a form of recognition of their struggle both domestically and internationally. The international component enhances domestic survival and contributes to the resilience of an organization. Although there was limited financial assistance until the ethnic riots of July 1983, there were many Tamils who were sympathetic towards the Tamil cause and waiting for an opportunity to make a contribution for the advancement of Tamil nationalistic aspirations and goals. The ethnic riots deeply wounded the sentiments and galvanized the Tamils as a community. Past tragedies were brought to light and kept alive by the political leaders on both sides. The injustices upon the minority as a community by the successive majority dominated Colombo governments were rectified by two pacts - the Bandaranaike - Chelvanayakam in 1957 and the Senanayake - Chelvanayakam in 1965. But under pressure from sections of the majority community, the pacts were abrogated. A series of ethnic riots - 1956, 1958, 1961, 1974, 1977, 1979, 1981 and 1983 - scarred the memories of a substantial segment Tamils.

Many who left Sri Lanka as victims of the riots were made to believe by Tamil politicians that only a separate Tamil state can and would ensure permanent protection. The TULF and several other Tamil political and insurgent groups kept the campaign alive by bringing back bitter memories. The incessant waves of riots that destroyed lives and property of the Tamils were highlighted. Sinhala Sri, Sinhala Only Act, Sinhala colonization and standardization of education that had antagonized the Tamils formed the basis of the conflict. ***(note-4)*** Prior to July 1983, all efforts by Tamil insurgent groups and their representatives to raise money overseas to sustain a war had been unsuccessful. It was only after July 1983, with the exodus of over 100,000 Tamil refugees and another equal number of displaced persons that gave birth to a distinct Tamil Diaspora ***(note-5)***. By the end of 1983, there were over 100,000 Sri Lankan Tamils in Tamil Nadu alone and this number would swell up to nearly 200,000 with the escalation of the conflict. The exodus to the West was equally intense. Many countries in the West, sympathetic to the plight of the Sri Lankan Tamils would revise their immigration and emigration policies vis-à-vis Sri Lanka. As a consequence, the number of refugees, mostly economic but in the guise of political asylum seekers, would bring the totality of the Sri Lankan Tamil Diaspora to over 450,000. Mid-1983 to mid-1987 witnessed Sri Lanka's international image at its lowest ebb.

Despite having an open economy, a model democracy and a major tourist destination, Sri Lanka's international image suffered irreversibly. TULF propaganda branded Sri Lanka as a state guilty of discrimination and perpetrating genocide against its minority. Sri Lanka harped on the fact that six of its top Ambassadors including those to the United Kingdom, France and West Germany were Tamils. Colombo also said that the Inspector General of Police, at least four Deputy Inspector Generals of Police, and the Chief Justice were Tamils. But, no attempt was made by the government to turn the events that would dampen the formation or hamper the operation of the network. Counter propaganda by Sri Lankan missions overseas and associations heightened the ethnic tensions overseas and polarized the communities further. Sections of the Tamils marginally involved or disinterested in communal politics were dragged into the center of a conflict in the making.

Formation of the Network

Although the TULF politicians spearheaded this anti-Sinhala and anti-government drive, it was not the TULF that reaped the benefits of their international and domestic campaign to politicize and mobilize the Sri Lanka Tamils. It was the Tamil insurgent groups that raised funds from a TULF - politicized and mobilized Tamil Diaspora to fund their war effort for an independent Tamil Eelam. Of the Tamil groups, the only group that developed consistency in conducting propaganda against the government and the Sinhala majority community and later even against the Government of India was the LTTE. It was also the LTTE that developed the systematic organization to collect money and use it with a high degree of honesty and efficiency to further their political and military goals. The LTTE has displayed mastery in generating funds from the Sri Lankan Tamil Diaspora spread over 50 countries. Soon after the July riots of 1983, the LTTE international representative K. Balasekeram, a radiographer working in a London hospital, convened a meeting under the banner of the Eelam Solidarity Campaign. After many speakers had aired their views, the voices from the audience asked, "What can we do?" Balasekeram said, "Those who want to do something about the plight of the Tamil people in Sri Lanka may leave your name and phone number."***(note-6)*** From that night, Balasekeram called many of the committed Tamils who had come for the London meeting.

After soliciting funds, Balasekeram developed a system to follow up on the contributions pledged by the community. Afterwards, he appointed a coordinator for each area and set out guidelines to develop a state of the art finance generation operation throughout the UK. His policy was not to request or receive a large donation at once, but to socialize the Tamils to donating a small amount of money every month. This became the first instance the LTTE collected money from a large public gathering. The LTTE firmly believed in compartmentalization to secure the vital element of secrecy. Attempts prior to 1983 had failed to raise funds from the Tamils as a community although individuals did contribute to procure weaponry ***(note-7)***. Pre 1983 period witnessed the politicizing of the Tamils at a low level. The first public organization of the Sri Lankan Tamil community to generate funds had been formed in London in 1978. TULF's Amirthalingam who was on a world tour, together with a London based Eelam activist S.K. Vaikundavasan, formed the Tamil Coordinating Committee (TCC). ***(note-8)*** The TCC was later used by the LTTE as a front organization to carry out propaganda as well as to generate finance.

The UK Net

The UK has always been the heart of LTTE overseas political activity. Since the riots of July 1983, the LTTE has expanded into Europe from London. To make its position secure, the LTTE has either established, absorbed, or infiltrated a number of LTTE, LTTE front or pro-LTTE organizations in the UK. Some of them are the Tamil Information Center at Tamil House in Romford Road in London, The Tamil Rehabilitation Organization in Walthamstow in London, and the International Federation of Tamils (IFT) in Birchiew Close in Surrey. From IFT, LTTE legal advisor N. Satyendran, a Cambridge academic and son of the late S Nadesan Q.C., edits Network. IFT also publishes a Tamil journal Kalathil. Among the other LTTE publications are Viduthalai Puligal and Tamil Land. Other Tamil newspapers are Tamil Nation published from Croydon, Surrey and Thamilan from Undine Street in London. More recently, an LTTE front in London, publishes Hot Spring, a journal hitherto published in the peninsula.

The LTTE International Secretariat located at St. Katherine Road has functioned continuously since its establishment in 1984. Among the other organizations through which the LTTE operate are the London Tamil Mandram and the World Saiva Council. The latter uses an address care of the London Meikandaar Adheenam on King Edward Road. The LTTE also maintains an information center in Albany Street, London, where the latest news from Sri Lanka is provided to any caller. The Tamil Eelam British Branch, providing this service could be accessed by calling 0171 387 4339. There are similar news services in a number of countries from Germany to the US. From the UK, the LTTE feeds propaganda to its offices and cells throughout Europe, North America and elsewhere. In turn the funds collected are transferred to a number of LTTE and cover bank accounts.

In charge of the LTTE propaganda and fund raising is John Christian Chrysostom alias Lawrence Tilagar, the international representative of the LTTE ***(note-9)***. With him, dedicated LTTE leaders from Shanthan, Shegar and Ramasar in London, Murali in Geneva, Rudrakumaran in New York and Suresh in Toronto work day and night. The LTTE propaganda and fund raising network is superior to other extant networks such as Hamas, Hezbollah, Kashmiris, or the Basques. Today, in the North Atlantic countries alone, there are over 40 Sri Lankan Tamil newspapers, of which over 80% are either managed by the LTTE or their front organizations. If the LTTE is unable to infiltrate a Sri Lankan Tamil newspaper, it would call the stores that sell the newspaper not to sell it or would call the Tamil public to boycott it. In mid 1996, the LTTE decided to kill Manchari, a Tamil newspaper edited by D.B.S. Jeyaraj in Canada. Therefore, the writ of the LTTE extends beyond the LTTE dominated areas in Sri Lanka, into distant theaters where they have made a significant political, economic and a militant presence.

Dynamics of the Network

To build support for their domestic struggle as well as to consolidate their position overseas, the LTTE has developed relationships clandestine with foreign insurgent groups. By studying how other revolutionary groups operate overseas, the LTTE learnt the importance of propaganda material. London, the hub of revolutionary representatives, cells and offices, helped the LTTE to realize this dimension. In 1978, the LTTE produced its first leaflet for international distribution - it was for a conference in Cuba where a large group of revolutionary leaders would meet. In 1978, a Sri Lankan delegation left to attend the 11th World Youth Conference in Havana, Cuba. The three member TULF delegation was joined by a LTTE representative who had hitherto studied in the Soviet Union. Hoping to join them, the then UK based LTTE international representative N.S. Krishnan traveled with LTTE literature from London to Madrid in Spain to obtain a visa for Cuba. The visa was not granted and Krishnan had to return to London. However, he managed to courier the propaganda material to Havana, in time for the meeting.

From 1977 onwards the LTTE international network made inroads to countries where there was a Tamil presence. From the mid-1970s onwards, the Tamil militant structures steadily grew in the West, with its nucleus in London. The linkages were mostly confined to the Middle East, for military development, and to Europe and elsewhere like Nigeria, Yemen and Zambia for financial assistance. By the 1980s, Tamil militant representatives had traveled far and wide. The Arab and Islamic world was important but so were countries where Tamils lived, worked and earned in substantial number. They were Libya, Iraq, Iran, Lebanon, Syria, Algeria, Morocco, Turkey and Yemen. They also had substantial contacts with Cyprus and Greece. The government in Colombo failed to keep track of Tamil political activities overseas.

The United National Party government of J.R. Jayewardene that came to power in 1977 reorganized the intelligence apparatus and as a consequence, intelligence and data collection and analysis on Tamil insurgency suffered. In 1984, one year after the riots of 1983, when the seasoned operatives were called back, Tamil network overseas by then had grown substantially ***(note-10).*** Very few in the national security apparatus at that time realized the importance of monitoring activities of the Tamil insurgents overseas, including the vibrant Tamil Diaspora - insurgent link. Although a number of Tamils left Sri Lanka in the aftermath of the 1977 riots, they were not sufficiently politicized or mobilized to make financial contributions to the LTTE but this dynamic changed after mid-1983. The expansion of the LTTE network after 1983 was meteoric. The LTTE focused not only in developing relationships with neighboring India, Tamil communities overseas, but other revolutionary groups. But unlike other Tamil groups, the LTTE was mindful in every step they took both domestically and internationally. Even in their relationship with India, the LTTE ensured that their other relationships did not suffer. While the LTTE developed new contacts, they also managed to keep the old contacts alive.

Until late 1986, Prabhakaran did not wish to antagonize India but neither did he wish to rely on India totally. This led the LTTE to develop alliances with other groups outside India and thereby not become totally dependent on India. However, many of the alliances the LTTE developed during the early years, just like those developed in the subsequent years, were not permanent friendships. They were temporary and tactical relationships, very similar in content and context developed with India from 1983 to 1987 and with the Premadasa Administration from 1989 to 1990. Prabhakaran never compromised his avowed dream of Tamil Eelam. Prabhakaran's primary task and primary goal was to advance his objectives and reach his goal. So, the alliances would not last for more than a few years.

LTTE Foreign Policy

Having established political links with revolutionary regimes and revolutionary groups quite early in their history, the LTTE realized the importance of such linkages. Gaddhafi, Assad, and Khomeni were their heros in a series of anti-US and anti-Israeli demonstrations in the peninsula in the mid 1980s. These regimes had pledged support to LTTE representatives while maintaining a relationship with Colombo ***(note-11)***. However, the LTTE was cautious not to have contacts with organizations for the mere sake of establishing links because that would draw the attention of foreign security and intelligence agencies. Therefore, if ever the LTTE established links, it was based either on advancing mutual interests or for military, political, economic or diplomatic gain. Every insurgent group passes through a critical phase where they require either an external sanctuary and or external assistance to survive. The LTTE was no exception. Geopolitics as well as domestic compulsions led India to support the Tamil insurgents of Sri Lanka. Geographically, India is only 22 miles away from the Jaffna peninsula. It is one hour by speed boat. Although Tamil insurgents benefited from this natural external base from the early 1970s, it was not until the riots of July 1983 that India became an active base for the Tamil groups to grow in number, strength and operational capability and capacity.

The India - Sri Lanka Tamil insurgency relationship has its origins in the 1970s. The initial contact between the Tamil Nadu government and Sri Lankan Tamil activists was established in 1972. A delegation from the Tamil Manavi Peravi, a group of Tamil students who believed in the armed struggle and committed towards securing an independent Tamil state in Sri Lanka, traveled to Madras and met E.V.R. Periya, the then Tamil Nadu leader ***(note-12)***. Periya told the four man delegation, "If you are unhappy in Sri Lanka come to South India. We will give you enough land to cultivate." During the 1970s, Tamil youth activists used Tamil Nadu as a sanctuary to evade arrest from the Sri Lanka police - this included Prabhakaran and many other politically as well as criminally active youth.

Relationship with India

From the late 1970s, the LTTE developed links with a number of Tamil Nadu political groups - they were comparatively small in organization and membership. The most significant of them were Dravida Kazhagam headed by Veramani, the Kamraj Congress headed by Nedumaran and the Pure Tamil Movement headed by Perinchintanarayanan. To date, the leaders as well as cadres remain strong supporters of the LTTE. Veeramani called a meeting of all his key party organizers throughout Tamil Nadu and asked them to support the LTTE. Nedumaran wrote a biography of Prabhakaran. Perinchintanarayanan gave his property for the use of the LTTE. Thereafter, the LTTE developed excellent relations with M.G. Ramachandran and M. Karunanidhi, who succeeded each other as chief ministers. Although Tamil insurgents had established a few training camps in Tamil Nadu in 1982, there was no official assistance from the Central Government of India prior to August 1983. In the eyes of many Indian hard-liners, Sri Lanka since 1977 had stepped out of the non aligned orbit and had become an ally of the West.

There were Israeli intelligence operatives, British counter insurgency experts, South African mercenaries, and rumors about offering Trincomalee, one of the finest deep water harbors to the US navy. Sri Lanka had good relations with Pakistan and China, two countries that had fought border wars with India and they were in the process of stepping up military assistance to Colombo. Further, President J.R. Jayewardene of Sri Lanka did not enjoy with Premier Indira Gandhi the same warm relationship he had with her father, Premier Jawaharlal Nehru. After Premier Indira Gandhi, also the leader of the powerful Congress (I) Party, took a policy decision to support Sri Lankan northern insurgency from August 1983. The need to have leverage over Colombo was adequately demonstrated by the Research and Analysis Wing (RAW), the agency also responsible for advancing India's secret foreign policy goals. Within her inner circle, the decision was justified. Geopolitics and domestic compulsions validated the rationale.

The Third Agency of RAW, a supra intelligence outfit, was entrusted with the task. Within a year, the number of Sri Lanka Tamil training camps in Tamil Nadu mushroomed to 32. By mid 1987, over 20,000 Sri Lankan Tamil insurgents had been provided sanctuary, finance, training and weapons either by the central government, state government of Tamil Nadu or by the insurgent groups themselves. While most of the initial training was confined to Indian military and paramilitary camps in Uttara Pradesh, specialized training were imparted by the Indian instructors attached to RAW to Sri Lankan insurgents in New Delhi, Bombay and Vishakhapatnam ***(note-13)***. The most secretive training was conducted in Chakrata, north of Dehra Dun, India's premier military academy for training service personnel, where RAW had also imparted training to Bangladesh, Pakistan and Tibetan dissidents ***(note-14)***. With the Indo-Lanka Accord of July 1987, RAW assistance culminated. Rajiv Gandhi ordered the Indian Peace Keeping Force (IPKF) to fight the LTTE, when it went back on its pledge to surrender its weapons. The LTTE-IPKF war, apparently deprived the LTTE of its invaluable base, India. But, Tamil Nadu assistance to the LTTE continued even after M.G. Ramachandran's death in December 1987. Tamil Nadu State assistance under the Karunanidhi Administration, despite the presence of the IPKF, continued for the LTTE. Although the LTTE was at war with India, Tamil Nadu still remained LTTE's main source of supplies.

The Indian Net

Throughout the IPKF episode and until Rajiv Gandhi assassination in 1991, the LTTE continued to maintain a substantial presence in India. When the law enforcement agencies stepped up surveillance, the LTTE moved a bulk of its cadres from Tamil Nadu to other towns such as Mysore, Bangalore and Bombay. Even at the height of the IPKF - LTTE confrontation, the LTTE had twelve sections in India to manage:

(1) Intelligence
(2) Communications
(3) Arms Production
(4) Procurement of explosives
(5) Propaganda
(6) Political work
(7) Food and essential supplies
(8) Medicines
(9) Fuel supplies
(10) Clothing
(11) Transport
(12) Finance and currency conversion

The LTTE had also converted Madras, the capital of Tamil Nadu, and nine other Tamil Nadu districts, into centers for war supplies to the LTTE. Each center was linked by a sophisticated wireless network. Individual units carried sanyo walkie talkie sets. The centers of war supplies and other activities were ***(note-15)***:

(1) Dharmapuri: Procurement of explosives
(2) Coimbatore: Arms and ammunition manufacturing
(3) Salem: Explosives manufacturing and military clothing

manufacturing.

(4) Periya (Erode) Military clothing manufacturing

(5) Vedaraniym: Coastal area from where supplies were dispatched for the LTTE

(6) Madurai: Transit area

(7) Thanjavur; Communications center

(8) Nagapattnam: Landing area for supplies from LTTE deep sea going ships

(9) Rameswaram: Refugee arriving area and recruitment

(10) Tiruchi: Treatment of wounded LTTE cadres

(11) Tutocorin: LTTE trade in gold, silver, narcotics and other merchandise goods.

(12) Madras: Liaison with Tamil Nadu political leaders.

Implications for India

The LTTE-India nexus did not secure the geopolitical security New Delhi needed from Sri Lanka. It weakened Indian as well as Sri Lankan domestic security. In many ways, the presence of a foreign military strengthened the fighting spirit of LTTE and weakened the anti-terrorist capability of the Sri Lankan forces, then engaged in an anti-subversive campaign in the South ***(note-16)***. The organization gained mastery of guerrilla warfare by fighting the fourth largest military in the world. The LTTE suffered heavy causalities but replenished their ranks and gained a confidence paralleled by the Viet Cong and the Afghan mujahidin. LTTE also innovated new weapons, mostly projectiles and mines. Johnny mine, the anti-personnel mine invented by Prabhakaran, has at least claimed 5,000 Indian and Sri Lankan war causalities. Many Tamil Nadu political leaders from Nedumaran to Gopalasamy and Ramakrishnan visited the LTTE jungle base - known as the one four base complex over the years - and expressed solidarity with Prabhakaran. The role of the IPKF in Sri Lanka became a politically sensitive issue. When the IPKF returned to India, under the National Front government of V.P. Singh, the then Tamil Nadu Chief Minister M. Karunanidhi did not visit the port of Madras to welcome the Indian soldier. Even after the IPKF departed the LTTE continued to maintain excellent relations with Tamil Nadu politicians. The LTTE had managed to preserve Tamil Nadu as a critical base by retaining the goodwill of the Tamil Nadu leaders. In fact, when the LTTE hit teams under the one eyed Jack Sivarasan assassinated the anti-LTTE EPRLF leader Padmanabha and his colleagues in Tamil Nadu, chief minister Karunanidhi asked the Tamil Nadu police and the state agencies to turn a blind eye. A few months later, the LTTE used the very same infrastructure of the LTTE in Tamil Nadu to kill Rajiv Gandhi ***(note-17)***. The LTTE penetration of the Tamil Nadu polity was so good that a decision reached at a high level meeting comprising intelligence agencies in New Delhi about anti-LTTE operations was conveyed to the LTTE within 24 hours. Investigations revealed that the culprit was the then Tamil Nadu Home Secretary and at the instruction of Karunanidhi. The dismissal of Karunanidhi did not prevent the LTTE from continuing to operate in Tamil Nadu. The LTTE made a statement during the subsequent Jayalalitha Administration, "If the Tamil Nadu leadership cannot support the LTTE, at least we expect them to be neutral to the LTTE." This meant that LTTE operations should continue unhindered in the state of Tamil Nadu.

In retrospect, the LTTE - India relationship has been one of love and hate. It is a relationship that will have its ups and downs but a relationship that will nevertheless continue. Despite the fact that the LTTE eliminated Rajiv Gandhi, the last of the Gandhi-Nehru dynasty, there will always be a segment of the Tamil Nadu leaders and people that will support the LTTE. The contradiction stems from India's own structure - the diversity within India, particularly, the disparity in culture between the Indian Tamils and the rest of India's polity. The assassination of Rajiv Gandhi was imperative for the LTTE. If the LTTE did not, the IPKF that withdrew would have returned heralding another period of bloody fighting. Prabhakaran's calculus was right. As a leader, he had done his duty by his rank and file. By assassinating Rajiv Gandhi, he prevented the reintroduction of the IPKF to Sri Lanka ***(note-***

18). Even for Prabhakaran, it would have been a painful decision. Antagonizing India at the southernmost point of peninsular India meant the permanent closure of the door for creating Tamil Eelam and Prabhakaran becoming its ruler.

Non-LTTE Actors

While the LTTE international network grew from strength to strength, the activities of other Tamil insurgent groups such as PLOTE, TELO, EPRLF and EROS dwindled. There were three reasons for it. First, their ideology was strictly not Tamil nationalism but a mixture of Marxist- Leninism ***(note-19)***. The LTTE had made the transition from Marxist Leninism to Tamil nationalism despite the fact that Anton Balasingham was a confirmed Marxist-Leninist and had extensively written and published on the subject. Whipping up Tamil nationalism and fighting the Sri Lankan security forces appealed to sections of the Tamil community over ideological indoctrination and limited or no action with only visions of a mass revolution. Second, with the Indo-Lanka Accord of July 1987 and the introduction of 100,000 Indian peace keeping troops to Sri Lanka, all the Tamil insurgent groups entered the political mainstream except the LTTE. Although at first it appeared unrealistic to fight India, segments of the Tamil Diaspora were committed to supporting the armed struggle of the LTTE against the IPKF.

Through concerted propaganda, the LTTE had projected into the minds of the Tamil Diaspora, that the LTTE could even fight India. Prior to mid 1987, the LTTE was the only group that projected itself both militarily and politically as capable of delivering an independent Tamil Eelam. Although many Tamils detested the IPKF - LTTE confrontation (because India had been a traditional ally of Sri Lankan Tamils) IPKF civilian killings highlighted by the LTTE international propaganda machinery generated resentment against India and the pro-Indian Sri Lankan Tamil groups and generated support for the LTTE. Third, LTTE was the only group that systematically lobbied for Tamil Diaspora assistance and developed the organization to sustain international activity. When the fighting against the IPKF resumed, the network was already in place. Although the proposition was unrealistic to many, the Tamil Diaspora could not refuse the LTTE it had been supporting and funding for years. The rival Tamil groups such as PLOTE, EPRLF, TELO, EROS and ENDLF did not have the international organization. It must be recalled that PLOTE started its international activities with a bang soon after the riots of July 1983. In fact, they purchased the first ship, Palavan. In 1984, a PLOTE delegation visited Mauritius and received a red carpet welcome from the government of Androo Jauganath.

On that delegation with Uma Maheswaran was Dharmalingam Siddharthan, the son of a TULF parliamentarian, and currently the leader of PLOTE. Further, PLOTE had the largest number of cadres living in India. According to modest estimates, there were at least 10,000 PLOTE cadres in Tamil Nadu alone. Initially, TELO enjoyed greater patronage than the LTTE in India. TELO also had better training facilities at the beginning. But the LTTE checkmated all these groups by keeping their numbers small and a tight control to maintain discipline. Ruthlessness and efficiency forced the LTTE to ban all the other Tamil groups and hunt their leaders and cadres from 1984 onwards. Today, the LTTE claims that they are the sole representatives of the Tamil people, not only domestically but internationally, thereby dampening even the activities of rival Tamil groups overseas. Coercion is not an uncommon tool among the LTTE cadres operating overseas vis-à-vis Tamil civilians. These international developments demonstrated the ever changing dynamic between LTTE domestic policy and its impact on their international activity.

Finance Generation

Modern insurgent groups are developing the ability to raise funds in one theater, operate in another and fight in a third theater.

Although the international intelligence and security community has yet to focus on the LTTE finance generation, the LTTE is the archetype ***(note-20)***. By late 1995, 40% of LTTE war budget was generated from overseas ***(note-21)***. Since the loss of Jaffna peninsula in early 1996, 60% of the LTTE war budget is being generated from overseas. The LTTE has been engaged in a number of ventures that continue to bring them a massive revenue. It is likely that funds generated this way will surpass the funds generated domestically or internationally from the Tamil Diaspora. This is not a trend confined to the LTTE but to other transnational groups as well. But the LTTE is a trendsetter in this arena. The LTTE has invested in stock and money markets, real estate and in restaurants throughout the West and East. Starting with restaurants in Tamil Nadu and Paris in 1983, the LTTE developed its business acumen. Thereafter, restaurants sprang up from London to Toronto and Cambodia. Today, the LTTE has a large number of shops in a number of capitals, cities and towns. They sell LTTE videos, newspapers and Asian spice.

LTTE has also invested in a number of farms, finance companies and in other high profit ventures. Trading in gold, laundering money and trafficking narcotics bring the LTTE substantial revenue that is needed to procure sophisticated weaponry ***(note-22).*** The SAM missiles procured from Cambodia cost the LTTE US $ 1 million a piece ***(note-23)***. The gold that is collected in Jaffna - initially two sovereigns from each family for the war budget - is melted and ingots are formed and transported across the Palk Straits to Tamil Nadu. The ingots are sold by LTTE male and female couriers in Tiruchi, Coimbatore and Bombay markets. With the help of Thanjavur smugglers, the money is ploughed back to procure war materials. Supplies purchased in India are smuggled back to Sri Lanka from the Ramanathapuram to Thanjavur coastline to Jaffna and Talaimannar. The LTTE money laundering activities is not very different to the systems used by the Latin American narcotics cartels ***(note-24)***. Money is invested in legitimate ventures that makes it difficult for security and intelligence agencies to monitor their investments, accounts, transfers and investments. Although, the LTTE narcotic trafficking operations remain highly secretive, Western and Asian security and intelligence agencies have since recently made some significant detection's from the Philippines to Germany and from Italy to Canada. It is believed that the LTTE transports heroin on board LTTE owned ships from Myanmar to Europe ***(note-25)***. The LTTE also has their own fleet of vehicles in many countries from Tamil Nadu to Ontario. They also play a role in providing passports, other papers, and also engage in human smuggling. Like the Middle Eastern groups, notably the Hamas and the Hezbollah, the illegal and the legal components of the LTTE operation for the generation of finances overlap. Today, when money is collected by the Tamil Rehabilitation Organization (TRO), the rehabilitation wing of the LTTE, it is well known among the donors that the money is in fact spent not only on rehabilitation but also to procure weapons ***(note-26)***.

It is an unwritten understanding both among the collectors and donors. During their early years, almost all the Tamil insurgent groups were totally dependent on robberies, extortion (they use the term expropriation) and donations. Later the Tamil groups developed a taste for soliciting funds overseas from individuals and organizations. They were effective in organizing food festivals, film shows or other cultural activities. From LTTE controlled and dominated areas, they also began to levy a tax. The LTTE profit considerably from businesses and trade. They also tax through immigration and emigration, transportation of commodities to and from the northeast and wherever money changes hands in substantial quantity and frequency. Karikalan, the head of the political wing for the Eastern province, earned a reputation among Colombo-based foreign missions and development-oriented International Non Governmental Organizations (INGOs) working in the northeast for having approached their field representatives to make donations. At one point, the TRO, received a substantial donation from the Government of Germany ***(note-27)***. Thereafter, Karikalan would take a special interest in demanding for contributions from either the Colombo-based missions or INGOs.

Shipping Network

LTTE overseas department for clandestine operations, headed by Kumaran Padmanathan, is also responsible for managing the highly secretive shipping network ***(note-28)***. Padmanathan, a product of the Jaffna campus, uses over 20 aliases and an equal number of passports. This organ of the LTTE, also known as the KP department, has mostly militarily untrained cadres. Even Padmanathan has not been trained militarily. This makes the operation of their department much easier. There are virtually no records of members of this department in the files of domestic and foreign security and intelligence agencies. But they are trained in other skills from forging to gun running, secret communication to investing. KP department is also responsible for managing the LTTE shipping network. The LTTE shipping network, that has reached a high degree of proficiency, is a model for other insurgent groups. Except for the PLO and the IRA, the LTTE is the only insurgent group that owns and operates a fleet of deep sea going ships ***(note-29)***.

Equipped with sophisticated radar and inmarsat for communication, the LTTE built its fleet from small beginnings. Today, the LTTE ships communicate with a land based inmarsat in Sri Lanka. The LTTE ships play a vital role in supplying explosives, arms, ammunition and other war related material to the theater of war. The LTTE deep sea going operations began in 1984 after the purchase of Cholan from Singapore. Hitherto, the LTTE had only a naval capability to shuttle between India and Sri Lanka and a capacity to charter vessels. To finalize the Cholan purchase, Prabhakaran personally visited Singapore and Malaysia. During this period, the LTTE was also building a vessel called Kadalpura on the Kerala coast ***(note-30)***. Soranalingam, a double engineer, with expertise in aircraft/airframe and marine engineering supervised the construction ***(note-31)***. From 1985 onwards, the LTTE developed its fleet rapidly by actively purchasing vessels.

Tamil insurgents had decided to purchase their own vessels after experiencing difficulties of chartering vessels. From 1983 to 1985, they lost into the hands of authorities, three vessels carrying significant consignments. In Salonika, Greece, a Liberian registered plane with a load of arms, in Ras Garib, Egypt, the ship IVYB with two and a half tonnes of armaments ran aground, and in Madras, Palavan was seized with Chinese weapons sold out of Hong Kong by Alexander Urban, a Czech born Australian operating out of Singapore. Tamil militants have purchased explosives and weapons from a wide variety of sources - governments, from North Korea to Myanmar and the Ukraine, and from middlemen operating from Europe to Asia and the Middle East. Intelligence agencies with a global reach continue to monitor LTTE shipping activity quite closely but operationally could detect or prevent less than 20% of the weapon consignments from reaching the target. In fact, Illyana, an LTTE ship that unloaded weapons off Mulativu in October 1987, was monitored by Indian vessels entering the Rangoon harbor. Similarly Indian submarines, ships and aircraft's have tracked LTTE ships over the years. Aware of this, LTTE has yet managed to keep most of its shipping fleet intact. The deceptive shipping operations, indigenously developed, avoids detection and surveillance.

Yahata transporting weapons and explosives changed its name to Ahat by painting off the first and the last letters of the ship's name upon nearing the South Asian wars. After the LTTE lost Tamil Nadu as a semi-covert base in late 1987, the LTTE established a permanent naval base in Twante, an island off Myanmar, until late 1995. This was vital, because a transshipment point, determines sound logistics to security. While operating out of Myanmar, the LTTE also used Thailand, particularly the Pukhet area, as a back up base. Today, a bulk of LTTE shipping activity is carried out of South East Asia. The LTTE will always need a naval base in South Asia or South East Asia for its operations in the Central

Indian Ocean Region. For generating revenue, the ships also transports fertilizer, timber, flour, rice paddy, sugar, cement and other commercial goods ***(note-32)***. During the PA-LTTE peace talks, there were three shipments. The ship Sweene transported 50 tons of TNT and 10 tons of RDX purchased from a chemical plant from Nicholave, a Black Sea port in the Ukraine. Only 300 to 400 kg of this quantity was used in early 1996 to devastate the heart of Colombo's financial district by the LTTE. Similarly, a consignment of SAM-7s procured from Cambodia via Thailand reached Sri Lanka. This was the most expensive military cargo, the LTTE had ever transported. On board was Padmanathan himself. The details of the third consignment are not yet known. To save high registration costs, the ships are registered in the flag giver countries of Panama, Honduras and Liberia, affectionately known as "Pan-ho-lib." The unchecked expansion of the LTTE fleet has implications for regional and international security. From late 1983 to mid 1987, it was a belief shared by Sri Lankan defense, security and intelligence official that as long as India was used as an external base by the Sri Lankan Tamil militant groups, it would be impossible to destroy let alone pressurize the LTTE ***(note-33)***. During that formative period, the LTTE, was dependent largely on Tamil Nadu for its supplies to northern Sri Lanka. After the decline of official support from India, the LTTE has successfully replicated that network internationally. Instead of an hour long speed boat across the Palk Straits, deep sea going ships transport supplies procured throughout the world for the LTTE.

Evolution of the LTTE

With the expansion of the LTTE network overseas, the LTTE domestic structure has grown in strength and sophistication ***(note-34)***. But, some features of the LTTE never changed. Despite several offers for international mediation and attractive propositions both by India and Sri Lanka to resolve the political question, the LTTE remained rigid in its stand on Tamil Eelam. In many ways, the LTTE did not evolve but revolved. At the heart of it was Prabhakaran, an innovative, calculating and a ruthless military genius. Although, he subsequently developed political sophistication, he never compromised his faith in violence as a means to reach a political goal. Unlike most other groups, the LTTE began as a military organization but in time developed the political structures. Like most revolutionary movements of today, the LTTE is not a political organization that developed a military capability. History has shown that it is a near impossibility for organizations that are inherently militant to enter the political mainstream.

The leadership of such organizations think and act primarily militarily and secondarily politically. By virtue of their structural compulsions, such organizations prefer to fight continuously and win militarily. Such organizations feel uncomfortable to compete in a political environment. At leadership level, Prabhakaran maintains tight control. He is the final authority on each and every major issue. Prabhakaran's decision has always gone unchallenged. If Prabhakaran is killed, will the LTTE die? Examining similar organizations, particularly the capability of their middle level leadership, after the death or arrest of their senior leaders, provide a vital clue. Did the JVP or the Sndero Luminoso die after the death of Wijeweera or the capture of Guzman? ***(note-35)*** Although the death of Prabhakaran will be a massive blow to the LTTE, the middle level leadership of the LTTE is equally or more motivated than its senior level leadership. History shows that organizations like the LTTE cannot be easily eradicated. Despite their inability to meet their avowed goals and the massive suffering they have brought upon the Tamil public, segments of the Tamil people still believe in them and support them. For some, particularly for those who had lost a loved one during an ethnic riot or killed by a soldier, Prabhakaran is a demi-god.

As much as the moderate Tamil politicians have failed, successive governments in Colombo have not done their best for Sri Lanka. Even the best of Sri Lankan leaders have faltered. Colombo has failed to understand the aspirations of the Tamil people, the equation between the Tamil insurgents and the Tamil public, and finally, the importance of non military dimensions of counter insurgency. These dynamics have also impeded the government from dampening the Sri Lankan Tamil insurgent - Diaspora link. Governments have miserably failed to develop and implement nonmilitary strategies primarily counter propaganda among the Diaspora and in the LTTE dominated areas of the northeast. To what degree has the Diaspora helped the LTTE to become resilient? The expansion of the Diaspora, the backbone of LTTE finance generation, has helped the LTTE to develop its range of contacts for procuring weapons too. What will be the outcome of allowing a Diaspora to expand and root in this manner? Will the LTTE become more confident and less amenable towards negotiation? The expansion of the LTTE network overseas has brought them closer in contact with other insurgent groups. The LTTE has developed ideological, financial and technological linkages with other insurgent groups. Technologically, the LTTE has established links with the Assamese ULFA, Punjabi Sikh insurgents, Andhara Peoples War Group, the Kashmir mujahidin and several groups within and outside the region. Such groups exchange and purchase weaponry from diverse sources thereby contravening the established international arms control conventions and agreements. As insurgent group develop their structures to raise funds in one location, operate from another location and fight in a third location, law enforcement agencies of governments are constrained from conducting extra-territorial operations.

Destabilizing Force?

Is the LTTE a destabilizing force in South Asia? Does LTTE interaction with foreign insurgent groups contribute to the instability and insecurity of nation-states beyond Sri Lanka? The region is fed from West, Central and South East Asia and Europe by small arms. In 1994, 50 tones of TNT and 10 tones of RDX were sold by a chemical plant in Ukraine to the LTTE. Did the LTTE share a fraction of these explosives with their South East

Asian and South Asian counterparts? In 1995, a consignment of Chinese manufactured Surface to Air Missiles were sold by a group of corrupt Cambodian generals across the Cambodian - Thai border with the knowledge of a section of the corrupt Thai military. The LTTE as well as Khun Sa's Mong Tai Army had access to the sophisticated Thai and Cambodian arms markets. While the arms pipeline of the semi-covert multi-national anti-Soviet Afghan campaign continues to feed South Asia the LTTE has established relations with Gulbaddin Hekmatiyar's Hezbi-Islami ***(note-36)***. The solidarity between insurgent groups was best expressed when a Sikh insurgent group in Germany collected money for the family of Dhanu, the assassin of Rajiv Gandhi. The Sikh's claimed openly, "We have killed the mother, and you the son." The LTTE has also established links with at least 21 Tamil Nadu separatist groups. Although, these groups have only an electoral base of three million out of 60 million Tamils in India, if members of these groups are sufficiently motivated, politically and militarily trained, the damage they could do in Tamil Nadu is significant. Some of these groups are ***(note-37)***:

(1) Tamil National Retrieval Force
(2) Peoples War Group
(3) Liberation Cuckoos
(4) Peasants and Peoples Party
(5) MGR Anna Dravida Munethra Kalaham of Thirunavakarasu
(6) Tamil National Movement of Nedumaran
(7) Indian Peoples Party
(8) Center for the Campaign of Tamil Education
(9) Thaliai Nagar Tamil Society
(10) Movement of the Educated Front
(11) Tamil Nadu Peoples Movement
(12) Thileepan Society
(13) Peoples Education Center
(14) Tamil Nadu Socialist Party
(15) Republic Party of India
(16) Peoples Democratic Youth Front

(17) Liberation Organization of the Oppressed People
(18) World Peoples Progressive Front
(19) Human Rights Organization
(20) Organization for Social History
(21) Marxist Periyar Socialist Party

Today, the LTTE is looking beyond India and South Asia. But the links established by the LTTE in Asia is not fully known. The security and intelligence cooperation between the Sri Lankan and other agencies in the region has not been adequately developed. In 1995, western intelligence and security agencies received information that the LTTE had established links with FARC (Revolutionary Armed Forces of Colombia), a powerful Colombian insurgent group dealing in narcotics. In fact, it was believed that for the first time the LTTE had purchased vessels that could cross the Atlantic or the Pacific and reach Latin America. Although the LTTE has exchanged and procured weapons from a number of insurgent groups including the Khmer Rough and maintained links with South Africa's ANCL, Namibia's SWAPO and Eritira-Ethiopia's EPLF and TPLF, very little is known about its Middle Eastern connections, except for the fact that Tamil insurgents had trained at least in Lebanon with Fatah, the militant wing of the PLO and in the Syrian controlled Bekka Valley with PFLP. At these training camps, Tamil groups came into contact with a number of other groups, including the Japanese Red Army and the Kurdish PKK operating from Turkey.

The LTTE has also the potential to develop close operational cooperation with the Brotherhood through its links with the Afghan mujahidin and the Kashmiri mujahidin, two groups with which LTTE has had substantial technological links. Interestingly, the Muslim Brotherhood and its South Asian counter part Jamaati Islami sponsor wars of Islamic revival from Algeria to Egypt, Sudan to Saudi Arabia, Bosnia to Chechnya, Afghanistan to Kashmir, and Central Asia to Mindanao in the Philippines. International Security Implications Internationally, the LTTE has not only been active politically and economically. Their extensive political and economic presence has enabled them to be militarily active as well. The LTTE understood quite early that in order to expand their political and economic powerbase, they will have to strengthen their legal as well as extralegal capability outside Sri Lanka. Although small in number, the LTTE has assassinated Tamils in Europe, North America and in South Asia. Today, at least the law enforcement agencies of three European governments particularly prohibit Sri Lankan Tamils from carrying weapons on themselves. Today, the main centers of LTTE activity are in London and Paris for Europe and New Jersey and Toronto for North America. The key propaganda centers using computers primarily the information super highway are in Texas (USA) and Norway. Although the LTTE has an international secretariat located on Katherine Road in London, the LTTE has decentralized much of its international activities and operations since 1991. The decentralization was due to the pressure placed on the LTTE by Britain soon after the Rajiv Gandhi assassination in May 1991.

After the assassination, RAW stepped up surveillance on LTTE international operations. Aggressive lobbying by diplomats of the Indian foreign office and operatives of the RAW, India's premier external intelligence agency, led to the deportation of Sathasivam Krishnaswamy alias Kittu, the charismatic one legged one time Jaffna commander from London to Switzerland. The stepping up of surveillance by European security and intelligence agencies particularly at the request of the US on insurgent groups from the Middle East and the Kurdish PKK has made it difficult for the LTTE to sustain many of its operations in the West. As a consequence, the LTTE shifted most of its activities out of Britain. When Indian foreign service and intelligence service personnel began to mount pressure on the western government, the LTTE began to spread into Asia. Network's Implications Today, the LTTE has established offices and cells in over 38 countries, the latest being in Japan, South Africa and Botswana. For the survival of the LTTE, it is necessary for them to expand globally, because the LTTE had lost its most important external base of Tamil Nadu after the assassination of Rajiv Gandhi. Instead of LTTE speed boats shuttling between India and Sri Lanka for its supplies, today the LTTE ships navigate internationally bringing supplies to feed its fighting machinery. In many ways, the network developed by the LTTE over the years in India has been replicated, developed and sustained globally.

From about 1992, the LTTE has been shifting its international operations from Western Europe to Scandinavia, Eastern Europe and to South East Asia. From about 1995, based on information that Western operatives had gathered, the LTTE operations in the US as well as Canada has come under close scrutiny. While shifting their activities out of the North Atlantic area, the LTTE has also made attempts to win over key individuals in Western governments. As North America and Europe is so vital to the LTTE, they have hired some of the best lawyers, public relations agencies and lobbied political leaders into supporting them. In Canada when the LTTE leader Suresh was arrested for extortion and collecting money to procure weapons, the LTTE hired some of the finest lawyers and arranged for Western academics who sympathized with their cause to justify before the Canadian court that the LTTE is not a terrorist but a liberation movement. When the US was moving the anti-terrorism legislation that will affect LTTE activities in the US, a reputed public relations firm in the US was consulted by the LTTE to counter lobby the bill. LTTE manipulated Tamil communities from Canada to Australia have campaigned for host country political leaders with the hope that they will support the Tamil cause once in power.

The shift from West to East, particularly to South East Asia and the Far East has enabled the LTTE to grow in the Asia-Pacific region. In addition to the naval base in Twante, the LTTE also trained members of the Tamil National Retrieval Force, a high profile Indian Tamil secessionist group, and dispatched them to India. Under pressure from the Sri Lankan government, the military junta in Myanmar forced the LTTE to vacate Twante by

January 1996. The LTTE also developed difficulties of continuing their training in an island off Malaysia. This training, carried out in absolute secrecy, called "Singapore training" had helped the LTTE to compliment the RAW training in Vishakhapattnam. The LTTE had hired former Norwegian naval personnel to train LTTE cadres in underwater activities in the diving school. Meanwhile, the LTTE also developed a base in an island off Pukhet in Thailand. Surveillance in this area by RAW led an Indian submarine to mount surveillance on an LTTE ship Horizon operating under the name of Julex Comex 3 transporting weapons to Sri Lanka via Pukhet. Julex Comex 3 was destroyed near the Sri Lankan **coast of Mualtivu in early 1996.**

Fighting the network

Government of Sri Lanka has neither developed a systematic plan nor the organization to cripple the backbone of this network. The backbone, which is political propaganda, is aimed at building support for the creation of a separate state, the LTTE as an organization and Prabhakaran as its leader. Since mid 1986, the government has begun to reflect on the network and fight the network. Strategically, LTTE procurement operations can be restrained by generating an excellent counter propaganda network. Tactically, counter propaganda should be conducted with the support of Sri Lankans living overseas (individually or through their associations) by the Sri Lankan foreign missions ***(note-38)***. For this, Sri Lanka's classical foreign policy role of liaison with governments must change. Sri Lanka must aim for an innovative foreign policy to meet the current challenges and future threats. At least 40% of the foreign policy budget and 40 % of the time of Sri Lankan diplomats should be geared to fighting LTTE propaganda and building support among Sri Lankan and foreign governments against the LTTE. This has not happened primarily due to two reasons. First, policy and decision makers of the Government of Sri Lanka has not fully recognised the LTTE threat stemming from overseas. Many are not even aware that one out of every five

Sri Lankan Tamils, live overseas. Even, well traveled Sri Lankan diplomats see only a part of that threat. They see it individually and not collectively - often country wise, at best by region, very few the bigger global picture. It is because the Ministry of Defence or the Ministry of Foreign Affairs has not yet conducted a comprehensive study on the LTTE international network and developed a corresponding counter strategy. Towards this end an interministerial committee for defence and foreign affairs has been proposed ***(note-39)***.

The committee, if formed will (a) assess the threat, (b) review government progress, and (c) task relevant agencies to produce and disseminate counter propaganda ***(note-40)***. Creating an interministerial operations room to monitor and rapidly respond to LTTE international procurement, funding, and propaganda has also been proposed ***(note-41)***. Second, Sri Lankan diplomats have not been trained to conduct counter propaganda by personnel drawn from the Directorate of Military Intelligence and the National Intelligence Bureau. Although proposed, the Bandaranaike International Diplomatic Training Institute, established in early 1996, has yet to educate Sri Lankan diplomats on the LTTE history, organization, and operation. Most Sri Lankan diplomats are not aware that EROS has two factions. The EROS Raji Shankar faction support the government and the EROS Balkumar faction work with the LTTE. Sri Lankan diplomats cannot be expected to play a critical role without a thorough grounding in terrorism. If this is accomplished, Sri Lankan diplomats can play a leading role in building international support to fight terrorism, not only in South Asia but, throughout the word.

Government Response

The lack of international and regional interagency and security cooperation has brought about this predicament. Sri Lankan agencies have been weak in their efforts to develop frontline intelligence on the LTTE international as well as the domestic operations. The lack of political commitment to embark on high risk operations both overseas and domestic is seen as a major impediment to weakening the LTTE. At a military level, the government forces continue to fight an unconventional war, in a conventional mode. The need to transform the national security doctrine, training and weaponry to meet the growing internal threat has been long felt. But, to date a bulk of Sri Lankan troops are being trained to fight across clear battle lines. The pace at which, the counter insurgency component is being developed, is slow and inadequate to meet the growing threat. Further, the government continues to chase the military option. Government has failed to expand its activities in the non-military counter-insurgency spectrum. The government has failed to develop the political, socio-economic and international dimensions of counter insurgency. This has been largely due to the inability of the national security apparatus to integrate the military and non-military dimensions of insurgency. The development of an integrated and a unified strategy is seen as a major requirement.

Bringing the civilian and military branches to work together in the recently recovered Jaffna peninsula has met with internal difficulties. Many believe that the postings to the north of public officials are based on political colour or as a punishment transfer. On the contrary, the most able and the most dedicated public officials must be posted to the north. The militarily recovered north will be lost if the support of the Tamil public cannot be secured politically and economically. The half a million Tamils in the peninsula influence at least two hundred thousand Tamiils living overseas. At a political level, the government has failed to develop and implement political strategies to provide an alternative path to the Tamil people from being sucked into the gun culture. The package is attractive to many Tamils but even they question whether it will see the light of day? What is required is not grand plans but immediate measures to alleviate the suffering of the people of the northeast. The domestic Tamils continuously grade the genuine sincerity of the government's attitude towards resolving the current ethnic crisis. The international Tamil community reacts both according to the response of their kith and kin in Sri Lanka and to the plea of the LTTE. These are the very dynamics the government has failed to shift. As long as the staus-quo remain, the exodus of the Tamils from Sri Lanka should come as no surprise. If the insurgency continues more people will join the exodus. The alternative is an unhappy one, often a traumatic one. One generation has already seen and become influenced by nothing but war, anti-government and pro-LTTE propaganda, and anti-Sinhala and pro-Tamil nationalist views. A boy or a girl who was born in 1970, would have heard only of violence against the Tamils since he was ten years old. By the age of 15, he would have witnessed violence. By the time he reached 25, he or a member of his immediate or greater family would have experienced violence. Had the compulsions not driven him towards insurgency by that time, he would have actively or passively suffered from the day to day consequences of Eelam War I, II and III. One generation, has been completely wasted by war. The Sri Lankan political leaders and the bureaucrats have not done their best to end war in Sri Lanka.

Domestic Response

There has been no marked response of the non-governmental community to the internationalization of the Sri Lankan Tamil conflict. It has been, more or less, an extension of their attitude to the domestic developments. Some question whether they have been numbed by war. Others characterize this as a very Sri Lankan attitude. The non-governmental community - commercial, social and religious leaders, and academics, scholars and media personnel - has not realized that they have a major role to play when the security of their country is at stake. Economic diplomacy as a tool in conflict resolution is gathering momentum throughout the world. Economics can build broken bridges. Economics cut across ethnicity and religiosity. For ethnic and religious based conflicts, military solutions are increasingly seen as temporary solutions. Economics offer permanent solutions. Entrepreneurs and other business leaders can pressurize governments, communities and even groups committed to violence to end war. Most leaders of this category in Sri Lanka have decided to play a marginal or non role either in the prosecution of the war or in the peace and reconciliation process. In the Sri Lankan context, social and religious leaders have either not asserted their rights or they have chosen sides. They must be above ethnic polarization. What has adversely affected ethnic and religious communities are the very campaigns to advance their interests. A closer look at the plight of both the Tamil and the Sinhala communities demonstrate this fact. The era of working for "my community" is gone.

From Bosnia to Jaffna, religious and ethnic nationalisms have devastated people and their interests beyond comprehension. Social and religious leaders, must generate the will to rise above ethnicity and religiosity, in their endeavor to serve their people and their countries. There has been no effort by any of these leaders to address the Tamil Diaspora and lobby them into generating a negotiated settlement. A majority of Sri Lankan scholars and academics live in their ivory towers. They have not ventured out to capture the tragedy and trauma of the intermittent insurrections and analyze their causes. A vast majority of them have not made any in put to government policy. There is a dire need to fully assess the impact of the activities of the Sri Lankan Diaspora on the national security of Sri Lanka. This has escaped the minds of even the best of Sri Lankan scholars and academics. It is research that should be best conducted by independent academics and scholars because they would have greater insight into the Diaspora. Research in a nation like Sri Lanka, torn apart by conflict, must focus on dampening violence. The scholars and academics have a major obligation to contribute to the national harmony of their country if not the region and the world. Sinhalese and Tamil dons in particular, have not focused on the international implication of a domestic insurgency or the impact of the Diaspora on the domestic situation. Instead, many of them have continued to pursue their traditional disciplines of research and writing. Sri Lankan scholars and academics, instead of working on subjects that have no or little application to the national development of Sri Lanka, must conduct frontline research both on the ethnic conflict and its vicious byproduct - the insurgency. They must learn from other countries. Scholars and academics in the developed countries would work closely with the government. They will be formally and informally advising the government on the modifications required in their national policies to govern better and more effectively.

Working in isolation with data generated from newspaper accounts and published reports cannot produce first rate research. Field research is critical for penetrating analyses. While, departing from this monotonous tradition of working strictly in their disciplines and confined to their homes, libraries, departments and conferences, Sri Lankan scholars and academics must begin to explore ways and means of becoming more useful to the country. Some of the best minds in the government in the developed world are academics and scholars. They are not classical bureaucrats unable to meet the emerging challenges. They are innovative in their approach, multidisciplinary in their thinking and cross culturally amenable.

The mass media in Sri Lanka has improved dramatically in the recent years. They have been able to write accurate accounts of developments in the northeast and overseas on the ethnic issue. However, they have to move beyond reporting to analysis and advocacy. Although, media is not expected to take a rigid position and only report events as they occur, the media in a developing country has a more responsible role to play. The Sri Lankan media barons must reflect on this need . Sri Lankan news media has failed to educate the Sri Lankan public on terrorism. The average Sri Lankan is not alert to the destruction of terrorism. A civilian will often not be sensitized to alerting a law enforcement official to an unclaimed parcel in a public place. Similarly, the media has failed to educate them on the range of tools available in conflict management. The military option is only one road to combating rebellion. There are so many rebellions that have been resolved by negotiations. They have to be brought to light as well. The media, at the turn of the twentieth century, has role to guide leaders and lobby the public.

Peace Process

Organizations committed to peace have mushroomed in Colombo in the recent decade. Unfortunately, the focus of the peace industry has been "peace out of context." The leaders and members of these organizations have virtually no knowledge of the developments in the northeast. Therefore, they are vulnerable to manipulation by agents of insurgents or by insurgent propaganda. Many of these organizations have been infiltrated by other interest groups too. To retain their credibility, these groups must be politically neutral. To project their sincerity and commitment, they must work at the source of violence. Those leaders and members who are truly committed to peace must realize that being a peace activist is as risky as being a law enforcement officer. In context, the peace activists, have to venture out of Colombo and work in the war-zone, in the border villages, and in areas vulnerable to disruption. Staging demonstrations, rallies, marches and conferences, in the capital of Colombo, will not help. It will only make the government harden their stand towards war and advocate war as a strategy towards peace. Genuinely committed peace activists have to travel and live in the war zone, meet insurgent leaders and stress the importance of peace to them. They have to meet the parents, whose children have been committed to violence, to dissuade them from doing so. Similarly, they should campaign to move the government into bringing about policies of equality. The bravest of the peace activists must play a role on the ground. They could facilitate prisoner exchange. They could dissuade combatants on both sides from refraining from fighting in build up areas that produce civilian casualties. The macro view of peace is broader. Peace groups should be able to bring the government and the LTTE to the negotiating table. They should be able to pressurize governments that permit the LTTE to function in their countries, to exercise pressure on the LTTE to negotiate. Peace groups must reinforce the dialogue and the commitment of both parties to peace by participation.

International Community's Response

The International community's response to transnational insurgency has been weak. The LTTE along with several other insurgent groups have established offices and cells throughout the world. Most of these offices engage in disseminating propaganda and collecting money. In most countries the LTTE would collect money for the purchase of armaments under the guise of supporting rehabilitation. The LTTE has organized over 30 rallies and demonstrations in 1994 and 1995 in the West, including in front of the White House in Washington DC and the UN in New York. Ironically, the placards hoisted included photographs of Prabhakaran, who has taken the lives of two heads of government. The US has played a leading role in the Middle East and since recently in Latin America to dampen terrorist activity. However, the US has played a key role only when it directly affected US security interests. Due to US interests in Turkey, Washington lobbied its European allies to close down Kurdish PKK offices in Europe, particularly after PKK firebombed Turkish diplomatic and tourist offices.

Similarly, the US extended assistance to the government in Peru after Sendero Luminoso began to deal in narcotics in a big way. The US, despite the poor human rights record of the Myanmar military junta, started supporting the military regime to fight the drug lords engaged in producing narcotics that is threatening US interests. US assistance to fight the LTTE has been small - the Sri Lankan government too has not lobbied the US government substantially to secure a high degree of US military, security and intelligence cooperation. However, the US has realized the emerging dangers of transnational terrorism. The Western world as a whole has suffered as a consequence of conflicts in the Middle East. With the recent developments in the Middle East, governments of the developing world are attaching a high priority to security. In the years ahead, antiterrorism legislation in countries of the developed world will make it difficult for groups like the LTTE to operate under the cover of political offices. However, the nature of terrorism is such that insurgent groups like the LTTE will develop new methods of operation to evade arrest.

The political dimension of insurgent groups have been equally hard to fight. How does a domestic government stop an insurgent group from transferring funds from a bank in Singapore to Dresden to buy explosives or from Westpack in Australia to a Swiss account to pay for an arms consignment? Modern insurgent groups are beginning to operate like multinational firms or like intelligence agencies with a global reach. Recent evidence confirm that the LTTE has manipulated a number of human rights groups in the West to supporting them. The LTTE has poured in money and requested its supporters to campaign for certain candidates in countries like Australia, England, India and Canada so that in the event they come into power, the LTTE could use them to advance LTTE goals. NGOs have been manipulated by the LTTE and their front organizations to pressurize the government. The LTTE has lobbied for the appointment of certain individuals who are pro LTTE to head the Sri Lanka NGO consortium.

Further, the LTTE has developed relationships with officials who determine the yearly aid package from Sri Lanka. The Paris Aid Group meeting has become a forum to lobby for and against aid in Sri Lanka both by the LTTE and government lobbyists. LTTE has also secured the support of a number of intellectuals in the West like Peter Schalk of Uppsala University and human rights lawyers like Karen Parker to support them. Many of them have expressed their support to the LTTE at several meetings. The LTTE has also gained excellent access to media organizations from the newspapers in Canada to the BBC in London. The LTTE has also gained access to some world leaders through powerful business friends and other connections. In the legislative and legal fronts, the international community is preparing to develop frameworks to regulate and dampen activities of groups like the LTTE. Individual governments are realizing and they ought to take action, either to step up surveillance or ban organizations with a transnational reach like the LTTE. Despite the fact that the LTTE is not a banned organization in Sri Lanka, the LTTE has been proscribed by two governments - India renewed its two yearly ban in May of 1996, and Malaysia indefinitely. In Switzerland and in at least another two European countries, LTTE activity has led governments to ban Sri Lankans from carrying weapons on them. Australia came close to banning the LTTE in 1995, but the unwillingness of Colombo to ban the LTTE in Sri Lanka, precluded the Canberra government from moving in that direction. This is a security paradox - the government in Colombo has to leave its doors open for the LTTE to enter the mainstream while fighting them. Several countries have revised their anti-terrorist legislation and others are in the process of reviewing their legislative loop holes.

The line between political action and military activity is very thin - this is a phenomenon that most political leaders both in the East and West have failed to understand. Many of the modern conflicts are ethnic or religion-oriented. Often they cannot be resolved militarily. Third party mediation is required because such culturally based conflicts are deep rooted and protracted. Is peace making a line in the non political spectrum of counter insurgency? Peace is the absence of war but interludes of peace as a strategy has been used both by the insurgents to regroup, rearm and retrain themselves and take on the state exploiting the element of surprise. Governments in the Asia-Pacific region believe that the LTTE is emerging as a major destabilizing force. As a group, the LTTE is at the cutting edge of technology. In Sri Lanka, the first rocket propelled grenade launcher was recovered from a LTTE camp. Similarly, night vision glasses were used for the first time in the Sri Lankan battlefield by the LTTE. The LTTE, at the forefront of insurgent technological innovation, has gained mastery in the use of dual technology. Before the Sri Lankan military, the LTTE purchased Global Positioning Satellite systems, to accurately target its projectiles. The LTTE also used a land based satellite system to communicate with its overseas cadres. The LTTE has used the world wide web and the internet to establish a sophisticated state-of-the-art propaganda as well as a communication system within its members and supporters. LTTE suicide bombers have been trained both in France and in Britain to fly light aircraft. These ultralights do not carry sufficient metal for radar detection. Further, they could take off from a short runway. It is likely that these aircraft laden with explosives will be used to take vital economic, political and military targets, reminiscent of the Kamikazis ***(note- 42)***. In many ways, the technology generated by the LTTE has been a model for many other groups. There has been technology transfer or technology emulation.

Today, suicide bomb technology is used by the Hamas, Algerian FIS, Kurdish PKK and the Punjabi Sikh insurgents. The LTTE body suit is more advanced than the body suits used by any of the other groups. The Western agencies watch a possible transfer of suicide technology from the LTTE particularly to the Middle Eastern groups, where the suicide bomb technology is still very rudimentary compared to their South Asian counterparts. Can the LTTE conduct a suicide strike for another militant group for ideological or financial reasons? Although the LTTE has not conducted significant military strikes outside Sri Lanka and India, it has the potential to do so. The LTTE has a worldwide reach and a worldwide presence. The LTTE has assassinated a handful of opponents in Switzerland, France, Germany, Britain and in Canada. Although it has not yet conducted transnational terrorist strikes to the scale of the Palestinian, Armenian, Kurdish and other Middle Eastern groups, it has the potential to do so. The LTTE arms purchasing operations to finance generation projects can become the model for some groups. To combat groups like the LTTE new security structures will have to be developed. The idea of developing transnational forces to combat transnational terrorism is fast becoming one of the post-Cold war security imperatives. Considering the recent organizational and operational developments, is the LTTE a destabilizing force in the

South Asian region? Is the LTTE a destabilizing force in the rest of Asia Pacific? Is the LTTE a destabilizing force internationally? Although the international community will never allow a major inter state war, the international community should realize that intrastate wars have significant spill over effects that can complicate regional and international security to a very high degree. The 21st century insurgent groups will be very different from the twentieth century insurgents. Until recently, technology doubled every 25 years. Today, technology doubles every year. If not regulated and controlled, insurgents empowered by subnational groups will begin to use technology the same way governments use them. After the end of the Cold War, the porosity of the boundaries has transformed the international system dramatically. Countries cannot live in isolation any more. What will ensure the security of a nation-state is not only internal stability but the stability of one's neighbor and the region. Therefore, security of the 21st century will have to be cooperative and collective and not isolationist and individual.

The LTTE in South East Asia with Special Focus on Thailand

Report prepared November 24, 2004

F. Rovik

Introduction

This report is assembled from information received from several newspaper articles, the SPUR news archive, Intelligence reports and from interviews made in Phuket in 3 – 18 November 2004.

Why LTTE and Thailand

Distance

There is only 2.200 kilometres from Thailand to Northern Sri Lanka.

Coastline

Thailand's long coastline, porous borders, modern infrastructure, corrupt officials and a history of gun-running since regional conflicts of the 1950s, make it an ideal location for weapons traders and buyers.

Experts say that some of the arms sold in Thailand are rusty left-overs from the Cambodian conflict, but brand-new weapons are also freely available, either smuggled from China or obtained illegally from legal manufactures. There are more than 10.000

trawlers and other vessels roaming the Thai seas. This makes it difficult to monitor weapon smuggling activities.

Corruption

The corruption is widespread in Thailand. During the visit to Phuket in November 2004 several business owners were interviewed and all of them talk about the corruption and extortion in the police. Corruption is a nuisance for the legitimate business owners, but corrupt police officers are a great asset to terrorist and criminals.

Corruption is a well documented problem in Thailand and substantial research[1] has been done. Needless to say the corruption problem is a problem for the fight against terrorism, narcotics and illegal activities.

LTTE and Thailand

LTTE has been active in Thailand for two decades and has used Thailand both to acquire weapons, training of cadres and a transit country for weapons smuggling. LTTE has established several front companies and has a broad net of contacts in shipping, military, police and arms dealers. The front companies includes shipping companies, trading firms, restaurants and hotels[2]

Jane's Intelligence Review said in May 2002 that despite the ceasefire declared in February in northern Sri Lanka, regional intelligence sources believe the LTTE is continuing to re-supply the Tigers' guerrilla army.

"While Cambodia is the hub of the LTTE's East Asia network, Thailand continues to serve as the most important country for trans-shipment of munitions and co-ordination of logistics," it said.

"Its excellent communications infrastructure, proximity to

former war zones in both Cambodia and Myanmar, and its western coastline facing the Bay of Bengal and Sri Lanka beyond have made Thailand the crucial interface between the LTTE's war and its relentless procurement efforts in the region."

LTTE has very limited support, if any, among Thai politicians or the public in general. The fact that they have operated in Thailand for so long is purely due to corruption and the Thai liberal policies.

LTTE front companies and sympathisers in Bangkok have provided an extensive logistics network. Munitions have moved not only through Phuket, but also Ranóng and Krabi on the Andaman cost, as well as Sattaship on the Gulf of Thailand.

In January 2000, Thai police seized a trawler near Ranong, carrying Carl Gustav rocket launchers. The incident, which was hushed up, involved a link-up among the LTTE, anti-Yangon Karen guerrillas and the Arakan Liberation Party. Intelligence sources[3] say LTTE has moved arms through Haadyai and Songkhia on the Gulf of Thailand after April 2000.

Thai Army Chief General Surayudh Chulanont claimed the Tigers were running front companies in Thailand as smokescreens for arms purchases[4].

LTTE operatives arrested in Thailand

Three LTTE operatives was arrested in the Ranong province in Thailand May 12th 2003. The arrested men were Sujit Gunapala (27), Sasiljaran Teverajah (27) and Satiepawan Arseawatap (34). They were arrested with 10 Glock pistols and three HK Mark 23 pistols. The LTTE operatives plead guilty and received in November 2003 a five years jail sentence.

Following the arrest 14 Thais were arrested, whereof 8 were police and military officers. They were believed to be in the same gun smuggling ring.

The weapons confiscated from the LTTE operatives in Thailand are similar to those used by the Norwegian Special Forces and SWAT teams around the world.

LTTE Weapons confiscated in Thailand

In 1998 a number of fishing vessels carrying weapons, mostly machine guns, were impounded in Thailand and at in least two cases were linked to the Tamil Tigers a Thai military source was quoted by the Kyodo News service.

LTTE and Phuket

The LTTE has been present in Phuket since the late 80's. In 1990, port authorities at Penang impounded the Sunbird, a LTTE commercial vessel, and seized diving and communication equipment and some ammunition. The Sunbird has called regularly in Phuket. When a LTTE base in Myanmar was closed in 1996 after protests from Colombo, the Thailand Andemans seaports became still more important. According to SLA Brigadier Sunil Tennakoon[5] the LTTE has been active in Phuket and costal waters along the Indian Ocean since 1996.

In December 1993 merchant vessel Yahata left Phuket with a large consignment of weapons destined for Sri Lanka. Krishnakumar "Kittu" Sathasivam, a close associate of LTTE supremo Vellupillai Prabhakaran, led the operation and when the Indian Navy intercepted the ship, Kittu blew it up and drowning along with several of his crew members.

The Cholakeri, a ship with a wooden hull transporting weapons to Sri Lanka, sank off the coast of Thailand due to excessive weight[6].

Lloyds list reported on March 26 2000 that the Tamil Tigers were operating a base on a island near Phuket and set up a shipping base in Thailand to smuggle arms and drugs after being forced out of Burma.

"Army Chief Surayud Chulanont has told reporters the military has known of LTTE operations in Southern Thailand for some time. The Bangkok Post reported that an Army Intelligence Unit had photographed Tamil rebels transferring weapons to the island of Koh racha Yai, 15 kilometres from Phuket on May 24 2000."[7]

Arrests in Phuket

July 3rd 2002 Thai Police arrested in the Muang district the Thai national Prachumphol Rangphung (30) and confiscated six rocket propelled grenades, two M-67 hand grenades and AK-47 bullets. It was believed the weapons were to be delivered to the LTTE or the rebels in Aceh Indonesia.

Norwegian LTTE Agent building Submarine in Phuket

Christy Reginold Lawrence was arrested the 9th April 2000 by the Phuket Marine Police. He was driving his 17 meter long speedboat loaded with food and petrol heading for international waters. When the police accompanied him to his shipyard Seacraft Co. Ltd. they found a half built mini submarine. The hull was 3,6 meters and the tail, which has a rudder and designed to hold a propeller was 1,6 meter long Total length 5,2 meters, capable of accommodating 2-3 persons.

The Thai police also discovered sophisticated sonar and GPS systems, satellite phones, combat training videos in Tamil, LTTE calendars and uniforms. Sri Lanka's ambassador to Thailand Karunatilaka Amunagama said the submarine was similar to one sized by Sri Lankan Government Forces from the LTTE in Jaffna in the early 1990's.

Lawrence was released on Bail put up by the Norwegian Government[8].

The LTTE agent Christy Reginold Lawrence was found guilty by the The Phuket Criminal Court. The Court imposed a fine of 6000 Bath on Christmas day 2000 and deported him to Norway.

Norwegian Ex-special Forces training the LTTE in Thailand.

Norwegian ex-Special Forces have provided underwater demolition training to the LTTE in Thailand. Norwegians living in Phuket has verified Norwegian divers were in Phuket at the time this training allegedly has taken place. However they could not confirm these divers has been in the Norwegian Special Forces.

Canadian Intelligence Services says in its commentary # 77 March 17, 2000 written by Dr. Peter Chalk[9]:

"A small island in the Andaman Sea also serves as an important LTTE naval base used to train the group's Sea Tiger Wing. It is alleged that Norwegian ex-special forces instruct LTTE frogmen at this base, providing particularly useful lessons in the techniques and tactics of underwater demolition."

The LTTE cadres in Thailand have used the skills learned from the Norwegian ex-special forces to sink several Sri Lankan Navy ships.

LTTE Weapons smuggling Leader in Thailand

Shanmugam Kumaran Tharmalingham aka Kumaran

Pathmanathan (49) (KP) He is a key LTTE leader in charge of weapons smuggling and believed to live in Thailand and Cambodia.

He is one of Interpol most wanted terrorists. Wanted for participation in terrorism and the murder of Prime Minister Rajiv Gandhi.

"With more than 20 passports to his name, and possessing the ability to pass himself off as a middle class Tamil, Kumaran travels widely. However Sri Lankan intelligence sources believe his main bases has been Singapore, Rangoon, Bangkok and, more recently, Johannesburg; he is alleged to have held various bank accounts in London, Frankfurt, Denmark, Athens and Australia"[10].

LTTE arms deals in the high Seas

The vice-governor of Phuket province, Manit Nattanasaen, said improved intelligence gathering was expected to net more arms smugglers.

"Phuket is just the channel for arms shipments and mostly the deals are done on the high seas," he said. "Now we are trying to find a more aggressive strategy on the seas."[11]

LTTE Co-operation with other Groups.

The LTTE has allegedly been cooperating with the Free Aceh Movement (GAM), New Mon State Party (NMSP), the Karen National Union (KNU), The Chittagong Hill Tract (CHT), and the Shan State Army (SSA).

We also know the LTTE has cooperated with Al-Qaeda and to LTTE instructors has helped in the training of their terrorists. The attack against the USS Cole shows how skilfully the Al-Qaeda has implemented the Sea Tigers tactics in their terrorist attacks. Soosai, the Commander of the Sea Tigers, the marine armed wing of the Liberation Tigers of Tamil Eelam told BBC's Frances Harrison that the terrorist group led by Osama bin Laden, the Al Qaeda had copied terrorist tactics from them[12]. According to Indian Intelligence reports in 1999 and 2000 the LTTE was monitoring and planning to attack Indian nuclear ålants in Southern India[13] together with Pakistani extremists.

LTTE and SAMS

We know the LTTE has been able to acquire several surface to air missiles and have successfully used several against the Sri Lankan air force. The SLA seized in June 1998 an IGLA launcher and two missiles during a search of a LTTE hideout in Mannar.

The LTTE also tried to buy this system in Laos in February 2003 from Rosboronexport. Anton Balasingham allegedly raised funds in Germany to buy the Russian rockets. In the Tamil communities he asked them to contribute to funds for a "special project". The "special project" is believed to be the Russian IGLA rocket system.

The IGLA man-portable surface-to-air missile system is designed to engage low-flying approaching and receding fixed/rotary aircraft and to ensure pin-point anti-aircraft protection of installations and units in the battlefield. The system comprises a tiring set, target designation aids, maintenance facilities, and training equipment. The firing set includes a 9M39 homing missile kept in a launch tube, a grip-stock launching mechanism, and a ground power supply source. The missile`s optical seeker contains a logic selection unit to enhance system's acquisition capability when engaging targets using IR decoys. A man-portable electronic plotting board serves as the target designator for the IGLA system. It acquires data from automated theatre-range AD control posts and displays location, direction and identity of aerial targets within a 12.5 km distance. The plotting board is able to track up to four targets. The system can be interfaced with an IFF interrogator.

Basic Characteristics

Targets types	fixed-wing aircraft, helicopters, cruise missiles
Engagement range, m	500 ... 5,200
Target hit altitude, m	10 ... 3,500
Max. target speed, m/s	400
Max launch preparation time, sec	13
Weapon combat weight, kg	17
Warhead explosive weight, kg	0.405 (plus remaining fuel, 0.6 ... 1.3)
Missile tube length, mm	1,700

LTTE and Laos

In Laos two Sri Lankan citizens found to be members of the LTTE, approached the representative of Russian state organisation 'Rosboronoexport'[14] in order to procure small arms, anti-aircraft missile complex 'IGLA, communication means and other types of military equipment. The LTTE approached the Russian company in Laos in February 2003.

The Russian authorities have brought this to the attention of the

Interior Ministry in Laos. The Russian ambassador to Sri Lanka Mikhail G. Karpov has given the passport number and the name of one of these men to the Sri Lanka Foreign Ministry.

LTTE and Cambodia

The first LTTE operations in Phnom Penh were run out of the Rani restaurant, whose upper story was a virtual arsenal. Downstairs, a secretary handled professionally forged passports and visas. The LTTE's primary arms buyer, Selvarajah Pathmanathan, T.S. Kumaran, was seen in Phom Phen in the mid-nineties.

The Rani restaurant is gone, but similar establishments have sprung up along Sisowath Quay in Phnom Penh. It is believed that about 50 LTTE cadres[15] are operating from Phnom Penh, smuggling arms through the Cambodian ports of Koh Kong and Sihanoukville.

LTTE and Myanmar

LTTE has been connected to narcotics trade in both Cambodia and Myanmar[16]. Dr. Peter Chalk comments on the LTTE and drugs in the Canadian Intelligence report[17]: "LTTE is in a particularly advantageous position to traffic narcotics thanks to the highly efficient international network it has developed to smuggle munitions around the world. Many of these arms routes pass either directly through or very close to, major drug producing and transit centres, including Burma, Thailand, Cambodia, southern China, Afghanistan and Pakistan.

Moreover, a fair amount of circumstantial evidence exists which suggests at least some sort of nexus between the LTTE and narcotics operations. The Mackenzie Institute has documented the arrests, worldwide, of several Tamils with links to militant organizations for drug running since the early 1980s, including V.

Manoharan, the LTTE's present International Chief.[18] Indeed after Manoharan signed a petition challenging the US designation of the LTTE as a terrorist group in 1997, INTERPOL disclosed that he had been imprisoned in France for two years for possession of heroin. Suspicions that the narcotics had been traded on behalf of the Tigers were subsequently raised after it was discovered that Prabhakaran had authorized LTTE France to pay a monthly salary to his family while he was in jail."

The institute of Peace and Conflict studies estimate the LTTE annually is smuggling 1000 kilo of narcotics. The main drugs involved are 'mandrax' (methaqualone) and heroin.[19]

Terror treat in Thailand

Australia and several European countries issued a terror warning in travelling to Thailand in 2002[20]. Thailand can become a terror target and a terror attack could significantly influence the revenues to the huge Thai tourism industry. The Muslim separatist groups in the south might also pose a treat. Thai police has arrested four suspected members of Jemaah Islamiya[21] implicated in a plan to bomb numerous targets in Thailand.

Due to this it should be in Thailand's self interest to fight the LTTE and other terrorist groups currently operating in Thailand. International experts[22] say Thailand must improve its security mindset. In November 2004 the US Department of Defence held an anti terror seminar in Phuket for 57 Thai Police officers.

Conclusion

The LTTE has an efficient logistical network in Thailand and well established contacts with weapons dealers, suppliers and corrupt officials. Their front companies operate within the legal framework and work as a smoke screen for their illegal activities.

Thailand has become a safe haven for wanted LTTE terrorist and little has been done to track those down. LTTE has cooperated with insurgency groups in the South East Asia that pose a treat to Thailand, India, Malaysia, Burma and Indonesia.

The Thailand government or Thai political groups **do not** endorse the LTTE or support their terrorist activities. The fact that the Thailand has become an important country for the LTTE procurement and smuggling of supplies and weapons is purely due to the personal greed from individuals, police and lower level military officers.

Thailand authority's negligence to stop the LTTE and other terrorism group's weapons smuggling has probably cost thousands of lives in neighbouring countries and in Sri Lanka.

Thailand's soft policies on terrorism might come back to haunt Thailand. Terror attacks against key tourist destinations in Thailand were planned in 2003 and the resent unrest in the South increases the probability for terrorist attacks.

In order to minimize the risk for terrorist attacks in Thailand and in Asia it is of utmost importance to crack down on corrupt and criminal elements within the Thai police, military and public officials. The Risk/reward factor seems today too beneficial to those who choose to assist the terrorist acquiring weapons and supplies in or through Thailand.

End notes

1. Corruption in Thailand by Helsinki University of Technology www.hut.fi/~mwarsta/Corruption_in_Thailand.pdf
2. Bertil Lintner, The Week, April 30 2000
3. Asiaweek, June 16, Vol 29, No. 23 by Anthony Davis
4. The Nation 13 June 2000
5. Reuters 12 January 1999

6. Asia Times September 25 2002, Dr Rohan Gunaratna, Senior Fellow, Center for the Study of Terrorism and Political Violence, University of St Andrews, Scotland. www.atimes.com/atimes/South_Asia/DI25Df05.html

7. Indian Express 5 June 2000

8. Police Captain Pailin Jamjamrat of Phuket Town Police Station (Nation June 7, 2000)

9. Canadian Intelligence service commentary #77 http://www.csis-scrs.gc.ca/eng/comment/com77_e.html

10.Dr. Peter Chalk, Canadian Security Intelligence Service, commentary No. 77, March 17, 2000

11.Agence France Press, July 29 2002 Journalist Sarah Stewart

12.Source: Lankaweb journalist Walter Jayawardhana http·//www.lankaweb.com/news/items02/131202-1.html

13.Source: Sri Lankan Government www.priu.gov.lk/news_update/Current_Affairs/ca200003/20000309LTTE_threatens_India.html

14.Russian state owned weapon exporter www.rusarm.ru

15.The Week, April 30 2000

16.LTTE linked to narcotics trade in Myanmar www.apcss.org/Conference/CR_ES/020219ES.htm

17.Canadian Intelligence Service, Dr. Peter Chalk; http://www.csis-scrs.gc.ca/eng/comment/com77_e.html

18.Davis, "Tiger International"; "To Catch a Tiger," The Island, 25/05/98. One of the most recent apprehensions occurred in September 1998 when a 34-year-old Tamil was arrested at Maduari airport carrying 27 kilograms of heroin, worth approximately 54 million rupees. According to officials from the Indian customs Central Intelligence Unit, the quantity of heroin seized suggested that "very powerful people were involved in the deal." They also confirmed that they would be looking closely at possible LTTE involvement in the attempted smuggling operation. For further details see "Sri Lankan Carrying Rs. 54m. Worth of Heroin at Madurai Airport," The Island, 07/09/98.

19.Source: Institute of Peace and conflict studies, N. Manoharan

20.Source: BBC http://news.bbc.co.uk/2/hi/asia-pacific/2360209.

stm

21.CenterforDefenceInformationwww.cdi.org/friendlyversion/printversion.cfm?documentID=2391

22.Think Centre Asia: Thailand must improve it security mindset www.thinkcentreasia.org/opinions/improvesecurity.html

Eric the Viking: Deconstructing Solheim

Susantha Goonatilake

Sri Lanka (Sinhala, pronounced in Tamil as Eelam) in our long history has had many visitors. Some were received enthusiastically others thrust themselves unwelcome on us. In the category of the unwanted guests were various invaders, especially the marauding Portuguese, and less so the Dutch and British. The last invasion was the Indian experiment on destabilizing the country, presumably now abandoned.

We now have a visitor Eric Solheim from a small far away country Norway. Both our leading parties have embraced him as a savior as have separatists of all hues, specially the LTTE. This list includes presumed ex separatists like the TULF, and EPDP and TELO the latter two equally adept at handling guns and ensuring their "election". Our leaders, or for that matter our media, have said very little about this man Solheim.

Is he a man of simple good will? Or is he a new missionary to convert and subvert our country, as did earlier westerners? Is he as the Portuguese put it for the "spiritual and temporal conquest" of our country? Eric the pirate? In other words, is he a Western buccaneer in a priest's cassock. In those bad days of the Portuguese, there was no difference between the two.

"Deconstructing Solheim"

Searching for Solheim's name on the Internet gives many entries. (Surprising though, less entries than when I put "Goonatilake".) The entries unfortunately, are in Norwegian and my smattering of the language picked up when I taught in a Norwegian university was insufficient. I got a full-blooded Norwegian native to translate.

One prominent series of Internet sites had the title "Deconstructing Erik Solheim". These were unsavory exposures of the man that I asked my native guide to skip. I asked him to concentrate on the more respectable sites such as newspaper reports. And these public reports say some very interesting things about our savior.

He belongs to the small Sosialistik Venstreparti ("Socialist Left Party"). He admits that his party together with other parties inflates the number of its members, so as to get extra subsidies from the government. This would be like a public servant in Sri Lanka planting higher figures in a travel claim to illegally get extra money. This is an act that in Sri Lanka will bring in punishment, including dismissal. Solheim's expertise in manipulating figures would undoubtedly qualify him as an ideal election watcher in a future election. The LTTE under his guidance should then win even in Hambantota.

Solheim has supported the bombing of Serbia by NATO to help eliminate the dictator Slobodan Milosevic guilty among others of ethnic cleansing. He advocates a far more severe military solution for Serbia than Sri Lanka has adopted in its civil war. But Slobodan Milosevic's cruelties do not match those of Prbahakaran. No attacks on ancient religious institutions, no terrorist bombings like those of the Central Bank, no recruitment of child soldiers and no use of suicide bombers. But Solheim wants the elimination of Milosevic, while he embraces Prabhakaran in the jungle.

Solheim has also publicly called former American Secretary of State Kissinger a terrorist for his actions in Chile and Vietnam. Solheim says Kissinger should be charged as a war criminal at The Hague. But Kissinger's role in Chile led to the death of only a few in comparison with the larger number of deaths due to Prabhakaran. Prabhakaran was guilty of far more horrendous crimes than Pinochet's Chile.

Solheim instead should be suing the LTTE for two easily provable crimes against humanity. They are the ethnic cleansing of Jaffna of all Muslims and Sinhalese and the killing of the 600 policemen who surrendered to them as well as the killing of all the armed personnel at Mullativu. In addition, the Australian wife of Balasingham by recruiting child soldiers is guilty of child abuse. Crimes against humanity have no statute of limitations. They can also be pursued in third countries like Norway, witness the case of the Chilean dictator Pinochet. Solheim is said to be concerned about the spread of a racist party in Norway and wants to isolate it. But in Sri Lanka he befriends the most racist party, the LTTE.

Solheim bemoans that membership of political parties is coming down in Norway and that this is bad for democracy. But in Sri Lanka his government supports blatant brain washing of our population to believe in separatist falsehoods with his government's NGO money. This is a sneaky attack against both truth as well as democracy. When the journalist Frederica Jansz was dismissed from the Norwegian sponsored International Alert (IA) for telling the truth on Tiger fund raising in Norway, the pressure for her dismissal, had come from not only the LTTE but also the Norwegian government. Transparency is apparently only for Norwegians. Only fiction is good for us. The result is that a tin pot country like Norway now arrogates to itself imperial ambitions.

Solheim has also been against Norway joining the European Union (EU). He campaigned heavily against Norwegian entry when a referendum was held on it. But the EU today backs this political enemy of the European Union in his intervention in Sri Lanka. They consider him their representative. Apparently it is not his ideas that count for EU support but like the colonialists of yore, him being European. Europe *uber alles*, Hitler might have echoed.

But the real window to his mind is his recent autobiography. It gives an insight into this modern neocolonialist. The Norwegian embassy should translate this book into Sinhalese. It is the biggest aid they can give us. This book describes his escapades with pretty girls on his trips to Czechoslovakia. But, these are his private doings and should not concern us. But more interestingly he says, he used his own children in the media as part of his political image building. This is a contrast to politicians like Clinton who have gone to great efforts to hide their children from the public eye. But his use of his own family for profit does not stop there. He has had a divorce, again his private affair. But he had sold sordid details of his divorce to the gutter press for money. In Sri Lanka, the practice of the sensationalist press does not exist. So Sri Lankans might not fully understand this act.

But his misuse of others extends beyond his immediate family. His fellow parliamentarians and his own party men have reacted angrily to the one-sided distortions in his book. Members of his own party wanted the party chairman to correct his distortions. The Chairman diplomatically refused to comment. This book's severe failings, it was suggested would prevent him getting nominated for parliament again. What a convenient time, one would say, for Solheim to announce that he will not be going for reelection as he has done, and say that he will now devote his life to Sri Lanka's problem. This man who has misused his own children, makes money out of his divorce, lies about his own party members and is mistrusted by them is now to be entrusted with our future.

Some development in Sri Lanka has been helped by aid that Norway has given, say in places like Hambantota. But Norway has also hindered development by supporting the enemy. Money that could go into productive development has been diverted to destruction of lives and property. This is the direct result of Norwegian sponsorship of the LTTE. They gave artificial life both literally and metaphorically to the LTTE. They gave a new kidney to the secretly smuggled out Anton Balasingham, the Tiger theoretician. The latter's wife is an Australian nurse. Against all nursing norms, she became like one of the death doctors of Nazi Germany. She trained Tiger women and little children as suicide cadres. Her deeds are documented in LTTE propaganda films as well as in the British newspaper *The Independent*. With Solheim's peace talks, he has also given artificial oxygen to a dying group. Instead of giving us arms to militarily crush a dictator far more ruthless than Serbia's, his actions give the Tigers extra life.

The Norwegian constitution demands that all its officials know the Norwegian language, forbid their citizens to change their religion from Lutheranism and its government restricts the economic rights of the Saami people. Sri Lanka has no equivalent for these discriminatory acts. But now Norway wants to interfere in our country. For our good they say, in their missionary zeal. "White man, he talk with forked tongue".

Missionaries have come on other occasions to our country with alleged good hearts. The excuse was the supposed betterment of humanity. But this was the same motivation of Quisling, Hitler and Stalin. So was the Pope's motivation when he divided the world in 1492 and allowed for the genocidal crimes of the Spanish and the Portuguese.

In the two World Wars, there were signs everywhere in Western countries to look out for spies and to be careful of what they might hear. There are many Norwegians working in the country, many in the aid business. Some of them genuinely love this country. But in their misguided goodness, they might be working for the enemy; in the same manner that old missionaries were trying to "help" us by supporting the Portuguese, Dutch and the British conquests. Till this war is won, every Norwegian has to be seen as a potential spy. We must treat them politely, but look at them with suspicion.

As suspiciously as we should look at the latter day Viking interloper, Eric Solheim.

Chase the Norwegians! Bring in their Constitution.

The report into Kumar Rupesinghe's International Alert by a Norwegian Institute termed the type of "conflict resolution" Norway is doing now "a new form of imperialism." And, as Norway interferes, let us first learn about our new imperialist.

The Constitution of Norway says that the "Evangelical-Lutheran religion" is its "official religion" and that "inhabitants professing it are bound to bring up their children in the same". The Executive Power is vested in the King, who must be a member of the official religion and must "uphold and protect the same". The King's Council itself should have a majority of this sect. Senior state officials must speak Norwegian; and an international body can exercise on internal affairs on the country only with a prior "three-fourths majority" of parliament, but will "not" have the "power to alter the Constitution".

If that were Norwegian state theory, let us see her practices.

Norway put the Nazis' theory of selective breeding into practice, and like the Nazis sterilized people as racial policy these experiments continued up to 1994. These racist ideas gave rise to Quisling, the Norwegian leader under the Nazis. Even now, minority Lapps – Samis - suffer. Skulls robbed from their graves were used to show Samis as inferior. Young Sami children are encouraged to ignore their heritage and until very recently, were forbidden to learn their language at school. The use of the Sami language in the Church is banned. This year the Norwegian government ordered arbitrary reductions, up to 10% of reindeer herds - the livelihood of the Samis.

Let us now translate this Norwegian theory and practice to Sri Lanka.

Unlike today, Buddhism would be the State religion (now given only "foremost position"); there will be a ban on conversions; Chandrika Kumaratunga will be barred from baptizing her children; state officials must speak Sinhalese; foreign "mediation" will only be allowed after three-fourths of the parliament's approval; and will not be allowed for any discussion to alter the Constitution; Tamil children will not be allowed to pray in Tamil; and cultivation in Jaffna would be reduced this year by 10%.

It is with policies like this that this colonialist steps into our country.

Their present interference was preceded by a prior propaganda assault- PsyOps. Carefully selected, several university teachers were paid several times their salary by Norway to brainwash our youth. And those NGO employees who demonstrate against defeating the Tigers have links to Norwegian money.

The colonialist National Peace Council (NPC) is in the trenches with the new imperialists. Its chief organizer Ajit Rupasinghe, Kumar's brother marches with the LTTE in Geneva. When the troops were about to take Jaffna, Kumar Rupasinghe, a key backer of the NPC called on the army to stop. The NPC has propagated in foreign countries the traditional homelands hoax, at times calling for dismantling existing settlements. It's Media Director – read chief propagandist- Jehan Perera, at the time of the Indian incursion threatened Sri Lanka with dire consequences. He has several times questioned the need for our sovereignty and has called for a "shared sovereignty" and for "two near-states". Recently, his organization produced a completely unscientific survey – I saw the questionnaire - that falsely showed that the country wanted negotiations with the Tigers. They continuously brain wash the Sri Lankan public to accept a loss of sovereignty. The Norwegians would never allow any of this in their own country. In December, Jehan Perera was at a seminar organized by the German Cultural Institute on Sri Lankan history where many of his mistruths were implicitly under question. He did not say a single word.

Clear links between foreign funded so-called "Peace Groups" and Tigers and Tiger fronts are easy to establish.

This is not the first time we have been subject to Norwegian lies and interference. The then NORAD representative Arne Piertoff - who later formed Worldview Foundation - said in a Norwegian newspaper that in Sri Lanka three names were well regarded, the Buddha, Marx and himself. Thor Heyerdhal propagated the lie that the Buddha statues found in the Maldives - the heritage of the Sinhalese connection - were statues from the Easter Islands. And I had credible reports that their embassy or NORAD office in Delhi hid leaders of the Vikalpa group who were then waging their own war on behalf of Tamil separatism.

On the other hand, our ambassadors to Norway and Scandinavia have been "colorful" personalities. We had Neville Jayaweera who according to the BBC *Listener* had seen visions in the night; a condition I would have thought requires urgent psychiatric treatment. Instead he became head of a Christian propaganda unit in London and later our ambassador for Scandinavia. We had Lal Jayawardene in WIDER, Helsinki who left a deeply tarnished image, after sponsoring that book of partial fiction *Buddhism Betrayed* of Tambiah and whose wife Kumari Jayawardene was organizing a seminar at WIDER on alleged Sinhala chauvinism. (Source WIDER).

Our government (and opposition) is not like the sophisticated leaders of the Israelis and the Palestinians. In the last negotiations, they allowed the Tiger flag of the Cholas to fly side by side with the national flag. (Norwegians treat their national flag very properly). And when one of Chandrika's negotiating cronies was asked by the BBC of the problems at Elephant Pass, he said that it was no problem, because his "approach was scientific". And the negotiators at the last meeting with the LTTE were Uyangoda who is on written record justifying separatism and Charles Abeysekera whose NGO empires endorsed the fiction of traditional homelands.

With negotiators like this, we do not require Tigers as enemies.

From the beginning of the separatist war, Tamil migrants in Norway have pre brainwashed the Norwegians. Their University, Tromso already recognizes Eelam in their research grants. And, according to Tamil Net, which earlier leaked the Tiger agreement with Ranil; under Norwegian plans, ethnically cleansed land in the North will be left in Tigers' hand. Norwegians limit the Sami's use of their land but accept the completely fictional Tamil homelands.

After the Indian "Accord", the American Ambassador to Sri Lanka, James Spain said the Americans "still blame the Japanese, but ironically in Sri Lanka, the people do not blame India" And last week, a South Indian politician Subramaniam Swamy, aghast at our neo colonialism called for a halt to Norwegian interference.

Before coming here, the Norwegian Foreign Minister shook the blood stained hand of Balasingham of the LTTE, who is guilty of two easily provable crimes against humanity. They are the ethnic cleansing of Jaffna and the killing of the 600 policemen who surrendered to them, as well as of all the armed personnel at Mullativu. Instead of suing the Tigers like the Chilean dictator Pinochet, they now collaborate with it, putting on the Quisling mantle once again.

The Norwegian embassy should now make public, all those who got their money for ethnic "conflict resolution". They should announce whether - as being talked about - Norwegians are about to finance a new information technology facility for Kumar Rupasinghe. And, Foreign Ministry officials should also declare whether any NGO, they or their family is involved in, has received any Norwegian aid. This is a standard requirement in other countries to prevent possible conflicts of interest.

Courtesy: *Sunday Times*

Kissinger, Nobel Committee, Kissinginian Mutants, or how Norway became a Sanctuary for Terrorists

Mahinda Weerasinghe

With the publication of "The Trial of Henry Kissinger" by Christopher Hitchens, another violator of human rights is exposed; sorry, a human rights violator who is also a Nobel laureate. The work vividly portrays, how a super bureaucrat amasses power, cheats and manipulates his nation, and hoodwinks the world at large. The author remarks, "His single greatest achievement has been to get almost everybody to call him 'Doctor.' In the 70s, we recall the indispensable Dr. Kissinger's labours to achieve "peace with honour." Richard Nixon, surprisingly enough, "had only once, briefly and awkwardly, met Henry Kissinger in person," before he was awarded the top bureaucratic spot. His main qualification at that point in history for the job is that he leaked the Johnson administration's negotiating position with the North Vietnamese to the prospective president. Nixon used the information strategically to sabotage the peace negotiations. For that deceitful and unethical act the good doctor was well rewarded.

Bureaucrats such as Kissinger are never called to account. The President of USA appointed him, hence he is answerable solely to the President. The book illustrates the agonising repercussions when an unconstrained power thirsty bureaucrat grabs power. Most of us are under an illusion that politicians are the main culprits of the world. Yet in this information age the global citizen is becoming aware who really runs the ship of state. In democratic societies politicians are voted in, and if unsatisfactory, they're booted out, but mandarins who run the state machinery carry on regardless.

Nixon was found guilty and was expelled, but Kissinger just melted away un-sketched to a life of splendour. Indictments are piling up against him presently. Mass killings of populations in Indochina, collusion to mass murder and assassinations etc. etc. Surely isn't the doctor a Nobel laureate? Is it possible that his crimes against humanity went undetected at the time? Fact is, terror and mass death was inflicted on the Cambodian populace is a well-documented secret. It is said that as a result of his directives as many as 350,000 civilians in Laos, and 600,000 in Cambodia lost their lives. But then the Nobel Committee is wise - the reason why after Cambodia was bombed into the Stone Age, he was awarded the prize for "peace" and not the one for "war." In fact a mixed bag of characters had received this "prestigious" prize over the years. Among them we find, those who were earlier called terrorist such as Yasser Arafat and Menachem Begin. At least one who was a head of the Apartheid state, De Klerk, proselytisers such as Mother Teresa who was keen to get all Hindus to embrace the "true God." So how on earth did Dalai Lama end up in this category? It was given probably to teach China a bloody good lesson. Offering the prize to Mahatma Gandhi was never contemplated for obvious reasons. For at that point in history the Nobel committee totally agreed with Churchill, that he was just another "half naked Fakir." The global society is confused, and will soon query, is the Nobel Peace Committee, really a Noble one, or the handmaiden of the foreign office bureaucrats of Norway (called UD hereafter).

In order respond to this, we have to make a most subtle connection. We observe the well-known phenomenon such as in Kissinger's case. No matter who ascends to power, he also inherits the same intricate manipulative self-serving bureaucracy. Politicians, who are striving to make the system work, trying to implement this or that plan and make themselves popular, ultimately encounter a blank wall, which we term "bureaucracy." Surprisingly, we find a new mutation has occurred, among the bureaucratic species of Norway. UD bureaucrats has left the normal boundaries of conventional diplomacy and reached a new dimension of power and non-answerability. In order to grasp how this evolution came about we have to consider the special environment which exists in the country. Norway has a dilemma. It has loads of money. This flows out of pipes in the sea in the form of oil. Now here's the catch. According to Norwegian bureaucratic Pundits, this wealth must not be spent within the country because it will lead to hyperinflation. Infusion of too much money in to the hands of the ignorant masses will naturally make money as "valuable" as paper.

Norwegian politicians promise they will repair schools, help the old and the disabled, cut down the long hospital queues for the long suffering Norwegians, and even cut down taxes. But once in power, they water down their agendas. The result is schools are in disrepair, old and the disabled are neglected, pensioners are hardly able to make ends méet, hospital queues keeps growing. Vis-a-vis hospital queues, there are exceptions to the rule. Such as Anton Balasingham, spokesman of the racist terrorist group, fighting to create a ghetto state called Eelam in Sri Lanka. A non-Norwegian, he was allowed to skip the 3-year hospital queue courtesy of UD. What is to be done with this oil wealth was the quandary. Then a wise old bureaucrat in the UD got a 'brainwave. His idea was simple, daring, creative and most of all. profitable. Why not use these riches externally, hence without any impact on the Norwegian economy. I am sure you can guess by whom! Here we see the initial crawling of the peace industry. Norwegian people are blissfully ignorant how, millions are used for shuttle diplomacy to wine and dine and do other things necessary for themselves, and their terrorist friends in the name of "peace promotion." The genius of the plan lies in its non-answerability. No public to peep into its budgets, no need to seek approval from the masses for the expenditures. No need to seek a consensus from the people to speak to terrorist and murderers.

The rules of the game are set as they go along. Happily, they also pick and choose where to bring peace and harmony; such as corrupt and broken down Sri Lanka. As this is "sensitive work," all information is strictly confidential. UD's peace promotion activities in time have gone global. Thus this new species of bureaucrats came to hobnob with terrorist, ultra racist suicide bombers and have their rendezvous in thick jungle hideouts of murderers of prime ministers and presidents. There is an added momentum firing the growth of the peace industry. Earlier the white man went in search of conquest, colonisation and subjugation of backward nations for booty and plunder. Presently the colonies are hard to come by. It is hard to do that old trick of divide and rule, so the next best thing is to finance destabilisation. That is where the peace industry, human rights, NGOs and other scrounging groups get in on the bandwagon. Naturally during the colonial days there were no human rights. Come to think of it, no rights at all, when they were plundering these defenceless primitive hordes. Now we have such self-proclaimed European experts going round the globe to inspect and instruct these backward nations how to live in peace and harmony with their minorities. Gone are the days of the European gas chambers and pogroms of minorities.

Quite early, UD put its millions where its mouth is. To name a few of the countries the do gooders are trying to broker a peace - Haiti, Colombia, Sudan, Guatemala and obviously the Middle East where the famous Oslo process was set in motion. UD's boast of their non-colonial and un-imperialistic past. Not un-like Kissinger, their mentor, their working for arms control and detente, giving humanitarian aid and mediation. Emphasise is on being a "soft power" which has given them a formidable reputation. But disregard the adjective 'soft' and the real covert dreams of the UD becomes evident. In fact they do have an arms industry and whether terrorist get some of these arms after passing through second and third hands, history is sure to tell. The untold truth is that the UD bureaucracy stands alone today in getting to eat their pie and to keep it. They are not answerable to any mother's son for their actions. Certainly not to the Norwegian people. Presently they are the uncontested global arbiters of conflict. As the headlines of the Observer (Sri Lanka) reported once quoting Norwegian deputy foreign minister, "we have experience in solving the world's conflicts." What it essentially boils down to is, God has differentiated the nations at the moment of creation. There are the conflict solvers and the conflict creators, inspectors and monitors of the world and those need to be inspected and monitored. Indeed the good and the childish, or as the Jews would have it, the chosen people and the rest of the jokers. Let me break this down a little a bit further. Questions dealing with foreigners are split into two major bureaucracies.

The normal functions of the UD is basically the same as in any other country dealing with foreign affairs, and the UDI (foreigners office), the one controlling the life and destiny of any foreigner who wishes to enter Norway or reside in it. Split of the assignments is strategic. While one is involved with being a "soft power," the other one is exploiting all its bureaucratic might to make a red tape jungle for the third world foreigners. In the late 80s the Sri Lankan people showed their dissatisfaction of Norway for meddling in its affairs. By late 90s it has gone to the extent of burning the Norwegian flag and holding demonstrations outside the embassy in Colombo. Sri Lankans are unaware of the fact that Norwegian people are quite ignorant of Sri Lankan affairs and care less. Information concerning Sri Lanka is totally twisted by the terrorist supporting vested interest of Norway. Yet the Tamil terrorist-supporting alliance is negligible. The UD, elements in the UDI bureaucracy, a handful of politicians and the peace industry lobby (NGOs), the last again is also an affiliate of the UD. The LTTE terrorist penetrated the country using travel papers issued under the auspices of UDI starting the 80s. It is in the Embassy in Colombo that the two institutions, UD and UDI, merge.

The media has reported abuses, especially of the UDI. It's last head resigned recently, after the findings of incompetence by a commission. But the real misappropriations were not spelled out to the public. Norwegians still have not grasped how bureaucrats of these agencies operate. Sacking one of them is like removing a bucket of water from the sea. Criticising them is like pouring water on a duck's back - with zero effect. If we seam together the above subtle ingredients, a distinct covert pattern appears. It hints at how bureaucrats helped LTTE terrorists make Norway its sanctuary. Somehow I need to differentiate the vintage Kissinger from these new Kissinginian mutants, as there is a world of a difference in approach and rhetoric. Kissinger wished to be addressed as doctor, this species wish to be addressed as experts. He worked for "the balance of power," (crush those without it); these are working for human rights and minority rights, translated to the Sri Lankan experience, to create ethnically pure minorities with their ethnically clean racist ghetto states. Henry used raw military might on the unwilling Indo-Chinese people, whereas the power base of these mutants is money, aid money, the NGOs its army, and subtle manipulation its potency. Doctor only spoke with the high and mighty whereas these facilitators speak to the low and down trodden such as terrorist. He dined in fancy restaurants. These mandarins work low key and make their rendezvous in the jungle hideouts covertly. In fact, their media reporting style indicate why things have gone the way they did. When the terrorist Tigers attacked the civilian planes in Sri Lanka in July, according to the NRK (state run TV) it was termed a militant act. When a Basque terrorist left a bomb in the airport just a week later (but which did not kill or damage) it was declared a terrorist act. According to Herald Tribune (September 24), "the most precise word to describe a person or a group, who murders even one innocent civilian to send a political message is terrorist and not a militant."

UD with such fancy footwork probably believe it is cheating the world at large, but will eventually find they have cheated themselves. Indeed it is profitable to keep conflicts on the boil. Conflicts are the bread and butter of the NGOs (and UD), and business is presently booming. No conflicts, no business, no cosy jobs, no playing kingmakers. No playing the neo-colonial peace facilitators, no sway over the terrorised nations, indeed no badgering third-rate corrupt beggar nations such as Sri Lanka. Surely peace must have dawned at some place or other through such mediation? Not to Israelis or Palestinians who are at each other's throat like never before. Or observe how, the racist terrorists (militant to UD) bombed civilian planes in Colombo with impunity and we recognise the state of this "peace." Indeed peace may have not been achieved but suicide bombing has become fashionable. LTTE terrorist have even exported suicide bombing known how to Oasma bin Laden, according Times of India of 24 September. Then came the 11 September Islamic terrorist attack on US. Observe the strange situation.

UD adores one type of terrorist and hates another. USA is presently reaping the whirlwind sown through its financing of Islamic terrorists. History may well repeat this for Norway too for its covert buttressing of racist terrorist of Sri Lanka. As "nettavisen," a Norwegian web newspaper says in its Sept. 13 issue, and I quote "Norway is a Mecca for Terrorists." And as the chief of POT (translated as Police Surveillance Service) informs, he has worked a long time to get laws in place to forbid financing of terror from Norway. What he should have been doing instead is identifying the corrupt bureaucrats who helped make Norway a safe haven for terrorist. Truth like oil in water has a habit of surfacing. Kissinger's accountability is at hand. Terror co bureaucratic agents who never sought its people's approval will also be called to answer - ev I believe as far as the Sri Lankans are concerned, they are of the same view as the Americans. They do not wish to negotiate with terrorists, but only wish to eradicate them. And, don't be surprised if the terror price, oops I mean the "peace" prize is issued to one ambassador's terrorist friend in the Sri Lankan bush.

LTTE Child Combatants

Rohan Gunaratna

In defiance of mounting international opinion against the role of children in warfare, guerrillas and terrorists are increasingly using children in their military campaigns. As under-aged combatants are proving to be effective spies, couriers, suppliers as well as backup and frontline fighters, children in conflict-ridden areas are becoming a target for recruitment.

International and domestic conventions define childhood as life up to the age of 18. Currently, there is a debate as to whether compulsory or voluntary recruitment to the armed forces should be 15 or 18. Child rights activists are campaigning at international, national and local level to raise the age to 18. However, there is no international organization or mechanism either to regulate or lobby against guerrilla and terrorist organisations recruiting children to their ranks.

Child units have featured prominently in international and internal conflicts in recent years, serving both state and non-state forces in countries such as Liberia, Cambodia, Sudan, Guatemala, Myanmar. They featured in at least a third of the 50 odd internal conflicts that were ongoing in 1997, most of which have continued into 1988 and many with increasing intensity. Armed conflicts during the last decade left two million children killed, one million orphaned or separated, five million disabled, 10 million children killed, one million orphaned or separated, five million disabled, 10 million psychologically traumatised and 12 million homeless.

Cutting Edge

In the world's deadliest conflicts, children feature most prominently in the protracted guerrilla and terrorist campaign of Sri Lanka's Liberation Tigers of Tamil Eelam (LTTE). The United Nations Children's Fund (UNICEF) highlighted the Sri Lankan rebel group's practice of aiming its propaganda specifically at schoolchildren.

The LTTE is a leading-edge rebel group fighting for an independent Tamil mono-ethnic state in northeastern Sri Lanka. The LTTE - estimated to be 14,000-strong – employs adults and children as rank and file. Both male and female fighters participate in guerrilla and terrorist attacks against military, political, economic, religious and cultural targets.

Now in its 24th year of existence and 15th year of combat, the LTTE is assessed by the international security and intelligence community as the deadliest contemporary guerrilla terrorist group. It has built a tradition of senior personnel leading offensive operations and has a rapid turnover of new units. The LTTE is perhaps the world's first rebel group with cadres drawn from a younger age range. Sri Lanka's Directorate of Military Intelligence estimates that 60 per cent of LTTE fighters are bellow 18. Even if the figure is exaggerated, an assessment of the LTTE fighters that have been killed in combat reveal that 40 per cent of its fighting force are both males and females between nine and 18 years of age. Over the years, the combat efficiency, technological innovation, and leadership qualities of the LTTE have been integrated into the young fighting units.

Loyal to the Last

The Sri Lankan experience reveals that children are receptive to high levels of indoctrination, willing to engage in high risk operations and obedience. Modern weapons such as M16, AK-47 and Type 56 are light weight, easy to fire, and require minimum training. Conventionally trained soldier and policemen are also less likely to identify women and children as threats. In the Same way that the media and the legal system is sympathetic to children, humanitarian and human rights organisations reserve different rules for when dealing with a potential threat from this source. Such factors and conditions make the child a perfect target for guerilla and terrorist recruitment. Today, the LTTE deploys these units in direct combat against Sri Lankan troops both in Jaffna and Wanni in the north and Trincomalee and Batticaloa in the east. In addition to gathering first-rate intelligence and participating in ambushes, they also form the first wave of suicide groups, assaulting across the minefields and razor wire that encircle Sri Lankan military installations.

Origins of Child Cadres

After the ethnic riots of July 1983, sparked by an LTTE ambush of 13 soldiers, there was a massive exodus of civilians to India. The LTTE leader Velupillai Prabhakaran selected Basheer Kaka, an LTTE leader from the deep harbour city of Trincomalee to establish a training base in the state of Pondichery in India for recruits under 16. Initially, the child soldiers - affectionately referred to as "Tiger cubs" - received non-military training, mostly primary education and physical exercise. By early 1984, the nucleus of the LTTE Baby Brigade or Bakuts, was formed.

Until 1986, the LTTE had sufficient adult units in operation; as soon as a young recruit reached 16, he or she was put through the Tigers' standard grueling four-month training course. Many children from the Pondichery batch reached battle prominence. After the Pondichery stint, Karuna, a native of Batticaloa, received military training in Establishment 22, Chakrata, north of Dehra Dun. From 1984 onwards, Karuna rose through the ranks and assumed the mantle of District Commander for Batticaloa after the introduction of the Indian Peace Keeping Force (IPKF) to Sri

Lanka in July 1987.

Throughout, he displayed his loyalty to the LTTE leader Prabhakaran and showed a high level of commitment to the LTTE goal. With permission from Prabhakaran, he married an attractive LTTE female cadre Nira, and was thereafter relocated to the north to lead LTTE special groups in direct battle against the Sri Lankan forces. Several members of the Baby Brigade also served as bodyguards of Pottu Amman, the LTTE Chief of Intelligence responsible for planning the assassination of two world leaders. The LTTE began to seriously recruit women and children to its ranks only after it declared war against the 100,000 strong-IPKF in October 1987. Hitherto, the LTTE had trained only one batch of children in Pondichery in 1984 and one batch of women in Sirumalai, Tamil Nadu in 1985. The LTTE had to boost its rank and file to engage an overwhelming force in the India-LTTE war that lasted for two years. As an example, the Batticaloa 13th batch - trained in the jungles of Pondugalchenai, Pulipanchagal, comprised children under 15, some as young as nine years old. The only time that the LTTE engaged in forcible recruitment was just before and after the withdrawal of the IPKF, both to replenish its depleted ranks and to prepare for an impending offensive. After the March 1990 withdrawal and the resumption of hostilities between the LTTE and the Sri Lankan forces in June 1990, the LTTE continued to recruit women and children in unprecedented numbers. Today, a third of all LTTE recruits are women, and they serve in all units. Children too, serve everywhere except in leadership positions.

The child fighters were originally a part of the Baby Brigade commanded by Justin, a Pondichery-trained fighter. However, after 1987 the LTTE integrated children with other units to offset the heavy losses. Today, the overwhelming number of children in the fighting units has generated concern among many Tamils in Sri Lanka and overseas.

Since April 1995, some 60 per cent of LTTE personnel killed

in combat have been children. These trends are supported by, Olivichu, the LTTE monthly video release which announces its death toll. Unlike the government, the LTTE is prompt and accurate in announcing the death of its "martyrs". A study by a UK-based Sri Lankan researcher Dushy Ranatunge reveals that at least 60 per cent of the dead LTTE fighters are under 18 and are mostly girls and boys aged 10-16. Ranatunge also reveals that almost all of the casualties are from Batticaloa, but since the escalation in the fighting, the dead also include those from Jaffna. It is likely that the LTTE needs control of the Eastern Province to replenish both its supplies as well as its wastage in rank and file numbers.

Indoctrination

The LTTE focused on the politicisation of its people through propaganda (public events, leafleting, print media, radio, TV etc) to encourage them to support the LTTE campaign for an independent Tamil state. Almost all of the public events are attended by parading LTTE units. School bands play at the funerals of dead LTTE fighters and the LTTE has established spectacular memorial parks and beautiful gardens with monuments of its "martyr's." Striking features of these parks are the children's see-saws with toy automatic weapons mounted on the handles. During the heroes' week in October of each year, the LTTE invites families to attend the high-profile ceremonies in the graveyards of the "great heroes." The LTTE portrayed these functions as celebrations and the cemeteries as temples; attending children are welcomed and often leave with a strong sense of nationalism. The "great hero families" received a special status wherever the LTTE were in control. They paid no taxes, received preferential in job interviews, and were allocated special seats at all the public functions organised in LTTE-controlled areas.

Economically deprived families thus did not object to their children joining the LTTE.

"Sometimes, parents felt that they must let children go in order to be fed," according to UNICEF's Colombo representative Brita Ostberg, who is critical of LTTE's role. The LTTE has an unwritten rule that every family should give a son or daughter to the cause. Another feature that attracted the young minds to the LTTE was the glamour and the perceived respect it was paid by society. In the past, when a school teacher cycled in the narrow streets of the north, students would move to the side until he passed. Today, when a student who has joined the LTTE passes on a motorcycle or push cycle, the situation is reversed. Interestingly, the appearance of the young recruits was a strong factor in attracting youngsters to the movement. Tiger-striped uniforms, polished boots and automatic weapons acted as magnets to the children.

LTTE members regularly visited schools, addressed students of the need to participate in the "struggle" and screened films of their successful attacks against the Sri Lankan forces. Those fighters entrusted with indoctrination and recruitment would often ask that students supporting the struggle for independence raise their hand and, without giving them an opportunity to hesitate, would then drive them to a training camp. The LTTE system of maintaining everyone's records would prevent a teacher from refusing the entry of enlisted children to a classroom. In their book "Child Soldiers: The Role of Children in Armed Conflict" Guy Goodwin-Gill and Ilene Cohn (Oxford 1994) state: "Tamil children spend one or two hours per day out of school digging bunkers as a form of militarised civic duty and are eventually asked to join the LTTE. Enlistment is supposedly voluntary, meaning that no one is physically threatened. However, families are menaced with property confiscation or physical violence if they appear unwilling to contribute their sons for the cause." Other than projecting the military successes of the LTTE, a powerful image that attracted many youngsters to join the LTTE was the screening of films depicting Sri Lankan government atrocities. Although the state takes severe legal action against soldiers responsible for civilian atrocities, aerial bombing of LTTE public offices has damaged nearby churches, hospitals and schools. The LTTE has been partially successful in projecting these incidents as deliberate and calculated acts of genocide against the Tamil people.

In five years following the withdrawal of 100,000 IPKF personnel, the LTTE established its own administration in the Jaffna peninsula and in the Kilinochchi mainland. The Tamil Eelam Schools Board even introduced its own revised history. Separatist Tamil educationists, had a part to play in encouraging ethnic prejudice among children. The LTTE cultural section, headed by Puduvai Ratnadorai, supported the initiatives of the LTTE student wing - the Student Organisation of Liberation Tigers (SOLT) - giving a fresh impetus to its programs to build and sustain student support for the creation of an independent state. SOLT also set up branches overseas, producing an education syllabus and text books to teach Tamil and LTTE versions of history to all Tamil refugees, and also set up about 100 weekend schools, teaching traditional drama and dance, often with funding from host governments, local cultural and social bodies, and philanthropists.

Recruitment and Training

A typical unit of children is trained for four months in the jungle. Woken at 0500hrs they assemble, fall in line, and their leader raises the LTTE flag. Following this comes two hours of physical training, after which the recruits engage in weapon training, battle and field craft, and parade drill. During the rest of the afternoon time is spent both reading LTTE literature and performing more physical training. Lectures on communication, explosives and intelligence techniques continue into the evening. There is no communication between the camp and the children's homes during the training period.

There have occasions when parents have traveled even long distances, braving both Sri Lankan military and LTTE ambushes, in search of their children in LTTE jungle training camps. Having spent days waiting outside the camps for a glimpse of their children, parents have been sent back, told that the cadets have chosen not to meet them. During training, sleep and food are regulated to build endurance. Recruits receive crew-cuts to ensure that deserters may be easily identified. The LTTE code forbids liquor and sex and offenders are punished with death. Homosexuality, which also occurs, is a punishable offence.

The LTTE training curriculum is frequently reviewed and modified to meet the changing nature of battle. After 1990, when children were pitched into battle against Sri Lankan forces, the LTTE made training tougher. The military office of the LTTE headed by Wedi Dinesh developed a training programme that would make the child fighters more daring than the adults. This included the screening of Rambo-style videos in which the daredevil approach is invariably successful.

The trained young fighters are prepared for battle by attacking unprotected or weakly defended border villages. In these attacks, several hundred men, women and children have been killed by LTTE child combatants armed with automatic weapons guided by experienced fighters. The raids on these soft targets no police-defended forward defence lines. Thereafter, the trained fighters are deployed in camp attacks.

The performance of the LTTE Baby Brigade, under the command of senior commanders, has become increasingly dramatic. The daring and bloody attacks to capture weaponry and strategic ground produced heavy fatalities and injuries. The Tigers have built their expertise over a period of time, developing measures to eliminate failures and maximize successes.

Operations

The first major operation in which the LTTE deployed child combatants came after LTTE suicide bomber, Pork, rammed an explosive-laden lorry into the Mankulam army camp (north) on 22 November 1990. The pre-dawn LTTE attack from all flanks was initiated with indigenously produced Pasilan 2000 mortars, standard mortars, RPGs, machine guns and small arms and was followed by successive waves of LTTE fighters drawn from the Baby Brigade. The intensity of the attack led the commander to evacuate the camp at 1600hrs on 24 November. Of a total strength of 313 government troops, at least a third was killed and a few were taken prisoner. The LTTE lost 62 of their number, mostly child combatants.

The second major operation involving LTTE child fighters occurred on 10 July 1991 when the LTTE attacked the Elephant Pass Military Complex, located on both sides of the causeway linking the northern peninsula to the mainland. Improvised tanks - bulldozers plated with armour - were followed by waves of LTTE cadres drawn from the Baby Brigade attempting to penetrate the forward defence lines. The LTTE attempted to isolate the camp by building bunkers, trenches and other forms of strong defences around it. For the first time the child combatants who witnessed heavy casualties became reluctant to move along the open ground their positions and the target complex. The LTTE commanders shot their feet and humiliated them. At one point the camp defences were breached but the troops within the complex repulsed the LTTE by counter-attacking. The complex was then reinforced by a sea landing of troops. The LTTE lost 550 personnel, most of whom were children.

After the attack on the Elephant Pass Complex, the LTTE analysed their successes and failures. They then decided to develop small contained units for long-range reconnaissance and deep penetration to generate sound and timely intelligence on troop deployment and combat readiness. Equipped with this surveillance data on Sri Lankan government base complexes and detachments, the newly established LTTE map and model-making department built near life-size models of the targets to be used as practice exercises for their troops. To gain greater stealth, speed and surprise, the LTTE mixed Black Tigers - psychologically and physically trained-suicide units - with the Baby Brigade. The outcome shocked the Sri Lankan government, particularly when the LTTE overran two fortified base complexes in 1993 and 1996, killing 1800 troops and removing weapons worth about US$ 100 million.

On 11 November 1993 the LTTE launched an amphibious strike, destroying the Poonaryn army/Nagathevanthurai navy base complex. In preparation, members of the Baby Brigade were trained for night combat, swimming long distances and striking forward defence lines. Seaborne Tigers assaulted Sandupiddy pier and the Nagathevanthurai naval positions before dawn using improvised floats and weapons wrapped in polythene.

At the same time a land group staged a concentrated frontal assault, penetrating the forward defence lines, while a third group infiltrated the camp perimeter, creating confusion and overrunning artillery and mortar positions.

On 28 July 1995 LTTE units simultaneously attacked five camps in the Weli Oya military complex. Based on battle indicators, the Brigade Command alerted its troops to an impending attack. The predawn raid comprised at least 3000 Tigers, almost all from the Women's Wing and the Baby Brigade. Only one soldier and one home guard were killed and 22 soldiers injured. The military recovered 10 light machine guns, five light guns, four RPGs, 118 automatic weapons and ammunition. The aborted plan was to have concluded with LTTE vehicles and boats retreating with arms, ammunition and other equipment removed from the camps.

From October 1995, the Sri Lankan military launched a series of operations to deprive the LTTE of territorial control of the Jaffna peninsula: the Tamil heartland. The LTTE northern command engaged in a tactical repositioning of its troops, withdrawing the bulk of fighters to the Wanni mainland. The Baby Brigade was temporarily dismantled and it units were placed under the LTTE military intelligence directorate. The child forces were given training in small businesses - selling ice creams, newspapers, fruits, lottery tickets, and working in cafes and restaurants - and re-infiltrated into the peninsula. After a while, many of them began to live with the parents, relatives, and families of LTTE sympathisers, thus becoming the eyes and ears of the LTTE. With intelligence provided by members of the dismantled Baby Brigade, LTTE sparrow teams struck, killing Tamil informants and supporters of the government as well as Sri Lankan troops. Initially, it was difficult for counter-intelligence operatives to believe that the LTTE was using children to gather its intelligence on troop movements and dispositions. It was even harder for them to apprehend and prosecute children who were under 16 years of age.

From late 1995 to mid-1996 the LTTE recruited and trained at least 2000 Tamils largely drawn from 600,000 Tamils displaced in the wake of the operations to capture the peninsula. About 1,000 of these were between 12 and 16 years old and they were dispersed among the other fighting units. On 18 July 1996, the LTTE launched an amphibious assault on the Mulativu military complex. The LTTE operation, codenamed Oyatha Alaikal (Ceaseless Waves), deployed between 5,000 and 6,000 personnel both to strike the complex and to fight reinforcements. After fighting began, screaming waves of the Baby Brigade began to attack the complex. During the initial attack, to create confusion, many senior LTTE fighters were dressed in military uniform. Amid the fighting, an army major commanded his troops to surrender to the LTTE leader; after the Tigers had disarmed about 300troops, they were gunned down by the child combatants. The fighting killed 314 Tigers and injured at least 1,000.

Of the government forces, only two officers and 67 other ranks survived the attack. In addition to the loss of 1,173 officers and men, 37 elite troops engaged in a rescue operation were killed and

61 injured. An LTTE suicide boat rammed Ranaviru,a Shanghai class gun boat, killing 31 crew and vessel's captain.

Enter the Leopards

The physical and psychological war training of children as a formidable lethal weapon is an innovation of the LTTE. The high point of LTTE achievement in this direction was the formation of the elite Sirasu puli, or Leopard Brigade. The members of the brigade were children drawn from LTTE-managed orphanages. Within the LTTE ranks, this brigade is considered to be its most fierce fighting force. All LTTE recruits swear an oath of allegiance to the LTTE leader once every morning and evening but, Leopard fighters have an incomparable loyalty to Prabhakaran. Most see him as a father figure and equate a request from him to a directive from heaven. On 4 December 1997 the LTTE leopard Brigade encircled and killed nearly 200 elite Sri Lankan forces in Kanakarankulam in the Wanni, suffering heavy casualties themselves as well. Through the International Committee of the Red Cross (ICRC), the army accepted 113 bodies of soldiers from the LTTE; the LTTE buried 20 decomposed bodies. Uptil this point Sri Lankan infantry had been relied on elite troops - special forces and commandos - as its vanguard. The unprecedented loss severely demoralised whole sections of the government's frontline troops. The mutual annihilation also impeded the advance of Sri Lankan troops trying to open a main supply route linking the Jaffna peninsula with the South in time for the golden jubilee celebrations of Sri Lanka's independence on 4 February 1997.

The LTTE Baby Brigade lost heavily in two attacks: at the Weli Oya complex in July 1995and during an assault on the Wanni defences on 1 February 1998. The Weli Oya victory, according to Sri Lanka's National Intelligence Bureau, was the biggest defeat the LTTE had suffered. Major General Janaka Perera, the then Brigade Commander of Weli Oya, said that all of the LTTE casualties, apart from the leaders, were teenagers. Perera, trained at Sandhurst and at the Royal College of Defence Studies in the UK, believe that LTTE suicide wave attacks can only be fought by developing advance intelligence and preparing to meet an impending strike. 5 August 1995 an Economist story entitled "SriLanka's under-age war", commenting on the attack, stated: "There was little rejoice by the army. Most of the dead were women and children, sent in by the Tiger generals as cannon fodder. The Tigers said 128 women had been killed, but they did not mention their child soldiers."

When the LTTE assaulted the Kilinochchi, Paranthan and Elephant Pass defences on 1 February 1998, at least 200 child fighters were killed assaulting near impregnable defences with 10-foot bunkers. An LTTE-captured South African buffel armoured vehicle, laden with 800kg of high explosives procured from Ukraine's Rube zone chemical plant, toppled before it reached the target. The LTTE was not keen to accept the bodies offered by the northern commander, Major General Lionel Balagalle, via the ICRC, and so the Sri Lanka Army buried the dead children. The LTTE could sustain a loss up to 200 personnel not because the leadership considers child fighters dispensable, but because from every debacle the LTTE learns a lesson and improves. However, LTTE domestic and international thinkers, using computerised databases, have alerted Prabhakaran to the possibility of having insufficient members of both adult or child combatants to continue the campaign without expanding LTTE's geographic influence. To prevent the exodus of youth from LTTE-controlled areas, they effectively enforced a law to regulate departures.

Prabhakaran also directed that his eastern commands both expand their territorial control and recruitment. There are virtually no studies conducted by the government or foreign think tanks on LTTE kills and injuries as well as its potential for recruitment.

The International Response

The LTTE has been able to conduct its under-age campaign away from the international gaze. Like their adult counterparts in the LTTE, child fighters are required to consume a Phial of

Potassium Cyanide either when capture is imminent or when injured in the field. Enforcing the cyanide rule has, understandably, been difficult with children. John Burns of the New York Times, a regular commentator on Sri Lanka, highlights instances in which LTTE child fighters have failed to commit suicide. Acknowledging that the LTTE has been using "Tamil boys as young as 10" to counterattack the advancing government troops, Burns states: "Although the Tigers send their fighters into battle with cyanide capsules strung around their necks, many of the youngsters did not swallow the poison, as instructed by Tiger leaders, when shot." Burns also cites instances where LTTE units have withdrawn under fire "leaving wounded boys and girls lying in no-man's land, crying for help." As a result, there are more teenage than adult LTTE fighters in government custody. The exposure given by Burns and an anti-LTTE web site by Umberto Gui has hurt the LTTE most. However, on the whole, there has been no international response to the LTTE attitude towards children. For example, when the LTTE expelled Muslims from the north and staged a series of massacres of Muslim civilians in the east, there was no outcry even within the Muslim world. Before launching their anti-Sri Lankan Muslim drive, the Tigers butchered all the Eastern Muslim units, including the child children - some as young as 9 - in July/August 1990.

The UN has repeatedly expressed concern over the misuse of children but without an impact at ground level. The UN Special Rappoteur on Violence Against Women - RadhikaCoomaraswamy, a Sri Lankan Tamil - has been a critic of the LTTE for its use of women and children in warfare. After reviewing statistics of LTTE injured personnel, Garca Machel, former first lady of Mozambique and adviser to the UN secretary general, stated that 20 per cent were between the ages of 10 and 14 during recruitment. London-based representatives of LTTE fronts - the International Federation of Tamils, UK, and the Tamil Centre for Human rights, France - attempted to lobby Machel during the Commonwealth Heads of Government Meeting in Edinburgh in October 1997, but she evaded them. The LTTE has a vibrant global network neutralising anti-LTTE stances and promoting Tiger propaganda.

Sri Lankan Foreign Minister Lakshman Kadirgamar, a Sri Lankan Tamil, believes that an entire generation of young Tamil children is being systematically destroyed by the LTTE. In response to Kadirgamar's impassionate plea to the 52nd UN General Assembly in September 1997, Olara Otunna, the UN Secretary General's special representative for children and armed conflict, sought to persuade "foreign governments not to tolerate the activities of the LTTE in their countries due to the heinous crimes committed by the LTTE against children." To give the issue an international profile, Kadirgamar travelled to the US twice in a month and briefed the US first lady, Hilary Clinton, on 29 October 1997.The designation of the LTTE as a terrorist group by the Secretary of State, Madeleine Albright on 8 October, placed Kadirgamar, along with the Sri Lankan President and Deputy Defence Minister Ratwatte, high on the LTTE hit list. Meanwhile in the Sri Lankan press, the use of child fighters is not a serious issue. Sri Lankan propaganda, soliciting Western opinion, argues that the LTTE uses Tamil children as cannon fodder. However, the overwhelming success of the LTTE, means that the Sri Lankan state is failing against a ruthless adversary.

Domestic Response

Successive governments have failed to stem the exponential growth of the LTTE. To date, the LTTE's rate of recruitment of children is higher than its level of fatalities. The LTTE has concentrated on politically controlling or at least militarily dominating, Tamil areas in order to recruit. Government troops have lacked the right training and quality leadership to deprive the LTTE of this territorial control. Similarly, Sri Lankan defence decision- and policy-makers, as well as military planners and strategists, have failed to understand the importance of psychological operations (psy ops) to drive a wedge between the Tamil public and the LTTE. Although there have been proposals to broadcast in Tamil and to leaflet Tamil areas, exposing the use of children as cannon fodder, lack of priority to psyops continues to draw in children to join the LTTE. The only study on the role of the children in the LTTE is a sociological analysis by Peradeniya University's sociology student Chamarie Rodrigo. Her thesis, based on published literature and interviews, confirms the failure of the state to address the "misuse of children by power-hungry leaders."

The Sri Lankan Government has failed to take on the LTTE on child recruitment both domestically and internationally. The failure is integral to the overall inefficiency of a politicised Sri Lankan security and the intelligence apparatus of the government The replacing of intelligence and security professionals by novices to intelligence, along with the dismantling of the training branch of the National Intelligence Bureau, has prevented the state from correctly assessing as well as combating the LTTE. The bulk of the operatives posted overseas have lacked either the influence or the motivation to prevent LTTE propaganda, fundraising, procurement and shipping. According to a foreign intelligence agency monitoring LTTE money transfers, the bulk of the LTTE funds raised under the banner of humanitarian and children's welfare organisations have been channelled to fund the LTTE war effort. Unlike the Hamas rehabilitation and reconstruction programme, the Tamil Rehabilitation Organisation (TRO)engages in large-scale projects to alleviate the suffering of 600,000 displaced Tamils. Despite the US designation of the LTTE as terrorist, the TRO raises funds there. In permitting funds raised for humanitarian purposes, Washington has earned the criticism of its own operatives because of the difficulty of monitoring how the money will be used in the affected areas.

In most cases, the hard currency is not transferred but instead buys weapons and domestically raised money is used in humanitarian activity to show that the funds have been used properly. Since no mechanisms are available for monitoring expenditure in the affected areas, the US decision is perceived as naive. The TRO, registered as a charity in most Western states, has massive fund-raising campaigns in France, UK and Canada. inadvertently, the

German Government provided a substantial grant to the TRO. Similarly, only a fraction of the funds raised by other LTTE front and cover benign organisations - including those in support of San Cholai and Kantha Ruban child orphanages - have been channelled for humanitarian purposes. These two orphanages, founded and managed by the LTTE, received frequent visits by Prabhakaran himself.

In many Sri Lankan Tamil shops and ethnic restaurants throughout the world, the LTTE has placed charity donation boxes, ostensibly used for funding orphanages. In response, the Ministry of Foreign Affairs in Colombo released a book in January 1998 entitled "LTTE in the Eyes of the World" in which they request donors to channel their humanitarian aid through Oxfam, Save the Children's Fund, CARE, The ICRC, UNICEF and so on. One of the few respectable Tamil organisations that has fought LTTE infiltration and funded orphanages and other children's projects in the war-ravaged north and east of Sri Lanka is the London-based Standing Committee of the Tamil Speaking People (SCOT) founded in 1977.

In the history of the Sri Lankan conflict, 38 Tamil groups and three Sinhala groups that has advocated or used terrorism to achieve political goals. The LTTE remains the only rebel group to use children in warfare, stemming from the innovative capability and potential capacity of this resource. Those children captured in combat has been effectively transformed into non-combatants. The Sri Lankan Government has established a number of homes to provide education and vocational training After a period of time, they are released to their parents. Unlike the constraints precluding the transformation of criminals and adult rebels, child fighters can be rehabilitated. The fear invoked by the LTTE prevents the criticism voiced by the Tamils against the LTTE leader Prabhakaran from being heard Prabhakaran's unwillingness to bring his son Charles Anthony and Dwarka, his daughter, into the ranks of the LTTE is hurting the image of the supremo domestically and internationally.

The LTTE has fought the criticism at home and abroad by stating that these are the sacrifices the current generation of Tamils will have to make so that the future generations can live in peace and happiness. The LTTE has no qualms about the means used to accumulate political influence, military strength and economic power to advance its goals. In that light the LTTE will continue to disregard domestic and international pressure and continue its avowed goal fighting for a mono-ethnic Tamil state.

The Future

The ideological experiment of motivating children as combatants has been a highly successful one The LTTE has been able to enhance its performance in battle by deploying child units. Therefore, it is likely that other contemporary groups will now emulate the success of the LTTE.

The most devastating result of this practice has been the recovery of small-sized suicide body suites - denim jackets with concealed explosives to be worn beneath the garments of an innocent-looking guerrilla or terrorist to create heavy casualties. As these LTTE manufactured suits, recovered by the Sri Lankan security forces, could even fit a child, there is concern as to whether the LTTE will use children as suicide bombers. The LTTE, at the cutting edge of creation, innovation and invention, has deceived both the Indian and Sri Lankan security agencies by assassinating two heads of government. After garlanding the former Indian Prime Minister, Rajiv Gandhi, on the eve of the Indian elections in May 1991, a female suicide bomber killed him. A male suicide bomber, who infiltrated the presidential household, killed Sri Lanka President Ranasinghe Premadasa on May day in 1993. Security and intelligence agencies monitoring the LTTE claim that the faction retains the potential to use unsuspecting children as suicide bombers to target VIPs in the near future.

Unlike on governments, the influence of international organisations on guerrilla and terrorist organisations is likely to remain limited. The persistence of child guerrillas and terrorists, as a phenomenon is therefore likely to remain a feature use in the international system

Governments, both the weak and the influential, and the international community as a whole, have lacked the political will to change the status quo and to impede an emerging trend. By permitting their support structures for generating funds to weaponry to flourishing their cities, the West - the guardians of democracy and human rights - have tacitly supported many child-employing guerrilla and terrorist groups. For instance, the LTTE has a significant presence, by way of offices and cells, in the UK, Canada, France, Germany, Holland, Switzerland, Italy, Sweden, Denmark, Norway and Australia. These groups are all engaged in propaganda, fundraising, procurement and movement of weapons. The host states of the West retain the potential to instigate sanctions against them; until they do, the Tamil Tigers - and other groups witnessing some of their success - will continue to break accepted civilised standards in deploying child combatants.

Courtesy: *Janes Intelligence Review of July 1998*

Continued Abduction and Conscription of Children as Soldiers[1]

D.G.Harendra de Silva

"Peace" in Sri Lanka

One of the major events that happened in recent Sri Lanka, mainly during 2002, was the prospect of Peace that everyone had longed for so long. After all, not having significant deaths or casualties on both sides for over a year is a major achievement. After several futile attempts at peace previously, many feel that we have to make it happen this time. "Now or never" is the feeling. It is most significant to the people who are directly affected, whether we think of the populations in the Northeast, North-Central, families of the armed forces personnel or the business community. On the long term it is important to everyone in Sri Lanka. While we are thus overwhelmed with the romantic idealism of peace, we should also concentrate on the reality, logistics and other aspects, which are not visible but would be fundamentally important for building a foundation for sustainable peace.

Let us look at some underlying principles of peace. Initially we have to understand that peace cannot be achieved by the might of military power whether in Sri Lanka, Palestine, Iraq or Afghanistan. Nor could the process be *limited* to the leaders of rival factions, although they may have initially decided on "war". *Real Peace is a "bottom up" process*, which cannot be achieved by two signatures alone, nor imposed "top-down" on the people. At the same time leaders may not necessarily represent the views of their people. Although it is a fundamental necessity and an essential pre-requisite to have the consensus and the blessings of the leaders with or without signatures, what is more important is to build up harmony of all people towards peace. It is also necessary for them to look at the legal processes of peace.

We cannot afford to barter the social issues or rights of the people with the political power of any group. Peace is far from a process of "buying apples and selling oranges". Military strategists, "pure-bred" academics, businessmen, politicians or the International Community cannot decide on these issues on their own; though they could facilitate the process. Hence the need for *civil participation* at all levels of negotiations, but with the precaution that none are political or extremist's stooges nor harbour other ulterior motives. The strength and sustainability of the peace process would depend on how strong and committed we are to ensure civil contribution. It is unfortunate that some of the pure-bred Diplomats in the International Community and the peacekeepers are not pressing for civil involvement at negotiations. Apart from civil society why should we leave out the opposition at the discussions and, ironically, a majority of government Ministers and Members of Parliament.? This does not allow for broader consensus.

We have observed in Northern Ireland where signatures in a "Good Friday" agreement have meant little to a realistic peace process. This again demonstrates the futility of trying to concentrate only on symbolic signatures of politicians and extremist factions.

We expected peace through signatures and, in spite of Nobel Peace prizes as in the Middle East, real wars still continue to be waged. Ironically the same negotiators also mediated it. In the situation of the Middle East, peace has not been cultivated in the hearts and minds of the ordinary person at the grass root level, while politicians and warlords struggle for supremacy through the exploitation of poorly conditioned and cultivated minds of the community.

The sheer *necessity* of peace should not be confused with the *reality* of peace in an idealistic utopia. The one side, which may have other, ambitious agendas, may not reciprocate the sincerity of other side. Especially so when pressure, either military, political or International - such as "11/9" - has led to the "peace initiative" rather than it being achieved on its own; or when it is seen as an opportunity for a breathing space to regroup, double the cadres, strengthen the armory, and develop military strategies for an all-out offensive. Of the two Sri Lankan leaders who previously negotiated peace on a serious note, one was killed and the other permanently maimed in the eye. Let history not repeat itself. There could also be justifications to renew hostilities, especially those justifications that may be "created" by one side to inveigle the other side to attack - as in the Kalmunai incident where a group of protestors, allegedly backed by rebels, intimidated Special Police Task Forces to the point of retaliation; an age old standard strategy to *justify renewal of hostilities*. Incidents such as the very recent sinking of the alleged arms ship also have the potential for justification of rekindling of warfare. The "Jekyll and Hyde" stance of the rebels in often giving contradictory statements to the Tamil-speaking people on the one hand and to the government and International Community on the other, leaves room for justification and continuation of war with the *subtle beating of distant war drums within their community*. This would ensure the persistence of the polarization of communities with continued smoldering of emotions, within the potential community for possible mobilization whenever necessary.

The Idealism and Manipulation of Youth

It is also vital to recognize that a vast majority of persons actively fighting and dying in any war are the youth and children, and wars would be impossible if not for the ultimate sacrifice of youth and children for adults' agendas, as the decisions are made by adults who are powerful and are not willing to die in *their* quest for power. ***Wars will smoulder on as long as innocence and the idealism of***

youth are manipulated. This is quite obvious when we look at any propaganda material used for the conscription is targeting youth and children. The uniforms, guns, titles, of heroes and martyrs, clips of actual or simulated gun battles, and slogans of patriotism are all for the vulnerable but innocent and idealistic minds of youth before they have adequate experience and guidance from honest adults and a society in which to develop lateral thinking. *The value of youth is in the blend of honesty, innocence and vibrancy, and in no way should this be looked down upon.* They believe what is told to them because they are themselves honest and would expect others to reciprocate it. It is with experience in becoming an adult, and after being betrayed over and over again, that we start doubting something or think twice of what we are told. *As one develops into adulthood s/he tends to lose his/her innocence and honesty.* Adults, having faced negative experiences continue to doubt others, either develop lateral thinking or become dishonest frauds.

Youth can also be corrupted, especially when they are precociously exposed to adult abuse, exploitation and deceptions and violence, the responsibility of which falls on the adult. Exposure of a child to traumatic experiences early in life would make him or her develop coping mechanisms, especially when faced with similar situations, which would include dishonesty and guilt as part of the reaction. Let us look at suicide attacks; how many older persons whether in Sri Lanka or Palestine have blown themselves apart as “martyrs”? It is the honesty and idealism of youth that make them do it, and there are adults in this world that would exploit this honesty.

In the campaign to sign the UN optional protocol to the *Convention on the Rights of the Child* (CRC) on increasing the minimum age of recruitment, there was initially some resistance from several developed countries who were involved in the recruitment of children (below 18). One of the reasons against signing, stressed by *a* Western government official, was the issue of *trainability* of youth. The use of children and adolescents ***by***

proxy is related to this issue. Forcing them to fight and die, using them as cannon fodder, asking them to commit suicide all for the adult's thirst for power, on issues that the youngsters cannot even comprehend, are the primary concerns.

Child Soldiers and Peace

The continuation of impunity to International norms in recruiting and abducting children, leading to serious potential damage to the minds and bodies of youth, is a serious threat to the establishment and sustenance of peace. The continued manipulation of youth is a crucial facet that peacemakers and negotiators have to question if *the process of working towards peace is to be realistic.* What is the accountability of government authorities in addressing abductions of Tamil children and youth for armed conscription, or the use of youth and children for often-violent civilian "protests"? Are they not the responsibility of the legitimate government? ***Unfortunately the designed and prolonged alienation and polarization of communities has led to a feeling, by government/s, that the responsibility for Tamil children and youth lies in the hands of Tamil leaders, especially rebels; and hence, probably, the reason why their inaction or the fear of upsetting the abductors.*** Organizations such as the University Teachers for Human Rights (UTHR-Jaffna) have constantly reported names, addresses, times and dates of abductions which would be adequate for investigation of these occurrences that are alleged blatant violations of the Memorandum of Understanding and would fall under the obligations of negotiators and monitors to address.

In any peace process unless we focus on youth and give them some responsibility of the process, prevent them from being conscripted, move them away from violent alternatives to conflict resolution, and give them a vision for their future, we are unlikely to achieve much in terms of real peace.

Another paradox has evolved recently. There are Hartals i.e.

supposed agitations by the "people" as protests on arrest of child abductors while nobody (except the parents) is agitating against the abduction of the children. This raises the undoubted question "*Who is forcing and manipulating the 'people' to agitate?*" Is it to show the International Community that the "People" are for conscription or to focus away from the abductions?

The issue of child soldiers - often labeled as a "*sensitive issue*", which justifies not addressing the issue - clearly illustrates the insensitiveness of the responsible authorities, including International agencies, to social values, and to children and their rights, as opposed to their strong *sensitiveness* to political issues. Insensitiveness by some officials of certain organizations that may have obligations towards children demonstrates the immaturity of officials on specific children's issues rather than the official viewpoint of these organizations. Let us hope that the views are changing. The Western countries, especially the Scandinavians, are always hailed for their human rights records, their commitment to peace through peace prizes, impartiality and their commitment to children's rights. One has to embed these high standards and actions into the monitoring process and constantly close any gaps, especially when violations of child rights, in the form of abductions and conscription, are happening right under their (and our) noses. It is time for mature self-assessment, to take stock, before paradoxical behaviour would become all too obvious in the eyes of the world.

The allegation by the International community that the government is also recruiting children, especially as home guards has cropped up from time to time. *It is crucial, if there is proof to this effect, to make the government recruiters accountable,* since children are children irrespective of their ethnic identity and not an issue for political advantage. It appears in the absence of direct evidence other than hearsay accounts, some persons in the International community is trying to deny and avoid the child soldiers' issue and to justify not addressing it, by directing accusations (but not directly) at the government.

We need to deliberate on the following questions,

- *"Are children human too?"*
- *"Are they entitled to human rights or have they got to become adults before being entitled to it?"*
- *"Why do we prioritize violations of adult rights, including the abduction of 'peace' monitors?"*
- *"Why are we not addressing obvious human rights violations of children?"*
- *"Are 'Child Rights' and the Convention of the Rights of the Child (CRC) not on par with conventional human rights norms?"*
- *"Do we seriously consider the articles on child conscription in the CRC or consider it as a sensitive area and confine it to the book?"*
- *"Why are the cries of these children abducted and made into killing and suicidal machines not heard by the people, governments and, ironically, by some International agencies?"*

The continuation of child and youth conscription means the perpetuation of the conflict, preventing any chances of peace, since children form the 'backbone' of the rebel fighters. The plea from children by proxy to adults is, *"Get out of your shell and stop this vicious cycle of only looking after the interests of adults and their political and power agendas"*. Let us all challenge the impunity of child abductions and recruitment, not only in the best interest of the child but also in the best interest of society and a long lasting and sustainable peace. ***"Zero Tolerance" of child abductions and recruitment should be the rule, without any form of exception.***

The recent release of some child soldiers, **confirms** conscription of children, which ironically had been previously repeatedly denied by the rebels, while the release was probably a 'symbolic' show to the International Community, in the midst of continued conscription of children. The possibilities of either new conscription for the purpose of release, or release of recently recruited inexperienced cadres also has to be seriously kept in mind. It is alleged that there were 94 complaints of recruitment of children for training in combat for January 2003. What about the recruitment not reported?

[The latest reports confirm the failure of the demobilization of child soldiers supposedly by the recruiters themselves after Millions of Dollars were 'spent' on the process]

The Implications and Realities of being a Child Soldier & the Use of Children by Proxy

I still remember that in my childhood, immediately after watching a war film or reading a war comic (cartoon) book, how I used to cocoon myself in an atmosphere of war, how I hid behind pillows - the imaginary boulders, the "bravery" of my actions, the imagination of the number of "Germans" or "Japanese" I captured with my bare hands, the fantasies of daring escapades and those awards for bravery, the pride of being a brave fighter but still a child! The situation was such that most boys went through this phase without actually facing real danger and trauma, this is no different from today. The kids from villages with their imaginary swords idolized the past kings of Sri Lanka. The commercial and political ventures wanted children to develop ideas of "bravery" and they continue to do so. The profit-making establishments want to sell books, movies, videos, toy guns, toy soldiers and hundreds of other worthless but harmful gimmicks, while the politicians want the youth to be ready to sacrifice their lives in the name of bravery, and the "real" gun making industry is now ready to palm off those deadly weapons to those youth who were primed from boyhood with the "harmless" toy guns. The Sinhala people are proud of King *Dutugemunu* who defeated the Tamil King *Elara* over two thousand years ago. Over the years undoubtedly this 'heroic' story has been used to lift the heroic morale of the Sinhala people against the possible threat of invasions, a comparison parallel to this are the heroic Jewish historical stories of Moses or David who fought against the anticipated threat of genocide. Today the "enemy" would be Al-Queda, Palestinians or Muslim "Extremists". Similarly anti American, British, Bush would be instilled in the minds of Muslim children and youth leading to the process of polarization.

Hundreds of thousands of children are known to be used in warfare all over the world, including Sri Lanka. Way back in the eighties the public often interpreted children fighting alongside adults as heroes and martyrs. They are often depicted to be braver than adults. With the advent of lightweight, cheap but deadly automatic weapons, which can be easily handled, women and children appeared in the battlefield. It is ironic that adults with commercial objectives, but supposedly mature enough to know what is right and wrong, think through a mask of their childhood dreams that were also moulded by adults with other motives in perpetuating the cycle of war. The cycle would go on even though challenged, since the strength of money and power would always override the effectiveness of social justice, non-violence and peace. Yet the need to challenge this injustice is essential to check the Impunity of Global Violence.

During the early nineties, while looking at the definition of childhood sexual abuse, I realized that children cannot volunteer, even if they wanted to, whether it be in sexual relations or participation in armed conflict simply because they are unable to comprehend such complex acts, which even adults find difficult to understand (at least the adults are supposed to!). By this time there were indications of the detrimental effects of armed conflict on children with descriptions of Post Traumatic Stress Disorder (PTSD), the long-term psychological effects, especially on adults, and the long-term effects of PTSD on Vietnam War Veterans. The Convention of the Rights of the Child (CRC) had mentioned the prevention of children from being conscripted in 1989. However, ironically the CRC described a child as a person below 18 years but had the cut-off age for conscription at 15 years. Some Western Countries that have laws and systems in place to protect children from physical and other forms of abuse and exploitation still "idolized" heroism and paradoxically were recruiting children below 18 years! One of the official explanations mentioned at the time was; "It is easier to train youth". Of course that is why children are supposed to be "braver" than adults – they are unable to comprehend the dangers. Idealism of youth, before gaining experience or developing lateral thinking skills, with the flexibility to adapt to changing political tides, makes it easier to train them and get them to "listen" - without ever challenging orders - to the adults who want them to fight their (the adult's) power struggles. Apart from these reasons, the positive physical attributes, the *"trainability"* of the physique of youth, the ability to tolerate food shortage, changing environments, human rights violations, and their vital ability to coordinate body senses with actions, make youth and children the most sought after age group and, in essence, an unique choice for recruitment in war. The presence of 'hot' emotions makes them vulnerable to manipulation. They also have relatively less responsibility to family.

There were authentic reports, in the nineties, of children conscripted to fight in the war in Sri Lanka by the rebel groups[2]. At this time there were no parallels between conscription and child abuse described in the medical literature. I then decided, with the help of others, to document the use of child soldiers and to also establish the ways in which they are "abused" using accepted definitions of child abuse and adapting it to the context of child soldiers, a purely medically- oriented academic research study with a humanitarian aspect, but without political dimensions. Hence, this was the reason why there is/was no mention of specific rebel groups or even ethnicity in the original publication. The main objective was to classify the use of children in war as *child abuse* using standard and modified definitions so that the burden of responsibility is shifted to the adults who are the perpetrators. The children annot then be portrayed as criminals, but are mere victims of crimes committed by adults although they maybe viciously affected in their minds with potentially dangerous futures as adults. We initially studied nineteen former child soldiers recruited below the age of 18 years, based on the age of a child as defined in the CRC, and the results and interpretation of these studies are given below[3].

The mean age of child conscription to the armed groups was 14.5 years (range 10 to 17 years). The children reported performing a variety of manual labours, involving varied degrees of danger. Two children had performed radio communication tasks, and fifteen had carried out guard duty. Fifteen of the children had performed tasks such as digging trenches or doing kitchen work. Seven of the children had been engaged in front line fighting, five had manufactured bombs, and five had set land mines. Fifteen of the children admitted having had training in firearm use, and fourteen of them had been trained to commit suicide if captured. Most children had performed more than one of these tasks.

According to the nineteen children interviewed, life with the militants was not enjoyable. All of the children had to go through some form of indoctrination, designed at least in part, to create "hatred" of the enemy. Twelve of the nineteen had run away or attempted to run away at least once, and eleven of the nineteen reported arguing about or refusing to obey orders. Non-compliance led to different forms of punishment, including kitchen duty, beatings, imprisonment, blackmail, and even death threats. A majority of the children felt sad and emotionally upset when they remembered their mother or family.

Surprisingly only one out of the nineteen children had been abducted and forced to join; the other eighteen had all "volunteered". Why did the majority of the children "volunteer" to join the armed group? The "inside story" by the BBC[4], though not intentionally, illustrated many of the different methods adopted to encourage children to "volunteer" to join the Militants. Some of the methods include, public address systems where rebel radio and television stations continuously broadcast "reasons" and "justifications" for volunteering, and the production of literature, encouraging volunteerism that is targeted at children and adolescents. In one children's playground, model automatic rifles were attached to the seesaws. The dead are glorified as martyrs with monuments built in their honor, and their posters are on display. School children and school bands parade at funerals of the dead "martyrs". An excerpt of a poem addressed to a girl ridicules her ambition of becoming a doctor, and ask her to compromise: *'...study while fighting, fight while studying....'* A poem to an adolescent boy ridicules him: "... *you are idling and growing fat in your youth...*" Children, especially adolescents, "give in" to this ridicule. The effect of propaganda on the community would make them convinced of their duty to sacrifice for the cause of the liberation struggle.

Retribution for family members killed in action or from military assaults on civilians was another important reason given for joining. When there are such attacks it is easy to convince a child to join. It is an attack on civilians that result in the child experiencing destruction of property and life of either family or friends. Our later studies confirm this. A large number of child conscripts, especially from the Eastern Province, mentioned the atrocities caused by the government forces, which invariably pushed them to become child guerrillas. This is probably what is meant by the often-quoted Guerrilla propaganda maxim: "When one revolutionary is killed, there are thousands of others who emerge from his grave". ***Hence the reason why military forces should never attack civilians in retaliation.*** A vulnerable group that is at risk are children and women since they are 'soft' targets. Attacks on children, may have short-term military advantages but break the morale of the people. The "tit- for-tat"' retaliation by both sides, especially those targeting civilians, like the justification for retribution in the Middle East, is the only explanation I can offer as to why it is a never-ending conflict. The strategy of guerrilla warfare, hiding amongst civilians, compounds the issue and often justifies the attacks by governments on civilians. However the Militants retaliate, accusing the governments of attacking innocent civilians. Hence, another reason why there is a need to adopt International standards/norms on civilian attacks as well as the use of civilian shields. It is essential that these should be classified as war crimes.

Our interviews with the nineteen child soldiers suggest these strategies (or a combination of factors) are often successful in the recruitment. Nine of the nineteen said that they joined for the virtue of being a freedom fighter and martyr. They liked the respect accorded by society. Seven said they joined for fear of being abducted by the enemy, and five said they joined seeking revenge for the death of a family member who had been killed by the enemy (or surprisingly their own group or another group). Only three of the nineteen indicated that they had joined for economic reasons, to support their family. Unfortunately responsible persons in the International community may be convinced of justifications of poverty, hunger or lack of education as reasons for conscription. If so, these persons would also have to justify child labour and even child prostitution since the latter occupations are less likely to kill the child. It is also important to realize that rebels often withhold humanitarian assistance to those families that do not give a child conscript from each family. In other words, the rebels manipulate food to create the shortage.

However, it is important ***not*** to justify child recruitment and ensure that the blame lies squarely on the recruiters, while the atrocities caused by government forces - whether it be in Sri Lanka, Palestine or Burma - should be addressed by the governments itself, and if not, by International War tribunals. It is unfortunate that governments do not understand the long-term effects of civilian attacks. Pictures drawn by ex-child soldiers visualize mainly the destruction, trauma, violence and glorification of arms war and suicide.

Subsequent studies revealed that single parent-hood (especially when the father was killed in the war), domestic violence, extreme poverty (which pushes mothers to migrate to the Middle-East to work) were predisposing factors for conscription. Several of the recruits who had run away from home had been in orphanages maintained by rebels, and had undergone training for sometime before formal recruitment.

Conscripting Children is Abuse

Given the public's tendency to view these child soldiers as "heroes", it may be difficult for many to recognize the abusive effects of conscription. However, considering the different aspects of emotional abuse, a **conscripted** child would face the following: ***conscription*** *"corrupts" a child by making him engage in violent, destructive, and anti-social behavior, such as killing and destruction of property, thus making him unfit for normal social experience.* ***Conscription*** *"terrorizes" a child with verbal assaults, bullying, and blackmail and death threat all in the name of discipline.* ***Conscription*** *isolates a child from the normal social experience, and ignores his emotional and developmental needs by removing him from normal family life and schooling.*

Any of these circumstances would adversely affect the child's right to unhindered growth and identity as a child. Every child has a right to his or her identity; not only his or her birth, gender identity or name, but also an identity "as a child". **Conscription** removes that identity and with it the right to play and recreation, the right to associating with friends and siblings, the right to an education and the right to live with their parents. Apart from having a name, a child has to have an identity as an independent person, therefore becoming a "personalized entity" with self-esteem. The process of militarization with regimentation and indoctrination, often with convenient, short alias names, removes the element in a child as a person with an individual identity, "*who am I*?" Another aspect is losing track of time and individuality with conscription. "How old am I?", "Am I still a child?" these are questions that they are at a loss to find an answer for.

Moreover, **conscription** may *cause children to commit suicide*, an act of self-destruction that cannot be fully comprehended. Traditionally in Sri Lankan rebel conscripts, irrespective of age, wear cyanide capsules at all times, which they are trained to bite on during "suicide missions" or if they are captured[5]. An interesting observation was that some newly conscripted child soldiers had to wear poythene cyanide packets around their necks due to a shortage of glass phials. By wearing the glass phial they felt proud of the respect they got by being a *potential martyr*. The lethal capsule also gave them a *sense of security* from being tortured, as they have been previously told in the event of capture. What makes them bite on it? The prominent place given to martyrs and the oath taken by the child soldier in which, he vows to sacrifice his life, are likely to be contributing factors to this phenomenon. It is interesting to see the similarities between Hitler's oath and one of an armed group. Both talk about *sacrificing life, being obedient to the "master"* and *fighting for a cause,* all hallmarks of a "fascist" process. Indoctrinating and convincing a child to commit suicide for any cause should constitute both emotional abuse and intentional poisoning. These findings lead us to propose a new definition of child abuse.

What other Aspects of Abuse would a conscripted Child face?

The fact that many children "volunteer" is not relevant. Children's involvement in war, whatever the "justifications" may be, should always be considered as forced, as they cannot truly comprehend their action in war. The adult caregivers must take the responsibility. Another interesting phenomenon is that most of the suicide cadres are below the age of 25 years. Why is this so? The concept of Indoctrination is simple, adolescents tend to be more honest and therefore vulnerable, which is why they do not doubt nor question the adult's ultimate motives. They have their 'blinkers on' with no experience of lateral thinking, while an older person would think twice before deciding to blow him/her self up. It is also interesting to realize that a large number of non-war related suicides are also found in the same age group. Another interesting fact was the observation that the extremely high ***non-war*** related pre-war suicide rate in Jaffna had dramatically reduced with the onset of the war[6].

Moreover, we propose that conscription itself is a form of child abuse. Defining conscription as a form of child abuse does not require a great leap of imagination, as many of the traditional elements of child abuse are already contained within it. Severe physical punishment in the name of discipline clearly constitutes physical abuse. Getting a child to perform guard duty, involving the child in military operations, making the child manufacture bombs and set sea mines increases the likelihood that the child will suffer serious injury or death, and subjects the child to intense psychological and emotional pressure. The exploitation of child labour is yet another form of abuse, and was very recently introduced as one of the worst forms of child labour under ILO Convention 182.

Disallowing access to neutral information and dialogue with the outside world is itself a fundamental violation of the rights of the child (article 17 of the UN convention of the rights of the child – CRC).

Although sexual abuse was not a feature in our study in Sri Lanka, in a world where the rape of adults and sexual harassment of females are well described aspects amongst new conscripts of regular armies, the likelihood of sexual abuse of child conscripts within one's own ranks as well as when captured should be considered seriously. In African conflicts the sexual exploitation of girls is well known. In the Sri Lankan context, *celibacy* is a norm for all rebel soldiers, except for probably a privileged few, which has been introduced to maintain strict discipline in their ranks. Sexual abuse of captured child soldiers has been documented.

It would be appropriate to summarize some case histories of child soldiers to illustrate some of the long-term emotional and physical abuse they have suffered. Cases I & II were described by Prof. Daya Somasunderam, Professor of Psychiatry, University of Jaffna. He has described several other case reports in his book "Scarred Minds"[7].

Case I

"...He joined the militants at the age of 11. He was given extensive training & taught that those who do not support the struggle are his enemies & should be killed. ..... He was shown videos of killed women & children & told that his enemies have done this.

He felt no remorse when he described how he held a child by the legs & bashed the head against the wall till the brain matter came out, of how he enjoyed the mother's scream & how he hacked them to death later. He said they deserved to die.

He partook in 4 village massacres. When inactive he felt bored and restless. He longed to go into villages and brutally kill people. The sight of blood obsessed him. He became easily irritable and broke out in sudden violent outbursts at the slightest thing".

Case II

"...He joined the militants at the age of 14, and underwent extensive training. ... He caught 3 people whom he considered were informants and tortured them by cutting them to pieces while they screamed... He had nightmares of his dead comrades being blown to pieces. His insomnia worsened, & began to take diazepam...

His drug abuse practice was detected by superiors...he was physically beaten & kept in detention. He was obsessed with the urge to torture & see blood. When he was asked to draw a picture, he chose a dark red crayon, & drew blood drops, a hanging man, a knife stained with blood, a grave & ghosts".

We need to understand these pictures drawn by adolescents who may not be able to describe their inner feelings in words. What they have drawn is the trauma of war and mass destruction they have witnessed as children. It on one hand emphasizes the great need for rehabilitation, while on the other hand one could imagine the vulnerability of these children who can be used by power hungry individuals for their needs. This need not necessarily be true only for Sri Lanka but also other situations such as in the West Bank or Iraq; hence the need for discretion when governments decide to hit back to avenge an attack on them. It would mean the beginning of new recruitment and dragging on the vicious cycle.

Adults too could suffer from similar reactions of PTSD as a result of traumatic experiences. This was observed amongst Vietnam War veterans and many years later, even today; it has become a major burden on the US government to support them. Not every adult soldier gets diagnosed and this could continue to cause problems in society.

In the Sri Lankan perspective, there is no formal system to recognize psychological problems in government or rebel soldiers. We are, even today, faced with a major threat from deserters who have become the most violent group in civil society today and are involved in major crimes from rapes, robberies to even murder. Unfortunately research or official figures are not available and subconscious denial probably prevents us from addressing this major social problem. The official version of the armed forces is "they are cowards - and are scared to go to the front line". Is this true? They were the very people who previously fought in the front lines. The crimes they are involved in as deserters are often daring and are not "cowardly" acts. Therefore, it is reasonable to postulate that these young men who were "normal" people when they went to fight the war, have become anti social elements as a result of PTSD, on account of the traumatic experiences they faced. It is fortunate that all adult soldiers do not have the same consequences of being violently anti-social, although we do not know the numbers that are troubled with violence, including domestic, nightmares, addictions and anxiety states.

An interesting observation of the reaction of children who often witness trauma could be applied to most of these instances, including adult soldiers. When a child sees or experiences trauma, violence and pain frequently, he or she has to develop protective mechanisms to cope with this situation. He or she may "shut himself off" at the time (e.g. during killing sprees) and may subconsciously remove any personal feeling of psychological trauma and pain. When it happens over and over again, he or she may cut-off their feelings towards oneself or others. To them, violence is nothing abnormal. This effect could persist into adult life and they may not have any emotions or remorse when partaking in violent acts including murder. Village massacres of innocent civilians usually women and children, is a way of "priming" them. It is likely that Sri Lankan Army deserters involved in crime and contract killings, although not children, suffer psychological effects parallel to this phenomenon. In African situations it is known that rebels make the children to kill their own parents and siblings to "de-sensitize" them. Eating the enemies' heart has been documented in Africa.

We adults use children to fight a war for us so that we can gain power. What do the children get? They may be misled by titles of "major", "hero" or "martyr" but they more often are assured a coffin. The involvement "by proxy" of children in war should be raised as a humanitarian as well as a human rights issue concerning children, rather than as a political issue.

Conclusion

There is a need for the public in the affected areas and societies to recognize the long-term implications of childhood conscription on their society. There should not be any political bias when such a call is made. The objective should be to **protect children**, whatever the ***race, religion or political group,*** from the physical and emotional trauma, including death, and initiate a program to rehabilitate and re-integrate these children who suffer from deep emotional damage. It should be emphasized again that irresponsible bombing and killing by the armed forces is a factor that can be used to drive the children to "volunteer" and there is a need to make those responsible for civilian attacks be also accountable for such action.

End notes

[1] Adapted from a book by Prof Harendra de Silva *Power Games in War and Peace; the tragic impact of corruption, violence and impunity on the Sri Lankan Child* http://pay.lankacom.net/powergames

[2] Newsweek August 7th 1995; BBC, Inside Story 1991, Editor - David Elliot, Production - Stephen Lambert, Executive producer – Paul Hamann

[3] . *D G H de Silva & C J Hobbs British Medical Journal, 2001; 322:1372.*

Harendra de Silva, Chris Hobbs , Helga Hanks. Child Abuse Review*2001*, 10: *125-134*

[4] BBC, Inside Story 1991, Editor - David Elliot, Production - Stephen Lambert, Executive producer – Paul Hamann

[5] BBC - "inside story" 1991

[6] Personal communication with Prof. Daya Somasunderam, Professor of Psychiatry University of Jaffna

[7] Somasunderam D. 1998. *Scarred Minds –The Psychological Impact of War on Sri Lankan Tamils*. Sage Publications, New Delhi, India

The Political Timing of the Tiger Bombs

H. L. D. Mahindapala

The stunning results of the last Provincial Council elections proved that for once Ranil Wickremesinghe is correct: the political battles in the future will be the with JVP and not with the mainstream SLFP. Out of the 73 candidates fielded the JVP 71 were won by them. If the nine Wyamba Province councilors are added JVP has a total of 80 councilors. Political sources also stated that the JVP candidates have got the majority preference votes in the districts of Gampaha, Hambantota, Matara, Colombo and Ratnapura.

By any standards, this is an outstanding victory for the JVP which entered the democratic stream only the other day, compared to the UNP which has been in the political arena for well over half a century. Does this mark the beginning of a new era in politics, with the Third Force is leaping over the two main stream parties into first place? More importantly, why has the UNP with all its moneyed mudalalis and big businessmen – not to mention a well-oiled political machinery – failed to compete with the village boys? What are the new forces that are capturing the political imagination of the new generation of voters? The UNP's failure is astounding because it was not fighting alone. It had aligned itself with the minority parties, CWC, TNA (proxy of the LTTE), and SLMC. It is this combination that is claiming a mandate from the people in the parliament. But the ground realities in the last election have blown this myth sky high. The people are running away from the UNP-led coalition in droves. Why? Also, if the current trend continues what future has the UNP?

In the last century, the UNP managed to hold its head high. At the worst of times, it managed to hold its head above water. It never showed signs of sinking though the left relentlessly branded it as the instrument of the big business and the West. In the 21st century the signs are that the UNP is losing its grip and is sliding down the greasy pole into a bottomless pit, unless there is a mid-course correction. The history of the UNP reveals that it lost only when it abandoned the roots and aligned itself excessively with the right-wing forces of the chattering classes in Colombo 7 and the Western agencies, now represented mainly by the foreign-funded NGOs. The UNP sank to its lowest under the leadership of Sir. John Kotelawela – a name that is aligned to either eccentricity or alienation. Isn't this same "Kotelawela syndrome" that is dragging the UNP into its lower depths now? Would this debacle have occurred if there was a Senanayake or a Premadasa? The UNP reached the pinnacle of its power and popularity under the Senanayakes and Premadasa – two major political forces that flowed with the currents generated by the people. Its overall image was wrapped round these personalities. It was always difficult for the left opposition to undermine the power of the Senanayakes. It was easy to direct anti- Kotelawela and anti-Jayewardene campaigns.

Pieter Keuneman once told me that all what they could say against Dudley was that he had a "badey leday!" (stomach ailment) So they directed their attacks to project Dudley as a not-well person lying on the bed while "JR" – the "Yankee Dicky" – was under the bed up to his usual trickery and devilry. In other words, they couldn't undermine the mass appeal of the Senanayakes, who had a traditional rapport with the people, but they could easily demonize the Westernized Kotelawela and "JR". In the end, Kotelawela retired to a farm in Kent and JR's achieved his secret ambition of sleeping – at least one night -- on a bed in Buckingham Palace. Disregarding the sweltering heat of Sri Lanka, located just above the equator, JR even had the gall to place sentries at the Presidential House dressed up in the stuffy, sweaty, suffocating uniforms of the palace guards at Buckingham Palace! They both had their brief stints in power but they are remembered more for their alien ways than as leaders with links to the people. So are the successive defeats of the UNP at the polls, with no glimmer of light in the near future, a clear indication that it is going down the way of Kotelawela and "JR"? Another way of viewing the new political landscape is to ask whether the rise of the JVP is a passing phenomenon or is it on the up-and-up on its way to be another BJP? If it is the latter what are the political ingredients that are turning them into the next generation of power-brokers, if not the central force of power? If the UNP is fading out as the alternative source of power how can it turn the tide rising against it?

Its current strategy is to lean heavily on the minority parties, hoping to cobble up a shaky coalition to sustain itself in power. This is a recipe for disaster not only for the UNP but also for the nation. It has two major defects:

1) Minorities have always been an unreliable source of power because they bargain with both
sides for their benefit - and

2) It means that the UNP has abandoned the majority which is its elementary base.

Eventually, both mainstream parties have to depend on the majority. Periodically, they will have to come back to the electorate and depend on the majority to regain or to retain power. The life span of those who pretend to be with the majority is very short as seen in the last two elections. The minorities play their own games to extract the maximum from the majority and as long their games are played non-violently, within the democratic norms; they can be accepted as legitimate players. Political bargaining outside the framework of the democratic processes with the gun blurs the rules of the game. It will be like playing cricket without wickets and umpires. Anybody can dictate any rule or make up the rules as they go along to suit their self-serving fantasies. Any game or an act that affects the public needs rules. Where there is no rule of law the rule of jungle (or is it the Vanni?) that takes over? The tenth attempt on the life of Douglas Devananda, an elected representative and a Cabinet minister, is the latest attempt to dismiss with contempt the rule of law and impose the rule of the Vanni. There are two basic meanings of this brutal bomb: 1) the popular version is that it is a reaction to the increasing threat to the LTTE arising from the first formidable challenge led by Karuna and 2) the unexplored hidden meaning is that the "bra bomber" was sent on the suicide mission just two days before the Provincial Councils' elections to deliver a loud and fearful message to the electorate that there can be no peace with President Chandrika Kumaratunga. The first is merely a superficial excuse promoted by A. T. Ariyaratne's doppelganger, Johann Perera, the self-appointed spokesperson for "national peace" without any legitimate mandate from the nation to speak on behalf of all the war-weary people in al the communities. Nor does he have the intellectual integrity to address hard realities staring in his face with objectivity and an acceptable degree of honesty. For instance, his latest attempt has been to perversely misrepresent the one-man fascist rule of Prabhakaran as the emerging democrat of the Tamils. Ariyaratne keeps J. Perera's on his pay roll because the latter's role as an apologist for Prabhakaran – a criminal on the wanted list of Interpol, India and Sri Lanka – helps to rake in foreign funds in the name of peace.

But, more than this, it is the timing of the bomb that is more significant and reflects the hidden agenda of the UNP and the NGOs. On the eve of the election it was known widely that the UNP-led coalition was facing a humiliating defeat. This pro-LTTE coalition had played all its cards and there was nothing more they could do to save face. The last straw was to explode a home-made bomb (brand name: PRABHAKARAN) to swing the votes in favour of Ranil Wickremesinghe by frightening the voters. The objective LTTE was to kill two birds with one bomb: a) it would have got rid of one of its inveterate Tamil opponents challenging his claim to be "the sole representatives of the Tamils" and (b) to swing the southern votes to project the image of Wickremesinghe as the man with the mandate to negotiate peace on the terms dictated by the LTTE. But the bomb backfired on both counts. LTTE times its political assassinations to coincide with elections. Rajiv Gandhi, President Premadasa, Lalith Athulathmudali, Gamini Dissanayake, Chandrika Kumaratunga, Maj. Gen. Lucky Algama were all attacked on the eve elections not only get rid of their opponents but also to impact on the coming elections. For instance, two suicide bombers of the LTTE launched a two-pronged attack simultaneous on December 18, 1999. One was the President Chandrika Kumaratunga campaigning at the Town Hall. She narrowly escaped death but lost her right eye. The other was Maj-Gen. Lucky Algama at the UNP meeting held in Jaela. He died on the spot. Lucky Algama, the new Military Adviser to Ranil Wickremesinghe, was on the UNP platform as the election campaign in 1999 was reaching its climax. As the results showed chances Wickremesinghe winning against Chandrika were very slim. Chandrika won by 51%. In hindsight it is absolutely clear that the bomb at the UNP rally was not meant for Wickremesinghe. It was meant specifically for Lucky Algama – a committed soldier who had bravely confronted the LTTE in the east and cleared it. He was a hawk out to get the LTTE.

The LTTE has always targeted only those who were a threat to them and Lucky no doubt was one of them. Wickremesinghe was not a threat to the LTTE like Lucky. So the LTTE targeted Lucky before Wickremesinghe arrived on the scene. The timing was significant. The explosion had to take place before Wickremesinghe arrived to prevent any collateral damage to him. Nor could the suicide bomber have mistaken the identity because at public rallies when the leader arrives he is received with loud announcements and noisy greetings. Before Wickremesinghe arrived the suicide bomber got as close as possible to Lucky and detonated the explosive tied to the body. LTTE never wastes a human bomb on mistaken identity. The LTTE pre-plans its assassinations methodically and in great detail. But why was Lucky selected as a target and not Wickremesinghe? It would have been embarrassing for Wickremesinghe to have anti-LTTE "Lucky' as his military adviser. "Lucky" was useful to dig up information of the "Jayasikuru Operations" for Wickremesinghe to use in parliament. But he couldn't have pursued a lovey-dovey relationship with the LTTE with "Lucky", a heroic soldier committed to eliminate the LTTE, as his Military Adviser. "Lucky" had to go and he was taken out by the LTTE just before Wickremesinghe was de to address the election meeting.

Is there a co-relation between the two? The pre-planned movements of the suicide bomber, timed to go off before Wickremesinghe arrived on the scene, indicate that care was taken to protect Wickremesinghe from any harm, even from a flying shrapnel. To achieve this objective the timing had to be accurate. Here it must be emphasized that even with the combination of these factors it is difficult to come to a definite conclusion. However, without pointing an accusing finger at Wickremesinghe as an accomplice it is reasonable to assume that the elimination of "Lucky" would have helped Wickremesinghe to pursue a policy of appeasing the LTTE.

Besides, of all the southern leaders the LTTE has spared only Wickremesinghe. Why? This is by no means an argument to insist that he should be eliminated like the other southern leaders. This is merely a statement of fact, whether anyone likes it or not. The reality is that it is in the short-term and long-term interests of the LTTE not only to keep Wickremesinghe alive but also to back him to the hilt with all the violent means at their disposal. With the secret agreements worked out by both parties (like the signing of the MoU without informing the president, the parliament or the people) the LTTE has been banking on Wickremesinghe to deliver what they can't get through violence. He is their chosen man who is expected to hand over to them a share of "asymmetrical power", or the nearest to a separate state. It is in their interest to make him win elections. Judging by the current policies pursued by the political parties in the south it is obvious that Wickremesinghe is the only source through which the LTTE has a chance of getting all their demands. And Wickremesinghe has revealed his hand by going along with the LTTE all the way. Take the case of the latest bombing. As the leading opposition party it was the moral and political responsibility of the UNP to condemn it outright without any reservations. Instead the UNP spokespersons virtually blamed the government and exonerated the LTTE. The logic behind it is that the UNP could not have blamed the LTTE for the suicide bombing because it was aimed at helping the UNP win votes in the Provincial Councils' elections. But, as in the case of presidential council elections of 1999, violent tactics proved to be counterproductive in the Provincial Councils' election of 2004.

Consider also Wickremesinghe's partiality to go along with the ISGA of the LTTE. America,Sri Lanka, India, the people who had expressed their will in two elections, the Sri Lankan expatriate community etc have condemned the ISGA as a non-viable proposal. The UNP is the only political party that is backing it. Why? The answer is simple: Wickremesinghe relies on the LTTE to regain and retain power. His secret agreements with the LTTE (like the way he signed the pre-arranged MoU secretly without letting the president, parliament and the people know) binds him to the LTTE as its proxy to pull their chestnuts out of the fire. He has abandoned the traditional bases of the UNP and fallen among terrorists. It can be said of him that he is a good man fallen among violent men.

A big factor looming large in the horizon is the possibility of a war starting sooner or later. Absit omen! With the known track record of the LTTE any excuse is valid for them to abandon peace talks and unilaterally start wars. It is also known that the LTTE has been gearing to launch its next war for quite some time. If a war breaks out whose side will the UNP take? Anyone could bet their bottom dollar that Wickremesinghe will not side with the nation, not with the war-weary people, not with peace but with the LTTE aggressors. War is also most desirable to the UNP for them to score political points. The UNP will bleat saying that they gave "peace" without acknowledging that it was they who strengthened the hand of the LTTE to regroup, consolidate and arm themselves to the teeth. Of course, all this is done in the name of peace. The hidden objective behind the explosion of the bomb at the Kollupitiya Police Station was to signal the people that only the secret alliance between Prabhakaran and Wickremesinghe can bring peace. The failure of this tactic should open the eyes of the public and the UNPers that there is no future for them in the leadership of Wickremesinghe. Shortly after the electoral debacle last week, the internet edition of the *Daily Mirror,* in its running news flashes, reported that a "UNP strongman was challenging the leader". But the next day's *Mirror* did not run the full story. Does this mean that the days of Wickremesinghe are numbered? Or, if he is to remain as leader, does this mean that the days of the UNP are numbered?

– Asian Tribune

Is LTTE the Sole Representatives of Tamils?

Shantha K. Hennayake

The purpose of this short essay is to point out the fictitiousness of the LTTE claim that they are the "sole representatives" of Tamils. This "sole representative" cry was deliberately raised by the LTTE in the aftermath of the MOU signed by former Prime Minister of Sri Lanka Ranil Wickremasinghe and LTTE leader V. Prabhakaran. MOU treated both the legitimate government of Sri Lankan and the terrorist group LTTE as equal partners! The MOU was brokered primarily by Norway with the explicit approval of the "international community". Post MOU developments have amply proved that Norway is no "honest broker of peace" but naked supporter of the LTTE appeasing the latter. In the name of keeping the MOU alive both Norway and former government have overlooked the continuation of terror by the LTTE even in the areas under the government control including the city of Colombo where the Norwegian embassy is located. It is ironic that the LTTE's hold on the Tamil society reached its highest under MOU era.

Some speculate that Norway itself may have advised the LTTE to redefine itself as the "sole representative of the Tamils as Norway was a party to the discussions that lead to the preparation of ISGA which for the first time publicly declared this claim. The primary reason for the invention of the claim "sole representative" of course is to ensure that LTTE and LTTE alone will be recognized and thus their demands or rather aspirations will have to be addressed and that LTTE will not be made accountable and held responsible for all terrorist activities i.e. torture and intimidation, murder and assassinations, child conscriptions, fratricide, illegal taxing, confiscating property against Tamil citizens of Sri Lanka. The claim is nothing but hijacking a democratic concept and making mockery of it by a terrorist group unfortunately with the help of Norway and other members of the "international community". *(Note that this article doe not deal with any of the terrorist acts against the Sri Lankan state, the Sinhalese and other ethnic groups*).

Unrealistic Demands

Tamil ethnonationalist politics during both its democratic phase (1930s- 1980s) and terrorist phase (1980- to present) is crowded with unrealistic demands which contributed to the problem over the years culminating in the destruction of the Tamil society culturally, politically and materially by the LTTE terrorism. The "50/50" demand which Karuna- Eastern Challenge to LTTE were designed to artificially inflate the political representation the Tamil minority in the legislature was rejected by the British constitutional experts in the mid 20 the century. The "monolithic Tamil homeland" demand which limit the representation in the Northern and Eastern Provinces exclusively to the Tamils has been rejected by the Tamils in the Eastern Provinces as became evident from the most recent challenge by Karuna.

The "separatist state demand" which make Tamils the sovereign representatives of an imaginary Tamil state of Eelam has been rejected by the Sri Lankan state, US, India a the international community but also by the Tamils living outside the LTTE's grip. Had Tamil politicians in Sri Lanka been more realistic and less extremist and certainly respected democracy and human rights Sri Lanka would have resolved this crisis earl and peacefully sparing the agony created by the LTTE terrorism in the country. The latest in this series of unrealistic demands is the claim by the LTTE that it is the "sole representative of the Tamils". This is perhaps the most unrealistic claim made by the LTTE so far.

It is important to understand the sole representative claim is made by the present LTTE which is an internationally declared terrorist organization and not by a reformed LTTE which has practically renounced terrorism and embraced democracy. Many a times during the last two years LTTE has threatened to revert to war –"LTTE's own term for terrorism". The latest public threat on the resumption of terrorism was made by its London based theoretician (England too have declared LTTE as a terrorist organization!) in May 2004 in laying out conditions for the resumption of "peace talks".

Implications of the Claim "Sole Representatives"

Let us first examine the meaning and broad implications of this claim to Sri Lanka and the world? It first and foremost legitimizes terrorism of the LTTE as it has not yet renounced terrorism. Then, threats and intimidation, murder, assassinations, child conscriptions and violation of human rights will not only be institutionalized but also be accepted as legitimate means of governance of the Tamil society in Sri Lanka. Second, resulting from the first, violence will continue to engulf the Tamil society as those Tamils opposing LTTE will have no other means but to resort to violence to express their own concerns as already happening in Batticaloa (Over 300 Batticaloa Tamils have been reported killed by the LTTE). Third, it sends a very positive signal to world terrorists that terrorism pays when the rest of the world (except perhaps Norway as revealed by Svik organization based in Norway) is actively trying to de legitimize terrorism and eliminate it from the face of the world. **It is ironic that when countries like Afghanistan which helped nurture intentional terrorists now actively collaborate with the international community to establish democracy and human rights, countries like Norway allow their own soil to nurture and support terrorism!** Fourth, it simply denies to the Tamil people democratic freedom and freedom of expression both of which are projected as the hallmark of modern democratic societies. Fifth, it creates a dual society in Sri Lanka where Tamils will have to live under authoritarianism and gun culture while others enjoy democracy and a civilized life. Sixth, it will send wrong and dangerous signal to the rest of the world where minority ethnonationalist politics is intensifying in general and to India in particular proving that legitimacy can be derived from the barrel of a gun and terror if it invokes ethnicity/religion. Seventh, it simply make the international community which preaches high morals and democracy to the rest of the world a bunch of jokers and hypocrites who have willingly reduced the Tamils to second rate human beings as if they don't deserve democracy and human rights. Eighth, it will ensure the establishment of a permanent armed group within the Sri Lankan state creating a potentially dangerous and explosive situation in the country. Ninth, it will create and internal "hate boundary" manned, womened, chldrened by the armed LTTE carders. Tenth, it will also create an LTTE will resort to ethnic cleansing as they have done in the past in the areas under their control. Tenth, and lastly, it could instigate a mass exodus of people – to and from Tamil areas – similar to the post partition experience in the sub-continent. Those who are blindly supporting the LTTE's claim for sole representativeness should thus be held responsible and accountable for all these potential negative implications.

LTTE is not a Representative Body

The general meaning of a representative is "a person or thing enough like the other in its class or kind to serve as an example or type". (Webster's Dictionary). Going by this it will be an insult to the Tamil people to consider LTTE as their sole representatives. There are definitely enough differences between a gun wielding terrorist and an ordinary Tamil citizen of Sri Lanka and it is highly unlikely that given the opportunity the peace l ordinary Tamils would parade an armed LTTE terrorist or a suicide bomber as an example of a typical Tamil person in Sri Lanka.

The political meaning of a representative is "a person duly authorized to act or speak or another or others; specify, a) member of a legislative assembly b) a salesman or agent for a business firm" (Webster's Dictionary). The concept of representativeness is thus rooted in democracy and it should not and cannot be associated with terrorist leaders or organizations: Osama Bin Laden and Al Qaida are not representatives let alone sole representatives of Islamic world. Representatives are duly elected and free and fair election is the only means of electing representatives and if the world has forgotten, the Tamil people did not elect LTTE to its current dominance in Tamil society. LTTE established its dominance by decimating the rival groups (a conservative estimate put the number over 8000 -9000) and assassinating democratic political leaders such as the founder of TULF, Mr. A. Amirthalingam and the world renowned constitutional expert and TULF parliamentarian Dr. Neelan Tiruchelavam. Terror, intimidation are the only means by which LTTE maintains its power and hold in the Sri Lanka Tamil society. In this context, LTTE has no moral right to claim any Tamil representativeness let alone sole representativeness of Sri Lanka Tamils.

As a rule of thumb a party should receive the consent of at least 50% of the voting population to claim the representativeness in a democracy. Needless to say "sole representativeness" is a practical contradiction in terms in a democracy as 100% consent for a single party is simply unattainable in any democracy. Even if we accept the result of the election of 2004 which was blatantly rigged by the LTTE, the LTTE cannot claim sole representativeness for a number of reasons (see Table 1). First the LTTE proxy party ITAK received only 36% of the total registered voters in the two provinces which they claim as the "Tamil homeland". Only in Batticaloa ITAK was able to barely surpassed the 50% mark of the total registered voters and in all others including Jaffna where LTTE launched a massive election rigging campaign. Second, a large percentage of people (registered voters) have not voted at the election at all. The figure is 31% for the entire region while it reached the highest in Jaffna.

This can be explained in two ways. First that a significant number of people have clearly stated by deliberately refraining from voting for ITAK that LTTE is not their sole representative. Second, if the absenteeism is due to the fact that people have left LTTE controlled region, then their very action is a proof that they do not want to live under LTTE rule. Either way, the Tamils in Sri Lanka has rejected the LTTE claim that they are the "sole representative" of the Sri Lanka Tamils.

District	Jaffna	Vanni	Trincomalee	Batticaloa	Digamadulla	Total NE
Total Registered	644,279	226,604	224,307	303,928	379,044	1,778,162
Polled	305,259	151,003	191,657	254,023	308,625	1,210,567
ITAK	257,320	90,835	68,955	161,011	55,533	633,654
Others	386,959	135,769	155,352	142,917	323,511	1,144,508
ITAK % of Total Registered	39.94	40.09	30.74	52.98	14.65	35.64
ITAK % of Total Polled	84.30	60.15	35.98	63.38	17.99	52.34
Absentees	52.62	33.36	14.56	16.42	18.58	31.92

(Computed from Election Commissioner's Official Results)

Third, Eelam Peoples Democratic Party won a Parliamentary seat in Jaffna securing 6.55% of the votes against all odds and violence perpetrated by LTTE. Fourth, a number of election monitoring missions as well as the Election Commissioner have clearly stated the extensive nature of election rigging and malpractices in Jffna for which LTTE is primarily responsible. Two court cases have been filed by EPDP and the President of TULF Mr. Anandasangari who contested Jaffna as an independent candidate to nullify the election result in the North and East due to LTTE atrocities. Mr. Anandasangari complained to the Supreme Court LTTE and ITAK intimidated the supporters of his Independent Group during the election campaign. The petition said that the electoral registers in Jaffna were last revised in 1983 and thus the youngest voter in Jaffna would be over thirty five years of age at present. However, LTTE has been impersonating many voters with people as young as fifteen years of age. The Returning Officer for the Jaffna District was unable to prevent the election offences committed by the LTTE and the ITAK supporters. He alleged that the LTTE made several death threats against him, his candidates and his supporters even before the nomination. He also stated that the LTTE had intimidated and blocked the campaigns of the other parties especially the EPDP and alleged that the LTTE illegally forced the people of the two districts to vote for the ITAK.

The simple question one need to ask here is why would Sri Lankan Tamils political leaders go to court and some people are willing to testify against the LTTE taking a grave chance to annul the election results in Northern and Eastern province where LTTE's proxy party TNA apparently won, if LTTE are the sole representatives of the Tamils?

LTTE does not and cannot represent Tamils

"Tamils", "Tamils in Sri Lanka" and "Sri Lankan Tamils" are three distinct and separate categories. Often these terms have been used confusingly by most who are ignorant on ethnopolitics Sri Lanka.

Tamils are a distinctive ethnic group concentrated primarily in Tamilnadu province in India. The area falling within present Tamilnadu in India has been the historical homeland or cultural hearth of Tamils from ancient times. Tamilnadu has developed its own ethno politics since 1947 and today it is an integral part of larger Indian national politics. Tamil politics in Tamilnadu has been essentially democratic and the Tamils have not allowed it to deteriorate into terrorism. LTTE has little to do with Tamil politics but India has always feared of the possibility of LTTE potential to expand across the Palk Straight into Tamilnadu.

In contrast to Tamils in India, Tamils in Sri Lanka is a general term encompassing three distinctive socio-cultural groups (Sri Lanka Tamils, Indian Tamils and Colombo Tamils) and two prominent regional groups (Jaffna Tamils and Batticaloa Tamils). Sri Lankan Tamils are the descendent of the Tamils who had migrated to the island from South India throughout the history as meticulously argued by the famous Sri Lankan Tamil historian, Prof. Indrapala. However their permanent settlements in the northern littoral of the island date back only to the 12th century. They are also called Jaffna Tamils. During the immediate pre colonial and colonial periods, some Sri Lankans Tamils migrated from Jaffna into the East and they came to be known as eastern or Batticaloa Tamils with a strong regional sentiments in opposition to Jaffna Tamils.

Tamil ethnonationalist politics in Sri Lanka has always been sphereheaded by Jaffna Tamils as the so called grievances and the aspirations of the Sri Lankan Tamils are in reality those of the Jaffna Tamils. Tamils and the LTTE itself is very largely a Jaffna Tamil phenomenon. Batticaloa Tamils have over the years developed a contempt for the "Jaffna domination" and have always questioned the efficacy of Tamil nationalism of Jaffna Tamils as most recently manifested by the LTTE's eastern commander Karuna's challenge to the Jaffna dominated LTTE leadership. At the last election which was marred with rigging by the LTTE, the performance of the LTTE proxy TNA in he Eastern Province was 41.4 per cent while those who opposed LTTE obtained 58.6 per cent votes.

Indian Tamils were the descendents of the indentured laborers drawn from the poorer and lower caste segments of Tamil society in South India to work in the British plantations opened in the central highlands after forcibly confiscating the land from the Sinhalese in the 19th century. Still most of the Indian Tamils live in plantations but a large number of them have migrated into the cities in the rest of the country. Indian Tamils have over the years evolved their own political parties and have well integrated into the mainstream politics. They have held cabinet portfolios in all governments since 1970s. Indian Tamils have rejected the separatist politics of the LTTE. Colombo Tamils are the descendent of the Tamils who came from Jaffna to reside in Colombo after they were recruited by the British to work for them in the colonial administration and related services in the government. Some Tamils came to Colombo to take advantage of the expanding economic opportunities. These professional and business classes together comprise Colombo Tamils. Colombo Tamils have always voted with the two major political parties and have openly rejected separatism.

Then, LTTE simply cannot be the sole representatives of "Tamils" simply because Tamils live in Tamilnadu India. The LTTE is cannot be the sole representatives of the Sri Lanka Tamils as the Batticaloa Tamils have openly defied the LTTE. LTTE cannot even claim to be the sole representative of the Jaffna Tamils as a significant number of Jaffna Tamils have voted against the LTTE. The mere sharing of the same language by the LTTE and other Tamil groups in Sri Lanka does not qualify the former to be a representative let along the sole representative of Tamils. Thus, the claim that LTTE is the sole representative of Tamils is simply in error and a total fantasy without supportive empirical basis. The only argument in support of their claim is the baseless claim itself maintained by sheer intimidation and terror!

How LTTE (Mis) treats Tamils in Sri Lanka

Many have argued that LTTE is a political reality in Sri Lanka today. Yes LTTE is a political reality in many ways yet representing Sri Lanka Tamils is the least of them. What are the facets of political reality of LTTE? First they do control some territory of the Northern and Eastern Provinces. Second, they do control the life of the Sri LankaTamil people living under their territory. Third, the LTTE largely control the politics of Sri Lanka Tamils in the Northern and Eastern Provinces. LTTE continue to murder any Sri Lanka Tamil who question or opposes its agenda. Fourth, LTTE continue to recruit Sri Lanka Tamil children as young as 12 years to their terrorist cadre. Fifth, LTTE has been taxing the Sri Lanka Tamils in their territory and those who passes through their territory to fund the organization and its war/terror machine. Sixth, LTTE does not allow or tolerate any other independent Tamil political or social organization or institution to emerge among the Sri Lanka Tamils. Seventh LTTE does not allow any free expression political or otherwise among the Sri Lanka Tamils. Eighth, LTTE have violently repressed and ideologically subdued the Sri Lanka Tamils living within their territory to force total and unconditional support for them. Ninth, LTTE does not allow any potential political leadership to emerge from among the Sri Lankan Tamils. LTTE has simply assassinated the potential independent leaders among them. Tenth, LTTE in the name of "Tamil nationalism" has determined that violation of human rights of Sri Lanka Tamils as both necessary and essential and LTTE sympathizers both local and international have simply endorsed it and even encouraged it.

Who can better testify who their representatives are other than those who said to be represented?. In this case the Sri Lanka Tamils themselves. Given below are a few statements made by political and non-political organizations of Sri Lanka Tamils themselves which have braved the LTTE threats and intimidation. It is important to note here that not only the LTTE but also their local and international supporters and legitimizers have conveniently overlooked these Tamil voices as they do not subscribe to the LTTE as the "sole representative of Tamils" thesis. Their very presence undermines the LTTE's claim.

Eelam Peoples Democratic Party

This is the only political party which had survived all threats, intimidations, assassination attempts by the LTTE. Formerly a guerrilla group, EPDP entered democratic politics renouncing terrorism in early 1990s and have been represented in the Parliament ever since. LTTE find this democratic political party and its democratically elected Parliamentarians "traitors" of the Tamils cause! At the last election EPDP won 24, 955 votes and secured a single seat in the Parliament thus politically and democratically defeating the LTTE claim to the 'sole representativeness". EPDP win become more revealing and meaningful when viewed in the context of total voter intimidation and threat by LTTE to vote for its proxy ITAK and election rigging by the LTTE. EPDP has filed an election petition at the Court of Appeal complaining of intimidation of EPDP electors by the LTTE, in the Batticaloa district.

EPDP now represented in the Cabinet has by rejecting the concept of LTTE as the sole representative of the Tamil people arguing that. "No section has the right to claim to be the legitimate representatives of the people of the North -East,". It further said that legitimizing this concept is not only incorrect and undemocratic and but also it could lead only to the setting up of a dictatorship under LTTE in the Tamil areas (see the EPDP Website).

EPDP has published in its website the LTTE atrocities directed against the ordinary Tamils as well as Tamil political organizations since the commencement of the ceasefire in early 2002. EPDP argues that since then "hostile acts by the LTTE against democratic Tamil parties have systematically increased in intensity and form. What commenced with intimidation, threats, assaults, and forced conscription have now advanced to attacks, abductions and assassinations". Under what political system, can these acts be considered the activities of a sole representative of a people? The executive summary of the EPDP report is worth quoting extensively as it provides a comprehensive summary of the activities directed against the Tamil people in general and other Tamil political organizations in particular by the LTTE.

"This report covers 598 incidents of hostile acts by the LTTE against civilians, including democratic Tamil parties. In respect of the EPDP, members, activists and supporters of the party, and even their family members have suffered 50 cases of attacks or assaults, and 20 cases of abductions or attempted abductions. They have suffered 15 deaths. In addition, there have been 33 cases of intimidation.

In respect of the EPRLF too, members, activists and supporters of the party, and their family members have suffered 26 cases of attacks or assaults, and 18 cases of abductions or attempted abductions. They have suffered 12 deaths. In addition, there have been 2 cases of intimidation.

In respect of the PLOTE also, members, activists and supporters of the PLOTE, and their family members have suffered 14 cases of attacks or assaults, and, 1 case of abduction. They have suffered 4 deaths. The records in respect of civilians are in no way complete. Nevertheless, the information provided in this report is quite revealing, pointing to not less than 775 cases of child conscription, 199 cases of adult abductions, 197 cases of attacks or assaults, and, 91 cases of death."

The LTTE threat and intimidation and killing has not spared women and children, young and old, educated and less educated, farmers and government employees, and politically neutral and active. The common denominator in directing violence, intimidation and terror is simply the direct or indirect, real or assumed threat to the LTTE. These acts hardly reflect those of a sole representative of the Sri Lanka Tamils. If at all they reflect the acts of a sworn enemy of Sri Lanka Tamils!

The Human Rights Commission of Sri Lanka

The Human Rights Commission of Sri Lanka led by a Sri Lanka Tamil woman made the following observations regarding the LTTE. The relevant sections are reproduced as they are self explanatory and revels that LTTE behavior is anything but representative of the Sri Lanka Tamils.

"Since the ceasefire agreement and up to September 2003, there have been 38 so called political killings which relatives of the victims attribute to the LTTE. The victims of these political killings have been identified as members of Tamil political groups opposed to the LTTE and Tamils working with the Sri Lankan security forces"

With regard to continuing killing of Tamils by the LTTE the Commission stated "This situation led one of those who made representations to the Commission to say "the killings of Sinhalese have stopped but there is no ceasefire for the Tamils".... The impunity for these crimes following the ceasefire has serious human rights implications. The right to life is the most fundamental of all human rights and if that right is taken away arbitrarily and violently without due process of law, the most basic of all rights is violated"

On the issue of child conscriptions the Commission report states the following. "Of the 600 cases (of ceasefire violations reported by SLMM), 25% of the cases (around 150) related to chilled abductions. The SLMM also pointed out that their investigation lead to the conclusion that only 10% of the actual cases are reported to them. This is confirmed by the UNICEF figures that around 709 children have been known to be recruited by the LTTE in the past year."

The Commission also highlighted the abduction of adult Sri Lanka Tamils. "The abduction of children is also augmented by the abduction of adults, either for ransom or punitive treatment. The SLMM records around 130 such complaints of adult abductions for 2003. The Batticaloa office of HRC received complaints of 58 adult abductions for the year 2003..... As a result there is a great deal of insecurity and fear among the people living their daily lives, especially if they are from the middle class".

On the issue of illegal taxation, the Commission observed the following. "Until recently the government servants allegedly had to pay 5% of their salaries as taxes to the LTTE. .. with regard to agriculture they had to pay between 500-1000 Rs. Per acre per season, Rs.10-15000 a month for tractor use during the harvest season. Laborers have to pay Rs 25/= a month a part of their salary. Businessmen and fishermen also have to pay taxes on the goods they transform and on their earning and fisherman have to pay taxes on their catch. The arbitrary and unreasonable deprivation of property is a human right violation. (Taxes) They are also sometimes so exorbitant, crippling the economic and social life of the community". Given these accounts of the LTTE, one is compelled to ask the question how could a sole representative of a people engaged in a systematic violation of all conceivable human rights of that people.

On the issue of political freedom and freedom of expression the Commission report observed the following. " Complaints to the Commission from the eastern province, both written form and oral communication, point to a ear of harassment for voicing independent opinion as asserting one's freedom of speech or association. And in the Commission concluded with the following statement; " The LTTE displays a tendency to want to control all activity and programs in the areas under its authority with a tenaciousness that is very disturbing. This has major implications not only for the human rights of individuals living in these areas

University Teachers for Human Rights (Jaffna)

The University Teachers for Human Rights (Jaffna) was formed in 1988 by a group of Tamil intellectuals at the University of Jaffna. Its activities came to a standstill with the assassination of Dr. Mrs. Rajani Thiranagama, a key founding member, in September 1989 by the LTTE. Since then other UTHR(J) members were forced to leave Jaffna due to threat from LTTE.The following statement of UTHR (J) is a telling indictment against the LTTE's claim to be the sole representatives of the Sri Lanka Tamils.

"By combination of internal terror and narrow nationalist ideology the LTTE succeeded in atomizing the community. It took away not only the right to oppose but even the right to evaluate, as a community, the course they were taking. This gives a semblance of illusion that the whole society is behind the LTTE http://www.uthr.org/history.htm

A 2001 UTHR (J) report titled clearly states how and why LTTE has decided to make the sole representative claim. Given the behavior of LTTE within the Sri Lanka Tamil community, the human right activists perceived LTTE as an "oppressor" an appellation that directly contradict the LTTE's claim to the "sole representatives of Sri Lanka Tamils".

It has become clear that the LTTE will turn against any peace negotiations that do not recognize it as the sole legitimate representative of the Tamil people while giving unconstraint control of the North East. The LTTE's politics is primarily defined by its ideologically-driven military agenda and its ideology rather than by any concern for the civilian well being.

The LTTE has eliminated all opposition and exercises total domination in the regions it controls - i.e., it appropriates or directs the efforts of all organized forms of civil society-through an organic surveillance system. As a result, in their areas of control, sustained independent protest and public dissent has become impossible.

It appears the trend has intensified over the years to the extent that even the democratic political parties too have succumb to LTTE domination as clearly revealed by the performance of ITAK now in Parliament. UTHR (J) continued with a few questions to those who are too willing to accept the LTTE claim of sole representative of Sri Lanka Tamils.

Accordingly, NGOs pursuing peace must recognize the consequences of this climate of internal terror in the North and East, of the near complete control the LTTE exercises over all civil society activities within its domains of control. We need to face difficult questions: What political space is available for local participants in peace conferences who wish to continue to function in their respective regions, to engage in a free exchange of views? If we want to hear the views of the ordinary people of that region, how can we counter the climate of internal terror that already manages the stage and writes the script? What structures/ mechanisms must be instituted in such conferences to best produce a map of representative views? What is our responsibility when those we proclaim to be our sole representatives are denying this democratic space by engaging in activities ranging from forced child recruitment to political killings?

UTHR (J) further explains how LTTE tries to maintain its dominance among Sri Lanka Tamils both in Sri Lanka and abroad.

"We recognize that the LTTE as a group is rooted in narrow nationalist ideology bent on asserting its dominance through internal terror. It is a group that has made a virtue of political and internecine killings; It is a group that hassuccessfully established a robust international network that can provide resources for relatively long periods; It is a group that has extended its terror among the expatriate community to silence the dissidents and, most importantly, it has perfected suicide politics to a point where, the resulting ambience of fear, works subtly on decision-makers in the region."

UTHR (J) also warns the consequences of the acceptance of LTTE as the sole representative of the Sri Lanka Tamils in the peace negotiations.

"However, if a peace process primarily aimed at negotiations for a political settlement and opening up space, is not a feasible agenda for peace groups, and civil society organizations in the

Tamil community remained totally subservient to the LTTE, then peace is going to be a pipe dream. That would leave only the international community, if they so desire, to make the State and, particularly, the LTTE, accountable."

In a more recent report titled "*The Worm Turns and the Elections Where the People will Not Count*" UTHR (J) describes "both clear cases of political violence aimed at silencing electoral challenges to the LTTE's claim to be the Tamil people's "sole representative" as well as details of its ongoing campaign to root other less obvious challenges to LTTE authority". Sri Lanka's donors have encouraged the LTTE expansion under the misguided premise that the group could be eased into a democratic process; and they have failed to take responsibility for the abuse that has occurred as a result".

The LTTE has been able to push its theory of "sole representative "purely by terror. UTHR (J) contextualized this very convincingly in arguing that "Might is right has been the basis on which the Norwegian brokered MoU was framed. Repeated appeals by other that it needed revision because it in effect gave open sanction for the LTTE to consolidate its terror in the government controlled areas went unheard. Those who had to flee their homes into the abject misery owing to the LTTE's violence or to protect their children form its abduction gangs, were simply ignored".

It is sad indeed, if power hungry politicians within Sri Lanka and now international community all accept LTTE as the sole representative of the Tamils and continue with legitimizing and appeasing the LTTE purely to keep the so called peace process and MOU totally disregarding violence and terrorism perpetrated by LTTE on the Tamils. This tantamounts to denying the Sri Lankan Tamils democratic freedoms and even the basic human rights. The so called "sole representatives" of the Tamils have stolen the soul of the Tamil society with the open concurrence of the Sri Lankan political leaders and the international community as represented by such countries as Norway which has openly supported the

LTTE. A future democratic Tamil political leadership should hold not only the LTTE, the two Sri Lankan governments of the UNP and SLFP but also Norway and other members of the so called international community which flirted with the LTTE responsible for the injustice done to the Tamil society by legitimizing a terrorist rule and denying democracy.

Conclusion

In conclusion, the claim by the LTTE to be the sole representatives of the Tamils is flawed and untenable for a number of reasons. First, the "sole representatives" is a far fetched concept that cannot hold true even in the most repressive political systems in the world. Thus the concept cannot exit but in theory and fantasy. Second, LTTE is not an elected body and thus it cannot be representative let alone sole representative. Third, LTTE cannot be respected with a title of a representative given its long record of human right violations of Sri Lanka Tamils. Fourth, the LTTE cannot be representatives as they maintain their supremacy within the Tamil society only through sheer threats, intimidation and terror. Fifth, a number of Tamil political parties and human rights organizations have openly and successfully challenged the LTTE claim to be the sole representatives of Tamils. LTTE is better qualified to be identified as sole repressors than sole representatives of the Sri Lanka Tamils. Given this reality if an individual, organization, or a country continue to support the LTTE's claim to be the sole representative of the Sri Lanka Tamils, they are doing the greatest injustice to the Tamil people in Sri Lanka.

References

Report of the Human Rights Commission of Sri Lanka- Human Rights situation in the Eastern Province: Civil and political rights: — allegations against the LTTE http://www.island.lk/2004/05/12/featur02.html Reports of the Human Rights Commission of Sri

Lanka. *Human Rights Situation in the Eastern Province. Civil and Political Rights:- Allegation Against the LTTE.*

The Island http://www.island.lk/2004/05/13/opinio11.html

The Island http://www.island.lk/2004/05/12/featur03.html

The Island http://www.island.lk/2004/05/12/news11.html

http://www.epdpnews.com/A-Hostile%20Acts.html

The Daily Mirror

UTHR (J) Briefing No. 4: Date of Release : 4th December 2001: Peace activism, suicidal politics and civil society (http://www.uthr.org/Briefings/Briefing4.htm)

Peace within a Framework of Sovereignty, Territorial Integrity, Democracy, and Human Rights

Neville S. Ladduwahetty

Every state is a conglomeration of groups with distinguishing characteristics such as race, ethnicity, language, and religion living within a defined territory. Within each one of these distinguishing groups, further divisions such as social and class distinctions exist. If the conditions within a state are such that any of these groups is either excluded or affected by the process of nation building, ensuing discontent can lead to instability, and in general, if either the sense of exclusion or the degree to which they are affected is sufficiently extreme as to deny fundamental rights to a meaningful livelihood and a sense of well-being, it can lead to violence and civil unrest.

The inability of some groups within states to partake of the "good life" has been offered as the reason for most of the current conflicts in the world. Consequently, most dispossessed groups hope to redress their grievances as a right and an entitlement that is owed to them by virtue of universally accepted rights such as the "right to life, liberty, and the pursuit of happiness" as stated in 1776 in the American Declaration of Independence, and the right of "self-determination of peoples", a concept that emerged following World War 1, and is current in several of the more recent instruments of the United Nations following the Charter of the United Nations in 1945.

The fortunes of groups, however, can alter with circumstances.

For instance, during the colonial period minorities were favoured over majorities as a colonial administrative policy. Consequently, minorities in most colonial countries, (such as in Sri Lanka) enjoyed privileges that were denied to majorities. With the gaining of independence from colonial rule, the fortunes of majorities changed enabling them to redress the injustices perpetrated on them by the colonial powers. Instead of understanding that the processes at work were attempts to redress the injustices endured by the majorities during centuries of colonial rule and negotiating reasonable transitions, the dominant minorities often perceived the policies of the newly emergent majorities as deliberate attempts to discriminate against them.

This was the background in many countries of Africa, South and East Asia, and other parts of the world following the break-up of former Empires and decolonization. The newly dispossessed minorities perceived themselves as perpetual minorities. Their inability to negotiate arrangements that would help them to maintain their positions of advantage made them seek exclusionary arrangements such as regional autonomy or even separation. These reactions were in turn perceived by the new majorities as affronts to their sovereignty and to the territorial integrities of their states. The dominant minorities in most decolonized states then resorted to violence claiming entitlement to separation from the rump states, sanctified and sanitized by misplaced conceptions of self-determination.

The background to the conflict in Sri Lanka was no different. At independence in 1948, it is a universally acknowledged fact that the Sri Lankan Tamils who were about 12% of Sri Lanka's population, were a privileged minority community, having become so under a century and half of British colonial rule. To them, independence of a democratic Sri Lanka meant that they would be "... exposed to the danger of Sinhala domination" resulting in an erosion of their position of privilege. (Kearney, "Communalism and Language in the Politics of Ceylon", 1967, p.98). Quoting

Mr. Rasamanikam, Kearney states: "Sinhalese-Tamil problem in Ceylon is not a mere matter of language. It is one that affects our very existence as a national entity in the country."(Ibid, p. 97). This threat of 'domination' will persist as long as the Tamil community continues to maintain itself outside the pale by limiting themselves only to Tamil or even Tamil and English. On the contrary, ability to function in Sinhala would enable them to compete equally with the majority and yet retain their ethnic identity. It is NOT exclusion but inclusion that would prevent "Sinhala domination", as it has been with the Irish, the Welsh and the Scots in the UK, or for the multitude of ethnic groups that inhabit the United States.

The Two Nation Theory

Fear of Sinhala domination made the Sri Lankan Tamils come up with proposals that would make them as a group "feel equal" with the Sinhalese in the governance of the state, either as partners in the central government of a unitary state, or as a majority in a sizable portion of a federal state. Conceptually, the first option would have been acceptable to the Sinhalese because it would not have affected the territorial integrity of the state. However, the minority proposal for central power sharing was for equal representation, ("50-50" for the 25% minorities which included he Sri Lankan Tamils, and for the 75% Sinhala majority) in the Parliament of independent democratic Sri Lanka. The proposal was unacceptable to the Sinhalese because it was considered to be unreasonably excessive.

Upon rejection of their excessive and unreasonable proposal the Sri Lankan Tamils next sought a further audacious exclusionary arrangement of federalism based on a territorial unit in the Northern and Eastern Provinces, which encompassed 1/3 of the island's land mass and 2/3 of its coastline for 2/3 of the Sri Lankan Tamils residing in the region, i.e., 8% of the country's population. The unreasonableness of the extent of the federal unit demanded caused a valid concern on the part of the 75% Sinhala majority, that federalism was but a first step which would eventually lead to the division of the country.

Both arrangements sought by the Sri Lankan Tamils were with a view to "feeling equal" with the Sinhalese. A federal arrangement that included the Eastern Province in a Tamil federal unit was especially unacceptable to the Sinhalese because this particular province had for millennia been part of the Sinhala Kandyan Kingdom until the entire Kingdom was ceded to the British in 1815, as proven by treaties. Having failed to secure acceptance for an arrangement that would meet their expectations, the Sri Lankan Tamils then resolved in 1976 at Vaddukoddai, to establish a separate state in the Northern and Eastern Provinces of Sri Lanka, even if it meant a resort to arms, on the grounds of the right of self-determination.

Territorial Integrity and The Right of External Self-Determination

The issue of self-determination poses several questions that have not been answered since it was first introduced as a concept by U.S. President Woodrow Wilson at the League of Nations in 1918. Ever since the term "self-determination" was first incorporated into the United Nations Charter in 1945 there has been considerable debate as to what it means and to whom it applies, because Article 1 paragraph 2 refers to "equal rights and self-determination of peoples". What or who constitutes the term "peoples"? For instance, according U.N. Publication No. E.80.XIV.3, "it will be found that there is no accepted definition of the word "peoples" and no way of defining it with certainty....The various possibilities of interpretation and the consequent uncertainties could in many cases turn the right of peoples to self-determination into a weapon for use against the territorial integrity and political unity of states.... Improperly understood, this right could also lead to encouragement of secessionist movements in the territory of independent states, where any group whatsoever might believe that it had an immediate and absolute right to create a State of its own."

This lack of clarity as to whether the term "peoples" could apply to any group within a state has made minority groups aspire to statehood based on the right of selfdetermination in the hope that it is a right that can be claimed by any group. The Sri Lankan Tamils claimed the right of self-determination in 1976 and the most recent group to make a similar claim are the Kurds of Iraq. When groups within a state aspire to statehood they seek "external self-determination". The issue however, is whether groups within states have the right to exercise external self-determination, because it would inevitably disturb the territorial integrity of the state and in the process deny the right of self-determination to the others in the state who have a right to retain the integrity of their territory. Furthermore, if the principle is extended it would lead to endless fragmentation and chaos.

In the instruments of the United Nations, the term "peoples" applies to colonial peoples only. For instance, according to Antonio Cassese "Article 1(2) of the U.N. Charter was eventually perceived and relied upon as a legal entitlement to decolonization.....this was the first time that an international legal rule proclaimed self-determination qua the right of a whole population to democratic rule"(Self-Determination of Peoples- A Legal Reappraisal, 1995, pp. 65,66). Continuing, Cassese states: "The legal position..... summarized by the International Court of Justice in its Advisory opinion on Namibia (was that) if the population of a colonial territory is divided up into various ethnic groups or nations, they are not at liberty to choose by themselves their external status. This is because the principle of territorial integrity should here play an overriding role"(Ibid, p. 72).

In the opinion of Dov Ronen, a fellow at Harvard University's Center for International Affairs, "The Charter of the United Nations, the Covenant on Human Rights, the Declaration on the Granting of Independence to Colonial Countries and Peoples.....

are specifically aimed at colonized countries"(Ronen, The Quest for Self-Determination, 1979, p.5). A similar opinion is expressed by John Chipman. In an article titled "Managing the Politics of Parochialism" he states: "...neither in the instruments of the United Nations, nor in customary international law as a whole, does there exist any legal right to independence, by means of the right of self-determination for any noncolonial people or for a minority within an existing state" ("Ethnic Conflict and International Security", ed. Michael E.Brown, 1995,p.242).

In view of these and other similar opinions, external self-determination, meaning the right of secession unilaterally, is denied to groups within states. Even under conditions where human rights violations have taken place the international community has not supported secessionist initiatives. This has been the case with Kosovo and is the current attitude in the case of the Kurds in Iraq.

Claims to territory based on historical boundaries is also not recognized by the international community because the recognition of such a concept would mean that each contending party would select particular points in history that would be most advantageous to them. Similarly, refiguring states based on precolonial boundaries the doctrine of uti posidatis - would lead to chaos in Africa and South America. Consequently, the Organization of African Unity has accepted the principle of the inviolability of the colonial boundaries. Drawing a distinction between Eritrea and Sudan, Isaiass Afwerki, President of Eritrea states: "(South Sudan) falls within a category different from that of Eritrea in that the South did not have a history of a separate existence from the North during British colonization. The whole of Sudan, including the South, was a British colony until 1956 when the country formally obtained its independence"(Harvard International Review, Vol.XVII, No.3, Summer, 1995, p.21). Similarly, under the principle of the inviolability of colonial boundaries, the Sri Lankan Tamil claim for a separate state clearly has no legitimacy.

Since the right of external self-determination is recognized by the international community for colonized peoples, minorities have attempted to justify secession on the grounds that they are being internally colonized by dominant groups within the state. This argument was presented by the Sri Lankan Tamils at the International Conference of Tamil Nationhood and the Search for Peace in Sri Lanka held in Ottawa in May 1999.

The theory of internal colonialism is based on the premise that policies and processes of economic development controlled by the dominant group at the center is exploitative and is deliberately skewed. However, while such circumstances may exist in some countries, the reverse has been true in the case of the Sri Lankan Tamils. The Soulbury Commission (led by Lord Soulbury of Britain) acknowledged in 1945 that the Sri Lankan Tamils were a disproportionately privileged minority, and that the processes at work were not meant to discriminate against the Sri Lankan Tamils, but to redress decades of neglect and injustice perpetrated on the larger Sri Lankan nation, almost all of whom were Sinhalese. When attempts are made to redress past injustices through affirmative action such as those adopted by the US under the Civil Rights Legislation, it is inevitable that the privileged would be affected negatively. What took place in Sri Lanka was no different. Therefore, the Sri Lankan Tamil claim for the right of external selfdetermination on grounds of internal colonialism is also baseless.

Having failed to justify the creation of a separate state on the grounds of external selfdetermination, the Liberation Tigers of Tamil Eelam (LTTE), claiming to be the sole representatives of the Sri Lankan Tamils, "...agreed to explore a solution founded on the principle of internal self-determination...", during the peace negotiations in Oslo in December 2002.

Territorial Integrity and Internal Self-Determination

With independence, the "peoples" of Sri Lanka secured their right to external selfdetermination. This right gave them the freedom to choose the preferred structures and forms of government that would best serve them. These internal arrangements are what Cassese calls "internal self-determination" (Ibid, p.101). However, these internal determinations become valid only if they are established democratically. The ideal would be if there is unanimity in respect of these internal determinations. Since it would not be possible to assure unanimity in respect of all issues, internal determinations often would be based on the determinations of the majority. In such instances, either the dissenting minority should negotiate a compromise solution or accept the decision of the majority, but under no circumstances would they be entitled to indulge in determinations that are separate, independent, and outside the framework of the determinations of the majority.

These were the views of a group of individuals with no official status made up of academics, politicians, trade-union leaders, and representatives of national liberation movements who met in Algiers in 1976 and produced the document titled "The Algiers Declaration on the Rights of Peoples". The essence of this declaration is that for internal self-determination to be satisfied, the whole population must freely and democratically choose its preferred form and structure of government. They must democratically elect a government that is representative of the whole population, and it is the duty of the elected representatives to ensure that they reflect the will of the Peoples at all times. The Algiers Declaration also states that if the freedom to make the choices freely are denied, the right of internal self-determination is violated in addition to fundamental freedoms and human rights.

Therefore, since the Sri Lankan Tamils have never been denied the opportunity to be freely elected to the Sri Lankan Parliament on the basis of nationally legislated electoral laws, and also to freely participate in the internal self-determinations of Sri Lanka, they are not entitled to the right of a separate and distinct internal self-determination that is independent of the internal self-determination of the non-Sri Lankan Tamils in Sri Lanka. In 1975, 35 States constituting the Conference on Security and Cooperation in Europe (CSCE) adopted a declaration that came to be known as the Helsinki Declaration. This document affirmed that ".....the peoples referred to in the Helsinki Final Act are the whole population of each signatory State (and) by contrast, no right to self-determination is granted to any minority or ethnic group...furthermore, no right to secession is recognized" Cassese, Ibid, p.287).

Democracy and Internal Self-Determination

Despite the refusal by the international community to recognize the right of internal selfdetermination for ethnic or other minority groups within a state, minorities such as the Basque nationalist parties persist in demanding this right (The New York Times, August 15, 1999), as do the Sri Lankan Tamils. Granting one group a right that other groups in that territory do not enjoy contradicts the basic tenets of Democracy, and the principle that in a Democracy all are equal without distinction of race, religion, or regional belonging.

During the negotiations in Oslo, the LTTE as the self-appointed sole representatives of the Sri Lankan Tamils, demanded that the Sri Lankan Government recognize the right of internal self-determination of the Tamil-speaking peoples. Although there is ambiguityas to the composition of "Tamil-speaking peoples", since the LTTE represents only Sri Lankan Tamils and no other groups, it would be correct to conclude that the right of internal self-determination that is being sought is only for those they represent. If the right is to be enjoyed only by all Sri Lankan Tamils regardless of where they reside, it would be discriminatory by the other communities, because the latter would be denied a privilege that would be enjoyed exclusively by the Sri Lankan Tamils. On the other hand, if such a right is granted only to the Sri Lankan

Tamils residing in a defined region, it would be discriminatory by the Sri Lankan Tamils living outside such a region, as well as all the other communities in Sri Lanka regardless of whether they live within such a region or outside it.

One way to recognize the right to internal self-determination only for the Sri Lankan Tamils would be to create an exclusively homogeneous Sri Lankan Tamil region. However, the creation of such a region could only be accomplished by resorting to serious human rights violations resulting in ethnic cleansing. Aside from it being a humanitarian disaster, to create a homogeneous Sri Lankan Tamil region with the right of internal self-determination would to compel other communities in Sri Lanka to make their own separate internal self-determinations. This would institutionalize two or more separate internal self-determinations within one state; a condition that is totally unacceptable because it is tantamount to two de facto separate states with the potential for constant tension and instability.

On the other hand, if the right of internal self-determination is recognized only for the Tamil-speaking peoples within a heterogeneous region, it would result in discrimination being institutionalized, since all those who are non Tamil-speaking would cease to be part of the "self" in the process of self-determination. This would violate the basic tenets of Democracy because Democracy requires the participation of all "peoples" in the processes of government and in the processes that determine the collective "self". If the Tamil-speaking peoples exercise the right of internal self-determination it would compel other groups in Sri Lanka to make their own separate self-determinations, and cause the institutionalization of two or more separate and different internal self-determinations, as in the case of a homogeneous region. Internal self-determination is thus unacceptable for a heterogeneous region also because by implication it recognizes two de facto states. In fact, the proposals of the LTTE for an Interim Self Governing Authority (ISGA) approximates to this condition which is the justification for its rejection.

The territory over which the right of internal self-determination is to be exercised is to be Northern and Eastern provinces of Sri Lanka. The presumption is that Sri Lankan Tamils in both provinces are committed to the pursuit of this goal. The deep and distinct social and cultural separateness of the Tamils in each of the provinces make it an incorrect presumption (see Appendix 1 - McGilvray, Tamil and Muslim Identities in the East, Marga Institute, Monograph No.24, 2001, p.5; also K.M.de Silva, Separatist Ideologies in Sri Lanka, ICES, 1995, p.18). The most recent manifestation of this separateness is the split within the ranks of the LTTE into the Northern and Eastern factions. Internal selfdetermination under these circumstances must mean two separate determinations among the Sri Lankan Tamils themselves making a mockery of the demand for internal self-determination for Sri Lankan Tamils.

Therefore, the right of internal self-determination for a national or regional group is an unworkable proposition because aside from it being discriminatory by the rest who are denied a similar right, it would result in two or more self-determinations within the same territory giving rise to a multiplicity of de facto states. However, since the demand for such a right underscores the urge for regionally based groups to fashion their destinies, democracy and democratic practices allow regionally based groups who invariably are in the majority, to fashion the course of events to suit their priorities without the right of internal self-determination. No justifiable grounds exist for a right to internal selfdetermination to be granted to any single group while it is denied to other groups.

Democracy, Regional Autonomy and Federalism

Regionally based minorities look for political arrangements such as regional autonomy or federalism due to the narrow interpretation of Democracy as the "will of the majority". The will of the majority or majoritarianism often results in excluding minorities from the processes of governance. This is not only undemocratic but also violates the concept of internal self-determination that requires all to participate in defining the "self" of the nation. Therefore, for a Democracy to be stable it is necessary to create mechanisms to prevent simple majorities from ruling. Majoritarianism of one ethnic group, the Sinhalese, has been attributed to being the cause for the conflict in Sri Lanka.

Regional autonomy, devolution, or federalism are proposed as mechanisms to protect minorities from the excesses of majority rule or majoritarianism. They are viewed as opportunities for regional minorities to be associated with the governing processes relating to the region. However, under any of these arrangements national minorities are transformed into majorities in their dominant regions, and unless there are mechanisms in place to protect the minorities in those regions the excesses of majoritarianism would flourish unchecked. For instance, although the Sri Lankan Tamils are a national minority of about 12%(1981 Census), they are a 86% majority in the Northern Province, and a 65% majority in a combined Northern and Eastern Province. Regional autonomy or a federal unit based on a combined Northern and Eastern Province would create conditions for majority rule by the Sri Lankan Tamils. However, the other communities in the region would be greatly disadvantaged without safeguards to protect them. The oppressed, thus becomes the new oppressor.

If safeguards can be developed for the minorities of the combined Northern and Eastern Province to be protected from the excesses of Sri Lankan Tamil majority rule, the same safeguards should protect the Sri Lankan Tamils against the majority Sinhalese in the national context. The problem is therefore not with majority rule but in implementing safeguards against the negative effects that may arise from majority rule, because, in truth, no effective alternative to majority rule has been developed. According to Dhal "...the problem posed by majority rule and the alternatives to it is one of extreme difficulty for which no completely satisfactory solution has yet been found.... we are entitled to be just as skeptical about claims that an alternative would be clearly superior to majority rule or more consistent with the democratic processes and its values. For all the alternatives to majority rule are also seriously flawed". Continuing, Dahl states: "In a majority country, the protection of minority rights can be no stronger than the commitment of the majority of the citizens to preserve the primary democratic rights of all citizens, to maintain respect for their fellow citizens, and to avoiding the adverse consequences of harming a minority. So too in a democratic country with a nonmajority system, the protection of majorities against abusive minorities can be no stronger than the commitment of protected minorities not to abuse their opportunities to veto majority decisions they dislike" (Democracy and its Critics, 1989 p.110-162).

Nordlinger identified "six Conflict-Regulating Practices" in divided societies but did not include federalism as one of them, the reason being that in his opinion "...federalism may actually contribute to a conflict's exacerbation and the failure of conflict regulation. In some deeply divided societies it is impossible to draw state boundaries without including a large number of individuals belonging to segments whose territorial base is elsewhere. Federalism thus allows or encourages the dominant segment in one state to ignore or negate the demands of the minority segment. The possible consequences vary, but they may very well lead to the conflict's exacerbation, as happened with an Ibo minority living in Northern Nigeria" (Occassional Papers on International Affairs, January 1972, No. 29, "Conflict Regulation in Divided Societies, p.31). This could well apply to the Sri Lankan situation.

Ethnically based autonomous or federal units, as proposed for Sri Lanka, have the potential to be unstable to the point of secession because the exercise of constitutional privilege by one or more federal units could have adverse effects on a national majority in other units, in which event the exercise of constitutional privilege would be undemocratic. Furthermore, since powers to federal units are constitutionally guaranteed, the opportunity for consensus is remote. Consequently, ethnically based autonomous or federal units are prone to be unstable. Since regional autonomy or federalism in Sri Lanka would be ethnically based, either of these solutions as an antimajoritarian measure would lead to instability and eventual secession.

Federalism in the Sri Lankan context would mean creating an ethnically based federal unit for just one-half of the Sri Lankan Tamil population, and against the wishes of all the other communities. This violates all norms of Democracy and would lead to discontent and instability whenever such a federal unit adopts policies that are detrimental to the interests of the other federal units that make up about 95% of Sri Lanka's population. The converse could equally affect the federal unit in question. Furthermore, such a federal unit is incapable of internally generating the resources needed for it to function, and therefore would become dependent on the resources of the rest of the federation to maintain itself. Under such circumstances federalism is unsuitable in the particular context of Sri Lanka. Commenting on federalism as a conflict resolving arrangement, John Burton states: "...trying to impose some integrated structure such as a federation, has created more problems than solutions." (Global Conflict, 1984, p. 95).

Commenting on the durability of federalism, Nordlinger quoting Rothschild (The Limits of Federalism, 1972)states:"..... where federalism has been employed, as in Nigeria, Mali, East Africa, Ethiopia and the Congo Republic, the results have not been notable for their enduring qualities. Federal systems have remained operative for relatively brief periods of time, followed by fissure into separate, sovereign parts or movements towards unitary systems. Federalism has proved brittle". More recent examples of failed federal states are the Soviet Union and Yugoslavia, with the potential for failure in other federal states such as Canada and Belgium because the federal units in these states are ethnically based. On the other hand, federal states such as the United States and Australia are stable because the contours of the federal units are not ethnically based. Thus, ethnically based federalism is prone to failure, and is a lesson to be kept in mind when developing the road map for peace in Sri Lanka.

The Importance of The Eastern Province in a Federal Framework

Sri Lankan Tamils have laid claims to the Northern and Eastern Provinces as the political unit in all their deliberations. Without the Eastern Province federalism loses its appeal. Federalism with a federal unit consisting only of the Northern Province is too small for it to be economically viable. It is the potential of the Eastern Province that makes federalism attractive and which makes a separate state an economically viable possibility. These hard realities made the Sri Lankan Tamils go to great lengths to justify their claims to the Eastern Province.

The fact that it is the economic potential of the Eastern province that makes a separate state, or a federal unit with the potential to separate is conveyed by Amita Shastri in an article titled "The Material Basis for Separatism: The Tamil Eelam Movement in Sri Lanka". Shastri states: "...the greatest weakness of the Tamil argument for a separate state has been its lack of a viable economic base...The rural areas of the north and particularly the east had emerged as important paddy producing regions. The small holders in the Jaffna region had emerged as important producers of chillies and onions. Indeed, the locus of development in agriculture had shifted to the Dry Zone, and by the beginning of the 1970s, Trincomalee was recognized as holding the key to the next state of industrialization which would be export based"(The Journal of Asian Studies, 49, No. 1, February 1990, pp. 56-77).

As far as the history of the Eastern Province is concerned, records of treaties between the Kings of Kandy, the Portuguese and the Dutch, leave no doubt whatsoever that the Province had been part of the Kandyan Kingdom until it was ceded to the British in 1815 (see Appendix 1 - C.R.de Silva, The Portuguese in Ceylon 1617 - 1638, 1972, p.1; K.W.Goonawardene, The Foundation of Dutch Power in Ceylon, 1958, pp.32-33 ; K.M.de Silva, Separatist Ideology in Sri Lanka, 2nd.ed., 1995, p.32). In contrast to the authenticity to these treaties, the Sri Lankan Tamil claim to the Eastern Province is based on a single source - the Cleghorn Minute dated June 1799. Scholars such as K.M.de Silva, G. Iriyagolla, et al, have challenged the authenticity of this "Minute" because of its contradictions and inaccuracies. Under the circumstances, to even consider entertaining claims based on a single source, and a questionable one at that, would mean ignoring the authenticity of the existing treaties. Treaties made between rulers and representatives of sovereign states and the King of Kandy, that attest to the fact that the Eastern Province was unquestionably an integral part of the Kandyan Kingdom until it was ceded to the British in 1815, have therefore to take precedence over the "Minute" of an administrative officer.

The lack of archeological evidence is further testimony for rejecting Sri Lankan Tamil claims to the Eastern Province. By contrast, the abundance of archeological evidence of a Sinhala civilization in the province bears out the falsehood of the Tamil claim. Therefore, there are no grounds whatsoever for combining the Northern and Eastern Provinces into a single Tamil ethno-region on grounds of history.

Similarly, there are no grounds to combine the Northern and Eastern Provinces into a single autonomous or federal unit based on population concentrations, because the Sri Lankan Tamils are not a majority in the Eastern Province. According to the last authentic Census which was in 1981, the ethnic composition in the Eastern Province was: Sri Lankan Tamils 43%, Muslims 33%, and Sinhalese 24%, respectively. The Eastern Province is made up of 30 Administrative Divisions. Of these the Sri Lankan Tamils are concentrated only in 10 divisions covering 31% of the land area of the province. There is no justifiable basis for a minority group occupying 31% of the province to claim the entirety of that province.

Since no justifiable basis existed to back-up the claim for the Eastern Province, the Sri Lankan Tamil leadership contrived to "indoctrinate" the Tamils in the province and stated that the autonomous region or federal unit sought was for all "Tamil-speaking peoples" in order to include the Muslims as well. According to A.J.Wilson, "From the beginning Chelvanayakam concentrated on (as he put it) indoctrinating' the Tamil-speaking people of the Eastern Province. He quickly realised that they constituted thefrontline" (S.J.V.Chelvanayakam -A Political Biography, 1994, pp.32,33).

Despite all their efforts, the Tamil leadership failed to woo the Tamil-speaking people of the Eastern Province and win them over to their cause as amply demonstrated by the 1977 general election, when the Tamil leadership under the banner of the TULF sought a mandate to establish a separate state incorporating the Northern and Eastern Provinces. The acceptance of this election as being valid even by the LTTE is evident from their Application for Relief Against Designation as a Terrorist Organization by the United States to the Court of Appeals in the District of Columbia, USA, wherein they stated the they derived legitimacy for a separate state" ..pursuant to a mandate given by the Tamil people in the 1977 election, the last authentic election held in the Tamil areas of Sri Lanka".

(Polling Statistics - 1977 Election - See Appendix 2)
Conclusions from these 1977 election results are as follows:

1. 73% in the Eastern Province OPPOSED the mandate sought by the TULF.

2. ONLY 27% in the Eastern Province supported the TULF.

3. The voters who supported the TULF in each of the 3 Districts in the Eastern Province were 22664, 55120, and 39698, respectively. This means that ONLY 27%, 32.5%, and 22%, respectively, in each of the Districts in the Eastern Province voted for the TULF.

4. In the District of Batticaloa that has a 71% Tamil majority, ONLY 32.5% voted for the TULF.

5. Taking the two provinces together, 53% OPPOSED the TULF.

Therefore, those in the Eastern Province as well as those in the combined Northern and Eastern Provinces were OPPOSED to the establishment of a separate state. This is contrary to the claims made by the Tamil political leadershipand the LTTE.

With the escalation of hostilities between the LTTE and the security forces of the Government of Sri Lanka (GOSL), India intervened in the mid-eighties with the hope of resolving the conflict. The outcome of this intervention resulted in a negotiated settlement, the terms of which are contained in the Indo-Sri Lanka Accord of 1987. The most significant statements in the Accord are that the ".....northern and the eastern provinces have been areas of historical habitation of Sri Lankan Tamil speaking peoples, who have at all times hitherto lived together in this territory with other ethnic groups"(Clause1.4), and that the two provinces were required to be merged temporarily subject to a referendum within one year. The Accord required a referendum to held ".....on or before 31st December, 1988 to enable the people of the eastern province to decide whether: (a) The eastern province should remain linked with the northern province....or: (b) should constitute a separate administrative unit..."(Clause 2.3).

The requirement of a referendum to allow the "people of the eastern province" to decide clearly shows that the drafters of the Accord realized that the linkage between the two provinces was a questionable matter and was not be taken for granted. Despite the need to hold a referendum, successive GOSLs have failed to fulfil this requirement that is an integral part of the law of the land. The two provinces continue to remain merged since their merger in 1987. Both successive Sri Lankan and Indian Governments are responsible for violating their international agreement as well as Sri Lanka's law.

Eastern Province, Terrotorial Integrity and Regional Stability

Regional autonomy or federalism under circumstances where the merger of the two provinces has been allowed to consolidate is the source of much frustration and discontent because of its potential impact on the territorial integrity of Sri Lanka. Southern resistance to devolution of power to a merged Northern and Eastern Province is because of the possibility that it could lead to the eventual division of the country. They view the territorial integrity of the state as being inextricably linked with the Eastern Province.

The reason for the LTTE pursuing forced annexation of the Eastern Province is to create an economically viable region because as either an autonomous region, a federal unit, or even a separate state, a merged unit would be functional primarily due to the resource potential of the province and the rights to the yet untapped resources of the sea that extend over 200 miles from the coast. Furthermore, such a merged unit offers the potential to expand its extent and scope by eventually annexing adjacent regions with Indian Tamil concentrations such as the Province of Uva and the District of Nuwara Eliya. The fact that members of the Tamil community have already expressed such possibilities has caused deep concern among the Sinhalese, and furthermore, has caused the latter to adopt more hardened positions in respect of making concessions to all Tamils. From the Sinhala perspective, isolating the Eastern Province means protecting the country from serious disintegration which eventually would impact on the survival of the Sinhala nation and its civilization. From this perspective, for the survival of all that the Sinhalese cherish, it is imperative that the Eastern Province does not come under the control of the Sri Lankan Tamils of the North.

The Eastern Province is central to the prospect of a future Tamil state in Sri Lanka. The creation of a separate state in Sri Lanka also offers the prospect to link up with Tamil ethno-regions in India such as Tamil Nadu to create a federation of Tamil regions, possibilities of which have already been voiced by Tamils both in Sri Lanka and India. The political ambitions of the Sri Lankan Tamils are being spearheaded by the LTTE, who over the last two decades have succeeded in establishing close contacts in Tamil Nadu. The creation of a separate state in Sri Lanka would give the Tamil community scattered throughout the world, estimated to be about 50 million, who today are without a sovereign state, a springboard for the creation of a federation of Tamil states.

According to Maj. Gen. Karim "It is evident that a large number of people in Tamil Nadu and in Karnataka have been affected by LTTE propaganda. They support the objectives, not only in Sri Lanka, but also in India" (Maj. General Karim, Transnational Terrorism, 1993, p.61). Without this support base particularly in Tamil Nadu it would not have been possible for the LTTE to function and grow from strength to strength. However irksome the central government of India finds these developments, it is not free to take effective action to control their destabilizing influences because of the pivotal role Tamil Nadu politicians play in the coalition governments of India.

India is thus faced with a serious dilemma. To ignore the development of relationships currently taking place between the LTTE and its support base in Tamil Nadu would be at the peril of jeopardizing its territorial integrity. On the other hand, effective action has to be undertaken with circumspection because of the political consequences within India, while simultaneously engaging positively in the politics of Sri Lanka. India should not allow developments within Sri Lanka to drift to the point where it would have to invoke the theory of "defensive necessity" in order to protect its own territorial integrity. The key to the future of Sri Lanka's as well as India's territorial integrity and the future survival of both these states is the Eastern Province in Sri Lanka.

Eastern Province and Human Rights

The arbitrary merger of this province with the Northern Province would be a serious human rights violation of the Sri Lankan nation, and more particularly, of those in the Eastern Province. It is imperative that the people of the province are given the opportunity to decide for themselves their political future as well as their political associations; a right that is enshrined in the Universal Declaration of Human Rights and in several other instruments of the United Nations.

The concept of the "will of the people" is the very foundation of Democracy and to ignore it is to violate a fundamental human right. To merge the Eastern Province without first giving those in the Eastern Province the opportunity to decide freely and fairly whether or not they want to be a part of a single Tamil ethno-region, is to deny them the opportunity to exercise their "will". Article 21 clause (3) of the Universal Declaration of Human Rights states: "The will of the people shall be the basis of the authority of the government...".

The collective will of the electorate in the Northern and Eastern Provinces expressed their opposition to the creation of a separate state when 53% voted against the mandate sought by the TULF at the 1977 general election. The opposition was primarily from the electorate in the Eastern Province because 73% opposed the TULF and its mandate. Therefore, any attempt to forcibly annex the Eastern Province to the Northern Province, even as an interim measure, however temporary, goes against the "will" of the people in the Eastern Province. No administration has the authority to "govern without the consent of the governed" in the Eastern Province. The recent split between the northern and eastern commands of the LTTE further underscores the cultural and social separateness that exists between the Eastern Province and the North.

When the Sri Lankan Tamils resolved in 1976 at Vaddukoddai to establish a "free, sovereign, secular, socialist State of Tamil Eelam based on the right of selfdetermination" in the Northern and Eastern Provinces, they took for granted that the peoples of the Eastern Province would be part of their collective "self". The incorrectness of this presumption was confirmed when 73% opposed the mandate sought at the 1977 election. To persist in a claim that those in the Northern Province have a right to extend their right of self-determination arbitrarily over those in the Eastern Province against the latter's consent violates a fundamental human right and goes against the very tenets of self-determination, because the "self" is established by enslaving them against their "will". Fundamental freedoms and human rights require that the constituents of the "self" in self-determination are established freely and fairly.

Conflict Resolution Approaches to Peace

Despite the cultural and social cleavages that exist between the two provinces, the most recent manifestation of which is the split between the Northern and Eastern factions within the LTTE, the conflict resolution approach tends to discount them. The conflict resolution approach promotes the notion that the avoidance of war requires the acceptance of a single Tamil ethno- region involving both provinces even if it means abusing human rights and discounting the "will" of those in the Eastern Province. The Norwegians and other brokers of peace will exploit the threat of ar to prevent the holding of a referendum in the Eastern Province. A peace brokered on such a basis would be no different to peace brokered in other parts of the world, most of which have failed because they were based on expediency and not on principles of democracy and human rights.

Another aspect of the conflict resolution approach is to negotiate directly with rebels and terrorists. This has been the approach typically adopted in conflict zones such as Sierra Leone, Kosovo, and Angola. The absence of elected representatives may have left the negotiators with no option in these instances. However, this is not the case with Sri Lanka. Sri Lanka has elected representatives to represent Sri Lankan Tamil and LTTE interests. The 2004 Elections are openly acknowledged by election monitors as being flawed. However, Tamil representatives are in Parliament and act as proxies of the LTTE. Under the circumstances, at the very least for the sake of symbolism, in a democracy such as Sri Lanka, negotiations should have been conducted with the elected representatives and not with unelected members of the LTTE. Proper procedure was intentionally contravened with the cooperation of the international community to give recognition and legitimacy to the LTTE.

Yet another approach of conflict resolution is to negotiate with rebels and terrorists while they retain arms. Consequently, negotiations reward terrorists with legitimacy to exercise political power while retaining their ability to resume hostilities. By negotiations being conducted directly with the LTTE they have gained recognition over the elected Sri Lankan Tamil representatives. Granting the LTTE legitimate political power under an interim administration without any linkage to the issue of decommissioning arms, at least of the heavy weapons, would give them advantages over and above what they currently enjoy without any obligation of reciprocity. The entire approach is one sided and is doomed to failure as has occurred in other parts of the world where the approach enables rebels and terrorists with arms to keep demanding more and more because they have the ability to destabilize the peace at will. "As the 1990's spawned warlords from Yugoslavia to Haiti, from Cambodia to Africa, the principle was often sacrificed to the pragmatic goal of striking peace deals no matter how shaky. Diplomats look to the short term, they tend to think any agreement is good.....Diplomats like to export problems to the future"(The New York Times, May 21, 2000).

Therefore, in order to avoid repeating the mistakes committed in other parts of the world, and to prevent the LTTE gaining political power under an interim arrangement such as the ISGA while retaining arms, it is imperative that agreement is reached in respect of the final solution first. It is only after reaching such an agreement and the decommissioning of arms has taken place, that any interim arrangements should be considered.

A Framework for Peace

Peace, the future stability, and the territorial integrity of the Sri Lankan state are inextricably linked with the Eastern Province. The conflict resolution approach seeks to merge the Eastern Province with the Northern Province into a single Tamil ethno-region. The arbitrary merger of the Eastern Province with the Northern Province would not be acceptable to the larger Sri Lankan nation. What would be insisted on instead, is that the future of the Eastern Province be determined by the people of the province on the basis of a referendum as required by Sri Lankan law and by the Indo-Sri Lanka Accord. The key to peace in Sri Lanka depends on whether the future of the Eastern Province is decided on the basis of expediency and pragmatism integral to the conflict resolution approach, or on principles of democracy, human rights, and the rule of law.

The political sophistication of the Sri Lankan nation would not allow the conflict resolution approach to prevail. Instead, the nation would insist on an approach that preserves territorial integrity and is based on democracy and human rights. If the Eastern Province decides to be politically separate from the Northern Province, it is unlikely that the Sri Lankan Tamils would find federalism attractive as a political arrangement. In a federal arrangement, a politically separate Eastern Province in Sri Lanka would mean 7 federal units with Sinhala majorities, 1 Tamil federal unit in the Northern Province, and 1 mixed federal unit in the Eastern Province.

Federalism would remain attractive to the Sri Lankan Tamils and others who support federalism as a political arrangement, only if the Northern and Eastern Provinces could function as a single political unit. To achieve their goal democratically, the Sri Lankan Tamils would have to gamble on the outcome of a referendum; a risk they are reluctant to take because they are aware of the negative sentiments of those in the Eastern Province to be associated with the politics of the North. Consequently, every subterfuge would be exploited to combine the two provinces without holding a referendum. However, attempts to merge the two provinces illegally would be strongly resisted by the rest of the nation.

Federalism in the Sri Lankan context would be ethnically based. However, under federalism, most of the Sri Lankan Tamils would be outside the Tamil federal unit, thus depriving them of the opportunity to participate in regional politics in addition to the disadvantages of being ‘outsiders’ in other federal units. This would defeat the very purpose of federalism which is to create the opportunity for self rule and for serving the interests of most Sri Lankan Tamils. What would be more appropriate for Sri Lanka would be a political arrangement that assures extensive shared rule at the center with self rule for the regions, the most feasible being the districts, supplemented by safeguards to protect them and other minorities against possible majoritarian excesses.

Political arrangements should be based on three principles. The first is for all communities to have the opportunity to be represented and to participate in the governance of the Sri Lankan state so that all communities experience a sense of oneness and that they are an integral part of the collective “self” of the Sri Lankan nation.

The second is that the arrangement should guarantee the territorial integrity of the state. The third is the commitment to democratic principles and human rights with safeguards to prevent numerical minorities from the adverse effects of numerical majorities.

The concept of all communities participating in the processes of governance can be fostered by the following three arrangements. Firstly, to constitute the entire Parliament into a series of Committees called Parliamentary Committees (PC) with jurisdiction over defined policy areas and oversight powers to monitor activities of the related branches of the Executive. Thus, all members of Parliament would be involved in the Legislative processes of governance with powers to oversee Executive action. Secondly, to constitutionally guarantee that the composition of the Cabinet reflects the ethnic composition of Parliament. This ensures that all communities are represented in the Executive. Thirdly, to establish a National Planning Council whose representation reflects the political parties in proportion to their presence in Parliament. The Council would be assisted by competent persons from the public and private sectors. These arrangements should accompany measures to safeguard possible excesses from actions of numerical majorities together with constitutional provisions relating to fundamental rights.

Such arrangements proposed for the center are unique for Sri Lanka, in that they would create opportunities for all dominant communities represented in Parliament to collectively determine matters relating to Legislation, to collectively determine development plans for the country as a whole, and collectively participate in their execution. It is only through arrangements that foster the collective participation of all communities that a truly national self-determination can evolve.

With arrangements for the center as proposed, the regional unit should be the District. From a purely management and development point of view the District is better suited than the Province. Furthermore, it is more stable because it is better suited to accommodate ethnic, cultural, and social variations than the Province and with the provision that no two or more Districts could merge as in the Swiss and US Constitutions, the territorial integrity is assured. The District also offers greater opportunities for participation and representation of regional interests and for the center to help correct prevailing regional disparities. The District could be managed by an elected District Council with administrative and technical services being provided by senior personnel from an all-island service. Powers and functions could be assigned by Acts of Parliament similar to Municipal and Urban Councils.

Conclusion

Self-Determination is a right exercised by a "peoples". There has been much debate as to what or who constitutes a "peoples". Irrespective of how a "peoples" is characterized there is a territorial aspect to Self-Determination. The territorial aspect of the Sri Lankan Tamil claim to the right to Self-Determination is associated with the Northern and Eastern Provinces of Sri Lanka which amounts to about 1/3 the land mass and 2/3 the coastline of Sri Lanka. Since the international consensus is that external selfdetermination should be limited only to colonized countries, self-determination for the Sri Lankan Tamils has to be in regard to internal issues. Recognizing the right of internal self-determination exclusively to the Sri Lankan Tamils in a combined Northern and Eastern Province would mean that other communities within the region are denied this right. This would be discriminatory. In the alternative, if the region has to be occupied exclusively by the Sri Lankan Tamils - such an ethnically pure region could only be accomplished by committing unprecedented human rights violations.

Either in a heterogeneous or a homogeneous region, the exercise of the right of internal self-determination by the Sri Lankan Tamils in their region would result in the other communities in the rest of the country claiming the right to a separate self-determination because they are a different "self". Consequently, there would be two or more separate self-determinations which would amount to fragmentation into several de facto separate states. Under these circumstances, the right of internal Self-Determination is unworkable and unacceptable because of the democratic and humanitarian violations involved. Due to reasons such as these as well as other reasons, the Algiers Declaration as well as the Helsinki Declaration do not recognize the right of Self-Determination to "minority or ethnic groups".

Alternative political arrangements for minorities and ethnic groups are federalism or regional autonomy. Both alternatives claim to protect minorities against the excesses of majorities. However, the nett effect of both options is to transform former minorities into regional majorities and for majoritarianism to continue unresolved. A more positive way to resolve concerns of minorities would be to provide constitutional safeguards so that irrespective of whether the structure of the state is unitary or federal, minorities have institutionalized opportunities to protect themselves. Since no individual can be categorized as belonging to a majority or minority under all situations, e.g., a Sinhalese can be a minority in a Tamil region and vice versa, a Sinhala Christian would be a minority in a Sinhala Buddhist majority area and vice versa, and a Tamil Christian would be a minority in a Tamil Hindu majority area, and vice versa), the interchangeability of one's status from majority to minority and vice-versa makes safeguards a far more effective means of protection than the protection offered by federalism or regional autonomy.

Since the mind-set of the Sri Lankan Tamils is for a territory based on a combined Northern and Eastern Province under whatever political arrangement, they must necessarily gain acceptance for it democratically without violating the human rights of those affected. Sri Lankan law and the Indo-Sri Lanka Accord require that the people of the Eastern Province are given the opportunity to decide whether they wish to be associated or not with the Northern

Province, through a referendum. Would federalism lose its appeal if the outcome of the referendum is for the two provinces to be separate?

The election of 1977, accepted by the LTTE as the “last authentic election”, and the election of 2004 clearly indicate that the people of the Eastern Province wish to be separate from the politics of the Northern Province because of their cultural and social separateness from the Northers. The recent factional split within the ranks of the LTTE causing the Eastern cadres under Karuna to break away from the Northern LTTE on grounds of discrimination, is further confirmation of the Eastern Province’s wish to be politically separate from the Northern Province. These indicators further endorse the need for the political future of the Eastern Province to be determined on the basis of a referendum to establish the “will” of the people in the province. Not to do so would be a serious violation of their human rights

The reluctance of the Sri Lankan Tamils and the LTTE to hold a referendum is because they are conscious of the opposition by the people of the Eastern Province to the merger of the two provinces. The LTTE’s preference would be to merge the two provinces against the “will” of those in the Eastern Province. The conflict resolution approach would seek to sacrifice democratic principles and human rights in order to justify the merger for the sake of ground realities. A merger would divide Sri Lanka and lead to regional instability that would eventually threaten the territorial integrity of India. A forced merger has to be avoided at all cost if there is to be peace.

Peace is possible only when the Sri Lankan Tamils and the LTTE consent to resolve the future of the Eastern Province on principles of democracy and human rights. As Hurst Hannum states: “...there will be no peace in Sri Lanka until the Tamil community recognizes that it is, in fact, a minority - and a rather small one at that. No more than one-half of the Tamil population is included in the merged northern and eastern provinces, although

Tamil influence has long been disproportionate to mere population size. Nevertheless, Sri Lanka will inevitably be dominated by the Sinhalese, Buddhist culture of 75% of its population; so long as this does not imply discrimination against or denigration of Tamil culture and traditions. That is a reality that cannot be reversed by law or constitutional innovations" (Autonomy, Sovereignty, and Self-Determination, 1990, revised 1996, pp. 307-308).

Even if territorial claims are resolved on the basis of democratic principles and human rights, political arrangements such as regional autonomy or federalism in Sri Lanka would create ethnically- based territorial units. Proof of the instability of such political units abound, and Sri Lanka would be no exception. Peace is possible if greater emphasis is given to serious power sharing arrangements at the center among all communities, together with decentralized powers assigned to smaller units such as Districts. In anarticle titled "Constitutional Design For Divided Societies", Arend Lijphart states: "....establishment of democratic government in divided societies require two key elements: power sharing and group autonomy. Power sharing denotes the participation of representatives of all significant communal groups in political decision making, especially at the executive level; group autonomy means that these groups have authority to run their own internal affairs, especially in the areas of education and culture" (Journal of Democracy, April 2004, Vol 15, Number 2, p. 97).

Peace depends on whether the Sri Lankan Tamils decide to be an integral part of the collective self-determination process of Sri Lanka, or to forge a separate selfdetermination for themselves. The conflict arose because they chose the latter option with the hope of becoming "equal" with the Sinhalese by dividing the country between the two communities. For there to be peace the international community and those engaged in the negotiations have to convince the Sri Lankan Tamils and the LTTE that a separate self-determination is an unworkable pursuit, and instead, that it is the commitment to a collective self-determination that would bring peace to them and to the rest of the Sri Lankan nation. The focus of the negotiations would then be on how the Sri Lankan Tamils and the LTTE could become an integral part of the collective "self". It is only such a "self" that can commit to the preservation of the territorial integrity of Sri Lanka and to principles of Democracy, Pluralism, and Human Rights.

APPENDIX 1

Dennis B. McGilvray, T*amil and Muslim Identities in the East*, Marga Institute, Monograph No. 24, 2001 p. 5. “First, there are social, economic, political, and religious patterns deeply-rooted in the region that make the Tamil-speaking parts of Batticaloa and Amparai Districts, and even the southern parts of Trincomalee District, culturally and sociologically distinct from Jaffna and from the Upcountry Tamil region. The east coast Tamil and Muslim cultural complex includes joint cultivation systems and interspersed village settlements, matrilinneal clan-based temple and mosque leadership roles, matrilocal marraige patterns and total pre-mortem transfer of wealth (both houses and land) as dowery, non-Brahmanical Hindu ritual traditions and ecstatic Muslim and Sufi devotional performances by Bawas and faqirs, and a regional dialect of Tamil that preserves a number of older litarary forms. The high cast Jaffna Tamils, especially the aristrocratic Jaffna Velalars, look down upon the Batticaloa Tamils for their alleged lower caste and for their l ess Sanskritic forms of Hindu ritual”.

K.M.de Silva, *Separatist Ideology in Sri Lanka*, ICES, 2nd ed. 1995, p. 18. ”Thus the Tesavalamai, the customary laws of the Tamils, codified by the Dutch in 1706-7, and made operative in the Jaffna district by the British through Regulation 18 of 1806 was not applicable to the Tamils of Trincomalee and Batticaloa”.

C.R. de Silva, *The Portuguese in Ceylon* 1617 - 1638, 1972, p.1. ”In the early years of the sixteenth century when the Portuguese first visited Ceylon the island was divided into three major political units and number of lesser principalities...Nevertheless...it (Kotte) remained the strongest kingdom in Ceylon and the king of Kotte still claimed to be overlord of the whole island". Nearly a century later the treaty of 1617 between the king of Kandy and the Portuguese "...had granted the king of Kandy the whole of the eastern seaboard of Ceylon including the ports of Trincomalee and Batticaloa"(Ibid, pp.64,65).

K.W.Goonawardene, *The Foundation of Dutch Power in Ceylon*, 1958, pp.32-33. "On the 23rd May 1638 two copies of the Treaty written out in Portuguese, was signed by Raja Sinha on the one hand, and Westerwolt and Coster on the other...The treaty clearly stated that forts captured from the Portuguese could be garrisoned by the Dutch, only if his Majesty thought it fit"

K.M.de Silva, *Separatist Ideology in Sri Lanka*, 2nd ed. 1995, p.32. It was later, by the treaty of 1766 between the Kandyan Kingdom and the Dutch East India Company that the Dutch were granted control over some of the border territories. "Among the Kandyan territories acquired were Batticaloa and Trincomalee and the lands formerly dependent on these places"

APPENDIX 2

POLLING STATISTICS - 1977 ELECTION

NORTHERN PROVINCE

District	Total Voters	Valid Votes	For TULF	Opposed to
Jaffna	381591	310175	223463	86712
Killinochchi	26670	21258	15607	5651
Mullativu	24698	19596	10261	9335
Vavuniya	28450	23416	13821	9595
Mannar	31767	29352	15141	14211
Totals			278293	125504

EASTERN PROVINCE

Trincomalee	97417	83047	22664	60383
Batticaloa	132943	169422	55120	114302
Ampara	154831	181260	39698	141562
Total			117482	316247

(Information extracted from the Report of Commissioner of Elections, Sessional Paper IV, 1978.) Batticaloa electorate in Batticaloa District and Padirippu electorate in Ampara District were two-member electorates.

PART III

BACKGROUND DOCUMENTATION 2

The Norwegian intervention in Sri Lanka and other countries is being questioned in Norway itself as the following article from its daily newspaper reveals.

Morgenbladet 12.11.04

A Humanitarian Great Power's Growth and Fall

Simen Sætre

We grew up with the thought that we were a humanitarian Great Power. It gave us identity. It gave meaning to being a Norwegian. However, was it an illusion all this time?

In reality I cannot tell this story with any other starting point than myself. What I am about to tell is not really substantiated by irrefutable facts, but rather a feeling, which is genuine enough. I, and many others my age, grew up with a natural faith that Norway was a humanitarian Great Power.

Of course one can say that all the time it was an illusion, but the point is that we believed in it. When I think back to primary school it seems that all the time it was a lot of talk about "peace". At school we marked the UN-day. We participated in drawing competitions with themes around international solidarity, and the songs we song were about the same. When people in the class were to wish something, it was common to say "peace in the world". In children's TV we had small doses of the human rights; in between *Tøfflus* and *Jon Blund* ("… children's rights start now").

Many of us had civic confirmation (humanitarian confirmation?) and in the New Year speech at TV in 1992 we heard Gro Harlem

Brundtland say that "it was typical Norwegian to be good". In 1993, while we still were at high school, the Oslo-agreement came. Human rights were high on the agenda, Norway was world champion in aid and environment, the cold war was over and the notion "humanitarian Great Power" entered our consciousness.

Out in the world

In the newspaper-database *Atekst* we find the first use of the notion "humanitarian Great Power" in 1990. It is Jan Egeland who uses it. As young, dynamic, foreign chief in Norway's Red Cross, already author of "Impotent superpower – potent small state", he encourages the Norwegian Government to give 30 million Kroner to refugees in Jordan. And how is one to get somebody to give 30 million Kroner? "We earn enormous amounts at increased oil prices and of ethical reasons we ought to give properly. Norway ought to act as a humanitarian Great Power," Egeland said.

Since then we see a steady increase in the use of the notion. At the time when my generation came to political consciousness this was something which shaped us and our understanding of being Norwegian. When we were abroad on travels or studies, this was something which was referred to – I have many late nights discussed it with foreign study friends or with other Norwegians among foreigners (without now being able to remember whether it was the foreigners or the Norwegians who actually brought it up). Countless Norwegian students have looked at it in their dissertations at foreign universities. And that way it became a part of our identity.

An identity is shaped

In "*Power and Democracy*" (NOU 19, 2003) there is a chapter which gives nourishment to this feeling. "The image of Norway as a moral and humanitarian Great Power has become a new national symbol," it says. The authors point out that "the Church, the monarchy and the country are institutions and notions with great symbolic power", which create the core of the postcolonial Norwegian identity after 1814 and 1905.

However, some of these national symbols are about to be lost. The Church's power is on return. The national day and the flag are not adjusted to today's international, cosmopolitan world. The royal symbol has adjusted to "a democratized contemporary age", squeezed in between the exalt and the trivial.

And in the meeting with the world outside, in the era of the globalization, the thought about the humanitarian Great Power became a new identity-shaping symbol for Norwegians. They worshipped and believed in "Norway" as international brand name, circling around the international engagement for democracy, human rights, conflict solution and peace.

"The image itself of Norway both at home and abroad was shaped in a few moral projects… The image of Norway as an idealistic goodness-regime has become a new Norwegian national symbol which is part of shaping Norwegians' self-image and national identity," the research group writes.

When we won the world

I picture the 1990s as a flow of images. A front-page in *Dagbladet* which says that Thorvald Stoltenberg is to become peace mediator in Bosnia (we really believed he could do it!) An image of Yitzhak Rabin and Yasser Arafat who give each other the hand in front of the White House. Israel's Foreign Minister Shimon Peres who states that the Oslo-agreement "ends 100 years of conflict and begins 100 years of cooperation". Jan Egeland, untiring working all over the world. Knut Vollebæk in shuttle-diplomacy at the Balkans. Soon Norway is involved in peace mediating all over the world.

Not only in Guatemala, Colombia, Sri Lanka, but also in Sudan,

Haiti, the Dominican Republic, Mali, Ethiopia and Eritrea. And not only that. Now the countries come to us and want peace. "Norway can become mediator in the conflict between ANC and Inkatha in the Natal-province," a Norwegian newspaper writes. "Norway is asked to mediate at Corsica," another one writes.

Everywhere the mediators are followed by enthusiastic Norwegian journalists with unshakeable faith in the Norwegian heroes. They bring the stories home, and the stories warm us. Meanwhile the peace-nation goes back in history and finds an entirety in the peace-building: Nansen. Trygve Lie. Nobel Prize. The UN-engagement. The development aid!

At the end of the 1990s the notion "humanitarian Great Power" goes so naturally into the Norwegian language that it not only feels natural, it actually feels like it has always been there: In 1999 Prime Minister Kjell Magne Bondevik states that "since Fridtjof Nansen's historic effort for refugees in Armenia Norway has had reputation as a humanitarian Great Power… That is a hallmark Norway always has to be recognized on".

Hangover

It is difficult to say when the myth started to crack. Maybe the critics were there all the time, only I do not remember them. However, I think the first big battle was the Oslo-agreement, the pillar itself in the self-image we had built up.

Last spring a Palestinian comes to Norway. He is picked up at Gardermoen and just as we cross the border to Oslo his Norwegian host proudly says: "We are now entering Oslo!" Amazed he hears the Palestinian answer: "I don't like Oslo!" For a few seconds the Norwegian is surprised, an awkward quietness arises, before the Palestinian explains the joke. He explains that the word "Oslo" has very negative connotations where he comes from.

A Norwegian woman catches a taxi in Israel. The driver asks where she is from. She answers "Oslo". Not before has she said the word before the driver abruptly stops in the middle of an intersection, opens the door and commands the woman out. She never again says where she is from.

Out against the myths

However, that is not all. It is not only the question whether the peace process was realistic. Now Norway's role in the whole process is questioned. In the report "*Peacemaking is a risky business*", published this year, Hilde Henriksen Waage, researcher at the peace research institute PRIO challenged the whole Norwegian "truth".

"Norway appeared as the great peace creator when the Oslo-agreement got known. However, as an historian it is important for me to ask what this little country actually could do in the Middle East. This question was never asked. Instead myths and fairytales about Norway's contribution were created," Waage says.

An artificial impression was created?
"I refer to it as a fairytale, with strong person-focus, that "some Norwegians" pretty much alone could create peace in the Middle East."

How and why was this image created?
"It was created as much by the media, the political parties and the Ministry of Foreign Affairs, as by the participants themselves. It was a choir in unison which announced that Norway had created peace between Israel and Palestine. In this choir there was no will to analyze what kind of agreement Oslo was, or to analyze the process, or what kind of room for action a country like Norway had in such a situation."

Corpses in Sri Lanka

The fight about the history books' version of the Oslo-agreement had barely started before corpses started to appear outside the Norwegian Embassy in Sri Lanka. Sri Lanka was the new hope, the new task which was to prove that Norway still could create peace. In 2002 Norway and Erik Solheim actually managed to facilitate a cease-fire agreement. Still we had a sneaking feeling. It appeared when a demonstration march in Colombo's streets set fire to an effigy of the Norwegian envoy and called "Ugly Norwegians go home!" It appeared when President Chandrika Kumaratunga talked about "these busy-body, salmon-eating Norwegians". It appeared when *Dagsavisen* reported about the conspiracy theories which circulated around the Norwegian engagement: That Norway actually wanted Sri Lanka's cashew-nut farms. That *Norsk Tipping* wanted to take over Sri Lanka's state lottery. That the Norwegians sympathized with the guerrilla group LTTE due to "the Tamil Tigers Nazi-similar greeting". That Norway actually had neo-colonialist motives and was after oil on Sri Lanka's coast. That Norway not only supported terrorists but actually was a "safe haven for terrorists".

We could have ignored these reports; they are pretty strange and marginal. However, for us who have grown up with and built our identity around "the humanitarian Great Power", it feels sore, unjust. They would have been easier to ignore, if not the peace process was stalled. This summer Vidar Helgesen, State Secretary in the Ministry of Foreign Affairs, stated that the situation for the peace process is the worst since 2002. This week he travels to Sri Lanka together with Foreign Minister Jan Petersen and special envoy Erik Solheim to "investigate the peace will among the parties", which it is called.

"The security situation has calmed a bit, but the situation is still worrisome and the progress little," says Helgesen. He does not have any hope about resuming the process.

Challenged the system

And now we have still not talked about aid. Let us ignore that Norway now does not give one per cent of the gross national product to development aid, like we once did and which the aim was. Let us ignore that Norway and other rich countries have hold tight onto agriculture subsidies which shut poor countries out from the markets. Let us ignore the regular reports which call in question the aid's usage. Let us even ignore that much of the aid is channelled through missionaries with a totally different agenda than "development".

For the most thorough challenge to the Norwegian aid-system came last year with Professor Terje Tvedt's book "*Development aid, foreign policy and power*". "The aid researcher Terje Tvedt reminded us last year that the Norwegian model is distinguished by a broad agreement which is kept up by a tight power-political mixture of professional, political and journalistic expertise. The good Samaritan was again left without clothes," *Ny Tid* wrote this summer.

Tvedt describes a system, from the outside, which earlier only is described with the system's own words. That way he undresses it, exposes the myths it is built on and a powerful elite which draw nourishment from it. This elite have an "aura of moral-ideological irrefutability". Tvedt is the land surveyor in Kafka's *The Castle*, who, by asking questions and irritate, gets the system to fall apart. "The goodness-regime" is indeed moving along for billions of State Kroner each year, the Norwegian Samaritan keeps at it, but now without clothes.

The myth bursts

At the end of September another illusion burst. Not even the foreigners associated Norway with the humanitarian engagement. (Not even them! Why did they not say anything earlier?) A survey done by *Centenary-Celebrations-Committee*, where citizens from eight European countries participated, showed that "Norway is not perceived as a humanitarian Great Power in the European society".

Instead they said that they associated Norway with "magnificent nature" (44 per cent), "friendliness and openness" (8 per cent), and "nation's wealth" (8 per cent). The alternatives "a nation that shares its resources" (0 per cent) and "a nation with focus on humanitarian activity/operations" (0 per cent) were lowest ranked.

"The survey shows, in brief, that Norway's humanitarian effort and peace mediating effort with other words are not registered in non-aided associations," the *Centenary-Celebrations-Committee* could note with surprise.

Notion crisis

To really rub it in one could look at the notion itself which shaped our identity. The word-composition "humanitarian Great Power" is kind of a contradiction in itself, but now the word "humanitarian" has changed value too. The past decade we have seen "humanitarian" interventions with a few too many bombs, and a little too much blood, and now we do not buy the word's actual meaning anymore (*Bokmål* dictionary: humanitarian: charity work, human friendly, human loving).

The Norwegian "humanitarian" engagement in Iraq has not made the case any better. It has become more difficult to differentiate between "humanitarian" and "military" forces. "Norway's engagement in Iraq waddles like a duck, croaks like a duck, and swims like a duck, and it is depressing that the Government insists on calling it a peace dove," Niels Fredrik Dahl wrote in *Aftenposten*. (If this was "humanitarian forces" what is then a "humanitarian Great Power"?)

The word disappeared

Today the notion is removed in the Ministry of Foreign Affairs' papers. Then State Secretary Thorild Widvey did indeed use it, in parenthesis, in a speech about Norway's reputation last year: "We do not wish to hit ourselves at the chest and be conceited (I am therefore maybe a little bit uncertain whether expressions like "humanitarian Great Power" are very good, but it is still a notion which is interesting to "taste" in the discussion about reputation)."

However, State Secretary Vidar Helgesen is clear: The notion is not to be used.

"To take it away was one of the first things we did," Helgesen says.

But it appears again and again?

"It sticks; it is a catchy notion. In the beginning, when we took over, we repeatedly found it in drafts for speeches.

Is the notion a strain?

It involves a self-praising attitude which is in great contrast to the role it implies, which demands that one is low-voiced and confidence-inspiring.

Was it throughout the 1990s created an unrealistic image of what Norway could contribute with?

"Yes, and the "humanitarian Great Power"-notion in itself is a demonstration of that. The media, and the politicians who used it, kind of created an impression that Norway was greater than what we in reality were. We should not disallow Norway's role, but we are no Great Power, and to use such a phrase on the humanitarian area is not very tasteful. It is important to acknowledge when we can play a role, but we should not have ambitions about entering a role which is above our format.

Foreign Minister Jan Petersen also distances himself:

"I have never used the notion, which for me represents way too much Norwegian self-praise. When we do something on the humanitarian area, we can not communicate that we do it to bask in the sun, but because they are sensible things to do. There was an international survey now about what one associated with Norway and this is something which was not associated as much with Norway as some here at home maybe would have thought and hoped. I am not very surprised about that. However, I do believe there is some learning in this: We shall not believe we are the centre of the world the whole time".

The learning

The Norwegian humanitarian engagement continues with great weight. However, different words are used now. There are other expectations. One has learnt.

"We have learnt that effort for conflict-solution demands time, ability to be patient, long-term perspectives, one has to dare to se backlashes. We have learnt how important it is to keep the international society within the processes, draw from them. We have learnt about the use of aid to stimulate the peace processes. However, the main learning may be that a peace process has to be run forward and solved by the parties. One has to wait for the parties to mature. Moreover, it is not only the parties at the negotiation table which have to be included, but also the people they represent," State Secretary Vidar Helgesen says.

"Another difference is that in the 1990s it was often about "freelance activity". We have systematized the experiences, and combined the engagement with an own section which works with this within the Ministry of Foreign Affairs. In addition comes the acknowledgement, after the 11th of September 2001, that conflicts in remote places also have significance for our security.

Has the Ministry of Foreign Affairs become more selective with regards to entering into processes abroad?

"No, but we have gotten a better basis for evaluating whether Norway can and ought to play a role".

Out of proportions

PRIO-researcher Hilde Henriksen Waage believes Norway's role was "blown up to way too large proportions".

"If you read the 1990s media-reports it is much "Gloria hallelujah". And then the hangover came in the new millennium. I believe one has more sober perceptions now about how difficult it is to create peace, and how limited role Norway can play," Waage says.

Was Norway's self-image as humanitarian Great Power built on false conditions?

"I do not know enough about that, but I can say that the Oslo-agreement was Norway's break-through as peace mediator and as a consequence of that there were offers from all around the world about contributing to mediating. This became one of Norway's most important export-products, and served Norwegian self-interests. Norway received admission to decision-makers on the international scene. And that was important in itself".

Touched the bedrock

However, nobody should challenge the Norwegian self-image. When Waage presented her report she noticed an opposition with such a force that it had to be the result of something big.

"I was surprised about what kind of storm that report created. It was, the way I saw it, nothing controversial there. That Norway is a country without muscles, and that PLO was greatly weakened and would agree to pretty much anything… This should be obvious… I think I must have touched something totally different than the intention. I severely underestimated the storm which would occur after I asked some expedient questions about the Norwegian engagement. The only explanation I can find is that I had taken the "sledge hammer" and crushed a National myth".

Provocation

Least of all a Dane is to disqualify the national favourite myth. After the *Centenary-Celebration-Committee*'s survey, *Ekstra Bladet*'s editor Hans Engell wrote a provocation in *Dagbladet*. Norway has "a society elite which try to buy fame, and send people and cattle around the world on the pretext that they are to create peace. Norwegian politicians and their surrounding country appear as an assembly 'human rights' jetsetters. But all this is conceitedness," Engell wrote.

A cheap provocation in the tabloid spirit. But Engell had touched something. It resulted in a front-page. It resulted in comments. It resulted in debates. "Tasteless run down of Norway," Trond Giske said.

Competing myth

Maybe Engell's verdict was extra scorching, because it emphasized a competing "national myth". "The rich are seldom sympathetic… That also goes for nations. It is therefore, in spite of everything, a demonstration of a form for justice when the Norwegian oil money in itself can not buy the nation an image in the world as a humanitarian Great Power with great results within peace mediating," Engell wrote. He wrote that Norwegians are "rich, fat and conceited".

He hit a sensitive spot with that. This is a competing image of Norwegians in the world. We, who thought we grew up in a "humanitarian Great Power", woke up and instead heard that we had lived on "oil-drugs".

"It is typical Norwegian to be good," Gro said, while today's "Gro", Erna Solberg, says that "Norway is perceived as a rich, disgusting curiosity" in Europe. "We have become a nation of whiners," Finn Bergesen, chief in the *Confederation of Norwegian*

Business and Industry, said to *The New York Times*. "We are blessed and cursed with oil... The welfare systems have changed our attitudes".

Philosopher Kjell Madsen carried wood to the fire when he in *Dagsavisen* said: "It is naïve to believe that the Norwegian society becomes more human or pleasant due to the increasing wealth". While Jan Egeland in 1990 believed the oil-money came with a commitment to be a humanitarian Great Power, Madsen pointed out, thirteen years later, that "poor people [in contradiction to Norwegians?] have a remarkable generosity and willingness to share with others".

Requiem for a dream

Betong Pub, last week. Beer in plastic cups, scattered audience, Wednesday-debate. The title is "Ola peace mediator". "We are grown up with how Norway creates peace around..." the introducer says.

"We Norwegians like to think of ourselves as world champions: in cross-country skiing, when it comes to eating frozen pizzas, as well as when it comes to aid and peace mediating. The Oslo-agreement has been an enormous success, in Sri Lanka they burn effigies of Erik Solheim in pure pacifistic joy, and now Hilde Frafjord Johnsen has in addition secured the peace in Sudan," it says in the invitation. Norwegian self-irony. However, here is also a deeper resonance: People laugh.

This night, in the basement under *Chateau Neuf*, Norway's humanitarian engagement has become a joke. But for us, who grew up with the myth and believed in it, the joke is not funny. Maybe we were naïve. Maybe the thought about the humanitarian Great Power all the time has been a dream, an illusion. But it was nice to have. We needed it; it gave meaning to being a Norwegian. And if it was to disappear for good then we would miss it, because it is a part of us.

The Liberation Tigers of Tamil Eelam (LTTE)

US State Department "Patterns of Global Terrorism"

Other known front organizations: World Tamil Association (WTA), World Tamil Movement (WTM), the Federation of Associations of Canadian Tamils (FACT), the Ellalan Force.

Description

Founded in 1976, the LTTE is the most powerful Tamil group in Sri Lanka and uses overt and illegal methods to raise funds, acquire weapons, and publicize its cause of establishing an independent Tamil state. The LTTE began its armed conflict with the Sri Lankan Government in 1983 and relies on a guerrilla strategy that includes the use of terrorist tactics.

Activities

The LTTE has integrated a battlefield insurgent strategy with a terrorist program that targets not only key personnel in the countryside but also senior Sri Lankan political and military leaders in Colombo. Political assassinations have included former Indian Prime Minister Rajiv Gandhi in 1991 and President Ranasinghe Premadasa in 1993. The LTTE has refrained from targeting Western tourists out of fear that foreign governments would crack down on Tamil expatriates involved in fundraising activities abroad.

Strength

Approximately 10,000 armed combatants in Sri Lanka; about 3,000 to 6,000 form a trained cadre of fighters. Also has a significant overseas support structure for fundraising, weapons procurement, and propaganda activities.

Location/Area of Operation

The LTTE controls most of the northern and eastern coastal areas of Sri Lanka but has conducted operations throughout the island. Headquartered in the Jaffna Peninsula, LTTE leader Velupillai Prabhakaran has established an extensive network of checkpoints and informants to keep track of any outsiders who enter the group's area of control. The LTTE prefers to attack vulnerable government facilities, then withdraw before reinforcements arrive.

External Aid

The LTTE's overt organizations support Tamil separatism by lobbying foreign governments and the United Nations. The LTTE also uses its international contacts to procure weapons, communications, and bomb-making equipment. The LTTE exploits large Tamil communities in North America, Europe, and Asia to obtain funds and supplies for its fighters in Sri Lanka. Information obtained since the mid-1980s indicates that some Tamil communities in Europe are also involved in narcotics smuggling. Tamils historically have served as drug couriers moving narcotics into Europe.

Fact Sheet on Child Soldiers in Sri Lanka Human Rights Watch: November 11, 2004

- The government of Sri Lanka and the Liberation Tigers of Tamil Eelam (LTTE) were engaged in a brutal civil war from 1983 to 2002 that killed over 60,000 people. A ceasefire was implemented in February of 2002, but a final peace agreement has not been reached.

- The LTTE has used children as soldiers throughout the conflict. In the 1990's some studies found that 40-60% of LTTE soldiers killed in battle were children under the age of eighteen. Children have also been used as suicide bombers.

- The LTTE has continued to recruit children even after active fighting ended in 2002. UNICEF has documented over 3,500 new cases of child recruitment by the LTTE during the ceasefire. The true total may be much higher.

- Some children are forced or coerced to join. The LTTE often pressures Tamil families to provide a son or daughter for "the cause." When families refuse, they may be harassed or threatened, and the children taken by force.

- Some children join the LTTE because of they come from poor families, are orphaned, or have no access to school. Some have experienced abuses by government forces or want to fight for an independent Tamil state.

- Children in the LTTE receive rigorous and

sometimes brutal training. Children who try to escape are typically beaten in front of their entire unit as a warning to others.

- Children are typically 14 or 15 years old when they are recruited, though some are as young as 11. Over 40% of the LTTE's child soldiers are girls.

- In June 2003, the LTTE signed an Action Plan for Children Affected by War and agreed to end its recruitment of child soldiers and to release children from its forces. Between signing the plan and November 2004, the LTTE released 831 children, but recruited or re-recruited 1,700 more.

- International law sets eighteen as the minimum age for all participation in hostilities, all forced recruitment or conscription, and all recruitment by non-state armed groups. Any recruitment or use of children under the age of fifteen is considered a war crime.

Personal accounts from "Living in Fear: Child Soldiers and the Tamil Tigers in Sri Lanka:"

Human Rights Watch: *November 11, 2004*

Note: *The names used are not the children's real names.*

My parents refused to give me to the LTTE so about 15 of them came to my house—it was both men and women, in uniforms, with rifles, and guns in holsters.... I was fast asleep when they came to get me at one in the morning.... These people dragged me out of the house. My father shouted at them, saying, "What is going on?", but some of the LTTE soldiers took my father away towards the woods and beat him.... They also pushed my mother onto the ground when she tried to stop them.

— Rangini, a girl recruited by the LTTE in 2003 at age 16

I went to school to grade 5. I dropped out because my mother and father died. No one cared for me, I had no parents, so I was willing to join. I lived with my aunt after my parents died. I cooked for her family. I had frustration in my life, so I was willing to join the LTTE. I wanted to live in this world without anyone's help. When I joined the LTTE, I went to the political office, and told the LTTE I wanted to join. They agreed. I told them I was sixteen, but they didn't care.

— Vanmathi, a girl who joined the LTTE in 2003 at age 16

The training was very difficult. They don't care if it's a rainy or sunny day. If you get too tired and can't continue, they will beat you. Once when I first joined, I was dizzy. I couldn't continue and asked for a rest. They said, "This is the LTTE. You have to face problems. You can't take a rest." They hit me four or five times with their hands.

— Selvamani, a girl recruited in 2002 at age 15

After four months I was sent to a landmines unit. I learned to handle landmines, to place them. I did this for four months. I couldn't concentrate. Sometime a landmine would explode and children would be injured. Their fingers, hands, face. One time we were working in a line, and the last girl made a mistake when removing a landmine. It exploded and she lost a finger. She was 17. I was scared to handle them.

—Vimala, a girl recruited in 2003 at age 17

Lots of people tried to escape. But if you get caught, they take you back and beat you. Some children die. If you do it twice, they shoot you. In my wing, if someone escaped, the whole group was lined up to watch them get beaten. I saw it happen, and know of cases from other groups. If the person dies, they don't tell you, but we know it happens.

— Nirmala, a girl recruited in 2001 at age 14

The One-way Fighter-The Child Soldiers of Sri Lanka : As a Reward, Death is Waiting

Uwe Siemon-Netto
[Die Welt - 21st March, 1998

(Translation of an article from the "Die Welt")

The US government has put them on their list of the "most dangerous terrorist organisation in the world" - the Tamil rebels who have been fighting for 15 years for an autonomous "homeland". In their great offensive in February they unscrupulously sent children into the battle.

(Jaffna) - Child soldiers have unmistakable eyes: They appear to be without emotion and very old. The prisoner Elisaman Jenova has this look too. It seems to stand in a great contradiction to her girlish voice and immature body. Elisaman is only 17 years old and has already been an MG firer i the jungle. That she is still alive is only thanks to the fact that she was shot on 1 February near her heart, which led to unconsciousness. It prevented her from continuing to fight or to bite into the potassium cyanide capsule which all "Tamil Tigers" carry with them in order to prevent them from being taken prisoner. Now she is in the headquarters of the government troops on the Jaffna peninsula which was conquered back by them not so long ago. Elisaman is the daughter of Elias Jenova from chundrikulam in the district of Jaffna. Her father is a fisherman and therefore belongs to that caste from which Velupillai Prabhakaran, the 43-year-old leader of the "Liberation Tigers of Tamil Eelam", comes. At the beginning of 1995, when Elisaman was recruited, Chundikulam was still in the claws of the "Tigers". The LTTE cadres went from fisher hut to fisher hut in Chundikulam and said that every family owed Prabhakaran a child. Elisaman went voluntarily, "Because my elder sister was ill. One brother was too young, the other had just married. It would have been a pity if his young wife became a widow so soon." She knew that she would be sent to her death: "The recruiting officer explained to me that I would either fall in the battle or that I would die in a suicide command for the cause. The latter would be a particular honour." Elisaman Jenova went with the two LTTE recruiting officers without taking leave of her parents. "I thought at first that I would be taken to a politcal meeting, but I was taken into the jungle straight away." What happened then proved to the officers who were taking part in this interview the cynicism of Prabhakaran: The "Tigers" gave the girl no basic training. Elisaman only learnt how to use a machine gun of the Belgian type FN. A lieutenant colonel: "This girl was planned as a one-way fighter, she was to be used up at the first attack. Therefore there was no reason for a military training."

Elisaman lived in the jungle for one and a half years. In this time she hardly ever saw grown-up "Tigers", let alone Prabhakaran. The trainers of the 15-year-old girl were 16-year-old girls. Just like Pol Pot Prabhakaran lets children brainwash other children. The daily manta of the child soldiers: "The Sinhalese are oppressing the Tamils. We must free them. You have the great honour to die for this cause. You needn't be afraid of death." Elisaman and the other girls lived in a bunker, where they spent a life with unusually little contact. They were not allowed to put their arm around each other, they weren't even allowed to tough hands. There should be nothing to make up for physical contact with parents or brothers and sisters. The unkindness had a system: Elisaman was also not allowed to write to her parents; as it became apparent later on, they did not know either whether their daughter was alive or not. Not only was Elisaman a nameless member of a nameless unit of 90 doomed teenagers, they were in fact already dead, as their trainers told them. At night the girls lay next to each other on their mats, in the morning at 4 o'clock they had to jump up, one kept post in the bunker, the other two had to search the camp for possible infiltrators. "then we washed ourselves with water which we got from a source in the jungle, we had rice and curry for breakfast, sometimes fish or beef." Beef? In an area where most of the inhabitants are Hindus? How this worked is explained by the explosive expert Kurt Mohring from Wilhelmshaven, who searches for mines for the Society for Technical Cooperation", so that his colleagues can repair the water supply in Jaffna without being hurt. "Here are at least 300,000 mines", he explains, "therefore the farmers let the cattle go in front. If they trigger off an explosion, they have to be slaughtered, whether they are considered holy or not." Therefore beef is so often on the menu of the rebels. After breakfast Elisaman, who is the second MG markswoman, practised for hours on her machine gun - a Nato weapon, which the rebels had bought with the money which had been given by Tamil exiles, just like almost all their war gear, In Germany alone 40,000 Tamils live who give 1000 DM on average per year per family to the terrorists in their homeland. In this life between loading, shooting, political lessons and sleeping Elisaman's world shrank. She didn't know any more what was happening outside of her jungle existence; there was no radio or television. Once a week the girls were taken to a central bunker where there were televisions. There they were shown a documentary film, which was about a battle in which the "Tigers" had killed over 1000 governmental soldiers. Elisaman was prepared for a battle of this kind, when on 31 January her unit was moved to the dense jungle of the district of Kilinochchi, where the five brigades of the armny division 54 had set up their defence line along the national route A-9; this road leads from Jaffna to Kandy, the cultural centre of Sri Lanka. It has not been able to be used for years because of the guerrilla war.

Around midnight the 90 girls took up their positions, from which they were supposed to attack the governmental troops, in order to break up their defence line. For the first time Elisaman saw her boss, a young woman who gave orders to the girls troop, but who herself was under the command of male commanders. At 13 hours the next day the "Tigers" attacked, and shortly afterward the offensive was already at an end, because the division 54 hit back with great force: With grenades, machine guns and with Kfir bombers which had been imported from Israel. "the first who died was our officer" says Elisaman, "then my first MG markswoman was dead. All around me I only saw dead people. I hid behind a bush. There I must have been hit. Out of the 90 girls five survived. Four of them tried to surrender. But according to the plans of the "Tigers" a capitulation is no option for one-way fighters, therefore they had nothing white with them with which they could have signalled their peacefulness. And although Tamils and Sinhalese have been on the island for thousands of years, the one ethnic group does not speak the language of the other, therefore the "Tiger girls" could not make themselves clear to the governmental soldiers. The military shot and after that only one of the 90 girls was still alive Elisaman lay unconscious with a shot in her chest behind the bushes. After days she regained consciousness in a military hospital. The military prisoner Elisaman Jenova is not thinking of going back to the "Tigers", who would not forgive her for not having lost her life for the Tamil cause. In such cases the LTTE gives people short shrift. But what does Elisaman, this traumatised fishersman's daughter with the black skin from Chnundikulam, actually want? "I want to return to my father and mother and to be a good child", she says. And then for the first time here lips move for the first time as if to smile. Her eyes do not smile

Tamil Nadu Law and order

Activities of LTTE and other Terrorist/ Extremist Organizations

The ban on LTTE for two more years with effect from 14.5.2004 has been notified by the Government of India. It has also been declared as one of the terrorist organizations under POTA. The LTTE cadres, who are identified on arrival or otherwise, are lodged in the Special Camp. During 2003 and 2004 (up to 1.4.2004), 4 LTTE drop-out cadres were lodged in Chengalpattu Special Camp.

After the ban imposed on CPI-ML(PW) under POTA on 5.12.2001, there were no significant open activities by the PWG in Tamil Nadu. Due to the relentless action taken by 'Q' Branch CID, 3 absconding accused in the Uthangarai encounter case were arrested.

Three persons having links with the PWG were arrested in Chennai City on 21.11.2003 when they pasted wall posters of CPI-ML(PW), condemning the then Chandrababu Naidu Government in Andhra Pradesh, and the alleged atrocities of the Andhra Police in Northern Telengana, etc.

- Asian Tribune -

"Colonel" Karuna: Money collected in Europe and North America by the LTTE for terrorist activities are banked in Denmark and Norway

Money collected in Europe and North America by the LTTE for terrorist activities are banked in Denmark and Norway – "Colonel" Karuna Amman.

Money collected for terrorism activities in Sri Lanka are banked in the monetary institutions in Denmark and Norway alleges Colonel Karuna Amman, in an interview he gave to the London based Thamil Broadcasting Corporation an independent Radio station on 10 of July in the Tamil language. Karuna Amman alleged that Norway Government has helped the Liberation Tigers of Tamil Eelam with banking the money collected from the expatriates Tamils and from other questionable sources, intended to be used in the future for violent terrorist activities against the Government and the people of Sri Lanka. Full text of the interview with Venayagamoorthy Muralitharan alias Colonel Karuna Amman that was aired over the London based Thamil Broadcasting Corporation on 10 July 2004 is given below. The interview was conducted by V.Ramaraj, Program Director of the TBC:

Regarding Muslims, especially the Muslims of the North, what is the position you are adopting?

The important thing is that the right of Muslims has to be safeguarded. In the Eastern region all three ethnic groups are living. There is a necessity to work with them together. In the future all the ethnic groups must coexist happily in the Tamil Elam enjoying equal rights and status. This is our contention.

In the past it seems that you too was involved in issues connected

with the Muslims. What is your comment about this issue?

We have no connection at all in this issue. It is only Prabakaran, the one who is anti-Muslim and involved in their killings. The biggest incident in the whole world occurred only in Jaffna. Prabakaran chase the Muslims through Kilali only with shopping bags in their hands. After the commencement of my issue, there were no incidents against the Muslims in the East. They live happily. It was Prabakaran who autocratically did the ethnic cleansing.

Earlier you have participated in the Peace Talks for more than six times. Every time, whenever you met the media you have told that there was marked improvement in the Talks. But the talks did not move after certain stage. Can you tell us the true position of the Talks?

In fact Prabakaran was not at all keen about the talks. He made use of the talks as an opportunity to get down lethal weapons and to amass funds from the expatriate Tamils. Whenever we met him, he did not show any interest regarding the Talks. He showed keen interest in purchasing arms and in the purchase of foreign goods for his wife and children. You would have already read in the papers that even Thamilselvan who attended the peace Talks as Prabakaran's dummy, use to carry several bag loads of things from foreign countries to Prabakaran and to t his favorite commanders. Peace Talks was a drama arranged by Prabakaran. At present Sri Lanka Government announced of finding a final solution to the conflict, even then Prabakaran had not shown any interest. The People in the Tamil Eelam underwent untold hardships for the last twenty years and wait for a final solution. Prabakaran is obstructing the final solution. He is not a peace loving person. By announcing that we will talk about the interim solution by that he intends to obtain more funds and make his life more flourishing and also he is ready to sacrifice the cadres by launching another war. He was never a peace loving person. Recently on the Black Tigers day, he had accomplished a suicide attack in Colombo. While a peaceful environment exist at present, but he sent a woman suicide bomber and saw that the human bomb blast. Prabakaran too has two children in the age studying AL (G.C.E.Advance Level) But, Prabakaran is not going to recruit them either as a Black Tiger or as a militant cadre. At this juncture, I wish to appeal to People Thamil Eelam: Please get back your children from the Prabakaran and his gang. Prabakaran remains very weak and susceptible now. It is certain he will meet his end soon.

What are the ways available to stop the killings that is going on at present in the Eastern province.

For this, the solution is only with Prabakaran. At first the extremist activities undertaken by him should be stopped. Peoples' frustration and opposition against this are gradually http://www.asiantribune.com/show_article.php?id=1602 (2 of 4)19.08.2004 12:15:14 Money collected in Europe and North America by the LTTE for terrorist activities are banked in Denmark and Norway – Colonel Karuna Amman. growing. At present there are weapons available all over in the Eastern province. Whenever Prabakaran gang let loose extremism, then the people were compelled to make use of those weapons. Initially the gang belonging to Prabakarn must come forward to put a halt to this. Otherwise, people has to take up arms and fight against them.

Recently, a Human Rights Unit was set up in the Vanni, what do you wish to say about this?

This is the biggest joke. How can a man like Prabakaran who is involved with extra-judicial killings could come forward to open up a human rights unit and this amount to shedding crocodile tears. At the same time when they open up the Human Rights division over there, here in the East - Sivarasa ,a father three children was summarily executed by them. This is a deceptive ploy to hoodwink the international community.

- Asian Tribune -

The interview with "Colonel" Karuna Amman was conducted in Tamil. The English translation is unofficial. http://www.asiantribune.com 19.08.2004

LTTE's Kattankudi Muslim Mosque Massacre

Mosque Massacres Revisited

On Friday August 4, 1990 over three hundred Muslims, men and boys, were prostrate in prayer at the Meera Jumma Mosque, fifty yards from the Kandy Batticaloa Road. None of them were armed.

It was seven twenty in the evening and the town of Katankudi was lit up. The prayers went on when there was a power cut throwing the mosque into darkness.

A stones throw away from the Meera Jumma is the smaller Hussainya Mosque. There was a smaller gathering of approximately forty people here -- prostrate in prayer too. The power cuut had been effected by the large group of LTTE cadres on their murderous mission.

According to eye witnesses the raiders were dressed in battle fatigues, others in sarongs and tee shirts. They drove up in several white Hiace vans -- armed LTTE cadres.

A. I. Ismail was 55 then. M.M. Akbar was 16. Two men who survived the attack as fate disposed and told the tale. It was appalling.

The most crowded place

In Katankudi the population is denser than in any part of South Asia including Calcutta. In one and a half square kilometres live 50,000 people.

In August 1990 there had been agitation in the Eastern Province of Sri Lanka. Security was sparse and the Muslim and Sinhalese civilians living in the area were exposed to the aftermath of Black

July 1983. LTTE attacks had accounted for 14 Muslims on August 1 in Akkaraipattu. The dead men had their hands tied behind their backs with their own clothes and then shot in the occipital (back) region of the head. Between August 2 and 3 of that year, fifteen other muslims were killed in attacks by the LTTE at Medawachchiya, Batticaloa and Majeedpuram. On August 4 they hit Katankudi.

I found the streets of Katankudi bare and all the shops closed. First impressions were that of a ghost town. Then when we reached the mosque everything changed. "This is a 'hartal'. We have closed shops to mark the ten years that our children and their mothers have suffered without the bread winners of their families. Some mothers lost very young children who had gone but to worship Allah", the trustee of the mosque, a tall, bearded middle aged man says in perfect English. On the walls of the mosque are the marks left by machine gun fire. The floor bears the markings of the grenades that were thrown at the worshippers. We spend some time listening to the voices that are strained with emotion. Young children and women cling to the windows of the mosque and wait to tell their stories.

Losses

Katankudi's narrow side streets are crowded with screaming children at play in the hot soft sand of eastern afternoons. They are as noisy as children anywhere in the world.

In 1990 Akram was the youngest most precocious at six, Ajimeel, Jaroon and Rizwan, were 10, Asroof the only boy who was 11, Dalhan Haris, Fauser Hassan, Arip, M. Ajimal, Makeen, Kamaldeen and Imtiaz were all 12 - Anas, Faizal, and M.B.Jawad 13 - Sameeen, Jaufer, Samath, Mohammed Fauzer, Safar, M. S. M. Jaufer were all 14, Fazlan was the oldest at 15. They went to the same schools and played together. Came to the mosque and prayed together. Each neighbourhood has its own little mosque to permit the faithful to pray as mandated by the Word -- five times a day.

Then when the public address system sounds, calling the faithful to prayer the streets empty in a few seconds. They come to the mosque and wash themselves before every prayer. On August 4, 1990 they performed the same ritual. In their innocence they knew that something was wrong for attacks had been carried out on peace loving, hard-working Muslims.

The hour was grave. Everybody looked for Divine Intervention. The LTTE were on the rampage murdering unarmed Muslim civilians. The men in Katankudi had filed into the mosques and no one was on the streets to warn of the danger that lingered. The witnesses say that while men stood guard at the doors of the mosques latecomers were herded and shut inside. Then through the windows they were mowed down, gunfire drowning screams of "Allah - hu -Akbar". They were shot in the back, killed by men who respect nothing not even a place of worship.

The Muslims continued to be attacked despite President Premadasa's attempt to stop them by increasing the armed forces personnel in the Eastern Province. Six days after the Katankudi massacre Armed LTTE men rounded up hundreds of civilian Muslims. Akin to genocide now.Their attempt at mass murder in Siyambalagaskanda failed when the Army turned up in numbers. On August 18, however the LTTE launched another attack on Eravur and murdered 31 children, 27 women and 115 men. They then raided other villages unhindered and continued their reign of terror throughout the Eastern, Northern and North Central areas. Mosques all over the country had now to be given armed protection. Then the State Minister of Muslim Religious and Cultural Affairs Mr. Aswer called on the Muslims to be calm and patriotic. God fearing and disposed to peace, the Muslims did remain calm. Sinhala villages came under threat; hundreds were brutally murdered in Tantrimale, Weli Oya, Padhavia while the security forces chased phantoms.

The election of the People's Alliance Government in 1994 saw a lull. Calling the bluff off the LTTE President Chandrika Bandaranaike Kumaratunga refused to budge in her conditions.The Security Forces now were given orders to protect the threatened villages from the LTTE. However on September 17, 1999 the village of Gonagala was attacked and 52 people, including a number of very young children, were hacked to death in the stealth of the night. A visit to that region was made recently by two British Journalists, veterans at covering the fate faced by children in a conflict situation. Former paramedical officer , now photo -journalist and Scotsman Martin Klejnowski - Kennedy and Madeleine Leeson of the Reuters Foundation toured Batticaloa and the Eastern province.

Both had visited every battlefield except Kashmir in the last four years. Gruesome scenes are nothing novel to them. One million people were murdered in 100 days in Ruwanda and they have seen fields full of 15000 Somalians killed by Erithrean soldiers piled up in the desert sun. But they were appalled at the brutality of the LTTE in the Meera Jumma and Hussainia Mosques and at Gonagala. To be fair by all ethnic groups they visited Katankudi and Batticaloa where they met Tamil children whose parents had been killed by the security forces. On the last leg of the tour they met the children of Gonagala. Kennedy and Leeson were very impressed by the professionalism and thoroughness shown by the security personnel at the check points. They came into direct contact with numbers of Tamil, Muslim and Sinhalese civilians and have seen clearly that the LTTE does not represent the Tamil people but form a micro minority of terrorists.

The LTTE – Al Qaeda link

Subramanian Swamy clarifies LTTE – Al Qaeda link

Liberation Tigers of Tamil Eelam and Al Qaeda rebel outfit were well connected alleges Dr. Subramanian Swamy' and he adds that both groups were involved in the business and dealing of arms and narcotics. Dr.Subramanian Swamy says that he came to know of the connections between the Liberation Tigers of Tamil Eelam - Sri Lankan Tamil rebel outfit and Al Qaeda in the year 2002 through the Afghanistan ambassador in India. A former Indian Minister of Commerce and Law, Leader of the Janata Party, a specialist in the political affairs of South Asian region - Dr. Subramanian Swamy who is also the author of *The Assassination of Rajiv Gandhi: Unanswered Questions and Unasked Queries* told the "Asian Tribune" that the Afghanistan ambassador in India was the associate of the former Ahmed Shah Massood.

Ahmed Shah Massood was a longtime commander in the 1979-1989 war against Soviet occupation of Afghanistan and a legendary guerrilla leader in the fight against the Taliban, who was killed by assassins on 09 September 2001, two days before the terrorist attacks on the United States. Northern Alliance leaders claim Massood known as the "Lion of Panjshir," was killed on orders by the Taliban and Osama bin Laden. It was reported that the Afghan ambassador to India was with Masood at the time he suffered bomb blast injuries and subsequently succumbed and the ambassador too sustain injuries caused shrapnel. In the latest article "Hanuman's Tail on Sri Lanka Again", written by Dr. Subramanian Swamy, for the

"Hard Talks" - a monthly Indian magazine for its August issue was published in advance in the "Asian Tribune." As the introduction to article "Asian Tribune" highlighted: *"LTTE has developed contacts with Al Qaeda in Afghanistan writes Subramanian Swamy, a former Law and Commerce Minister of India and Leader of the Janata Party of India, who is one of the Think Tanks of the India Foreign Policy and had access to classified intelligence reports. He adds LTTE developed contacts with Al Qaeda and also with ISI in Pakistan, and helped their drugrunning through India."*

Numerous readers and diplomats contacted "Asian Tribune" for further clarification on the Al Qaeda – LTTE link. "Asian Tribune" contacted Dr. Subramanian Swamy and he clarified as follows: As far as Al Qaeda is concerned, I came to know from Afghanistan's Ambassador to India, when I called on him in the Embassy in Delhi in late 2001 or early 2002, that when he was with the Massood's Northern Alliance, the LTTE was in Kabul shopping for weapons. "LTTE does a lot of drug running for narcotics gangs so there could be a quid pro quo with Al Qaeda. The Ambassador mentioned the year as 1997. As far as ISI is concerned, in mid 1995, many news items had appeared in Indian press that US Embassy had taken this up with Pakistan. I raised this with the Pakistani leadership when I was on a visit in 2000 to Islamabad, but I wonder how much control the political establishment has with the ISI to stop it," thus Subramanian Swamy concluded.

–www.asiantribune.com

Press release from ICJ, Human Rights Watch and Amnesty International asking LTTE to Stop Human Rights Violations

6 October 2004

On October 5, representatives of the Amnesty International, Human Rights Watch and the International Commission of Jurists (ICJ) met with a delegation of the LTTE at Geneva. Following is the full text of the press release after the meeting:

At a meeting with a senior Liberation Tigers of Tamil Eelam (LTTE) delegation visiting Geneva, Amnesty International, Human Rights Watch and the International Commission of Jurists (ICJ) called on the LTTE to end political killings and the recruitment of child soldiers and demonstrate how they will respect international humanitarian and human rights law in Sri Lanka.

The LTTE delegation, headed by S.P. Thamilselvan, leader of their political wing, is visiting several European countries to consider the Tamil Tigers' next steps in the stalled Sri Lankan peace process. International human rights organizations met with the LTTE delegation on Tuesday 5 October.

"We appealed to the senior LTTE leaders to show the world that they are both willing and capable of respecting the lives and rights of all Sri Lankans," said Nicholas Howen, Secretary-General of the ICJ. "We look to them to make a clear public commitment to international humanitarian and human rights standards and practical ways of putting them into effect," he added.

"At a time when we should be moving back to peace talks the LTTE seems to have dramatically escalated the killing of perceived

Tamil opponents and is still recruiting child soldiers," said Loubna Freih, Geneva Director for Human Rights Watch.

Victims of killings have included activists from Tamil political parties not aligned with the LTTE, members of a rival LTTE faction in the east, and alleged Sri Lankan military informants.

"This climate of fear, especially in the east, will make it even more difficult to find a lasting peace in the country," warned Peter Splinter, Geneva Representative for Amnesty International.

S.P. Thamilselvan said in the meeting with human rights organisations that the LTTE denies responsibility for such killings but that the LTTE would consider the development of confidence building measures to end killings that are threatening the peace process.

In the last two weeks reported killings have included: Valli Suntharam, a 61-year-old trade union activist and member of the Eelam People's Revolutionary Liberation Front (EPRLF), shot dead in Jaffna on 27 September; Selvarajah Mohan, a 22-year-old Eelam People's Democratic Party (EPDP) supporter, stabbed to death after being taken from his home in Jaffna district on 24 September; Rajadurai Sivagnanam, killed in Batticaloa district on 22 September; and Somasundaram Varunakulasingham, a central committee member of the EPDP, shot dead in Colombo on 23 September.

Recruitment of child soldiers also continues. UNICEF has documented that in May, June and July 2004 alone, the LTTE recruited 259 children, while releasing 106 -- and UNICEF acknowledges that they learn about only a small proportion of child recruitment.

The human rights organizations also met with members of the Northeast Secretariat on Human Rights, set up in July with the support of the LTTE. "Such human rights initiatives could be positive if they help to prevent serious human rights violations and give ordinary people a way of seeking protection and remedies," said Nicholas Howen. "We urge the LTTE to affirm publicly that they will cooperate fully with this Secretariat. The international community should assist any genuine moves towards a culture of respect for rights and the need for this new Secretariat to be independent and professional," added Nicholas Howen.

Source: *Amnesty International website*

International Convention for the Suppression of Terrorist Bombings

The United Nations in December 1997, adopted the "International Convention for the Suppression of Terrorist Bombings" which is applicable to attacks of this nature.

Abstracts from the "International Convention for the Suppression of Terrorist Bombing "adopted by the 52nd Session of the UN General Assembly on 15th December 1997..........

Article 2

1. Any person commits an offence within the meaning of this Convention if that person unlawfully and intentionally delivers, places, discharges or detonates an explosive or other lethal device in, into or against a place of public use, a State or government facility, a public transportation system or an infrastructure facility: (a) With the intent to cause death or serious bodily injury; or (b) With the intent to cause extensive destruction of such a place, facility or system, where such destruction results in or is likely to result in major economic loss.

Article 5

Each State Party shall adopt such measures as may be necessary, including, where appropriate, domestic legislation, to ensure that criminal acts within the scope of this Convention, in particular where there are intended or calculated to provoke a state of terror in the general public or in a group of persons or particular persons, are under no circumstances justifiable by considerations of a political, philosophical, ideological, racial, ethnic, religious or other similar nature and are punished by penalties consistent with their grave nature.

Article 15

State Parties shall cooperate in the prevention of the offences set forth in Article2, particularly; (a) By taking all practicable measures, including, if necessary, adopting their domestic legislation, to prevent and counter preparations in their respective territories, including measures to prohibit in their territories illegal activities of persons, groups and organisations that encourage, initiate, organise, knowingly finance or encourage in the preparation of offences set forth in Article 2.